THE GODS OF INDIA

A BRIEF DESCRIPTION OF THEIR HISTORY, CHARACTER & WORSHIP

THE GODS OF INDIA

A BRIEF DESCRIPTION OF THEIR HISTORY, CHARACTER & WORSHIP

BY THE

REV. E. OSBORN MARTIN

FOR 13 YEARS A WESLEYAN METHODIST MISSIONARY IN INDIA AND CEYLON

WITH

68 ILLUSTRATIONS AND MAP

GYAN

Published by

GYAN

Gyan Publishing House
5, Ansari Road
Daryaganj, New Delhi-110002
Phone: 011-47034999, 9811692060
E-mail: books@gyanbooks.com

Distribution Network
gyanbooks.com
India, USA, Canada, UK, Australia, France

ISBN : 978-81-212-2716-2 (HB)
First Published, 1914

2nd Impression 2021

Printed at: Gyan Press, Delhi.

The Gods of India
Author: Rev. E. Osborn Martin

THE GODS OF INDIA

A BRIEF DESCRIPTION OF THEIR HISTORY, CHARACTER & WORSHIP

BY THE

REV. E. OSBORN MARTIN

FOR 13 YEARS A WESLEYAN METHODIST-MISSIONARY IN INDIA AND CEYLON

WITH

68 ILLUSTRATIONS AND MAP

LONDON & TORONTO

J. M. DENT & SONS, LTD.

NEW YORK: E. P. DUTTON & CO.

MCMXIV

THE GODS

OF INDIA

PREFACE

ALTHOUGH many books have been written of recent years on Hinduism as a religious system, the number of works on Hindu mythology is extremely few, and scarcely one of these attempts to treat the subject in a popular way. Of this small number some have been out of print for many years, and others are intended solely for the student, as for instance Mr. A. A. Macdonell's admirable book on *Vedic Mythology*. One of the latest and best known of these books is Mr. W. J. Wilkins' *Hindu Mythology*, but this book appeared thirty-one years ago (the second edition in 1900), and excellent as the book is, it is not general in its scope. It confines itself to Vedic and Purānic deities, with special relation to the mythology pertaining to Bengal. The purpose of the present volume is to furnish an account of the deities known to India as a whole, a book which it is hoped, while of some use to the serious student, may yet be regarded of so simple a character as to make it interesting to the general reader. With the marked growth in our knowledge of the affairs of our great Dependency, and the increasing attention paid to all phases of Indian life, it is impossible to disregard the gods and goddesses who are the objects of worship of some 217,000,000 of our Hindu fellow-subjects, and it has been my endeavour to supply in small compass a correct though not exhaustive account of the most important and most representative of the many thousands of gods worshipped by the Hindus.

After two introductory chapters dealing with the development of Hindu mythology, and the relative value of the sources of our knowledge in the Sacred Books of the Hindus, I have ventured to classify and group the deities of Hinduism under three separate heads, giving a brief introductory chapter to the third section, and concluding with a chapter summing up the whole subject and defining the scope and value of Hindu mythology. The Gods of India are multitudinous, but they are capable of classification as:

(1) *The Vedic Deities*, worshipped many centuries ago by Aryan settlers on the plains of Northern India. With one or two exceptions the lapse of time has caused their worship to fall into disuse. I have therefore selected for mention only the deities still remembered, or in some measure recognised by modern Hinduism. Even these are not worshipped to any extent, but their inclusion is essential to the study of the subject as they mark a distinct stage in the development of Hindu mythology.

(2) *The Purānic Deities*, which are the great gods and goddesses of modern Hinduism, and at the present day objects of the worship of the Brāhmans, and of all the upper castes of Hinduism.

(3) *The Inferior Deities*, demi-gods and village godlings, a countless host which attract the worship of the great mass of Hindu peasantry. It has been possible to choose from these only a few deities representative of different stages of mythological growth, and the process of elimination rendered necessary for space reasons, has given more than ordinary anxiety.

Exhaustive lists of names of the Hindu deities are not given. Dowson's dictionary will supply this deficiency. Such a list would have little interest to the general reader whose requirements have been constantly borne in mind.

It must be clearly understood that this book makes no claim to be considered an original work. It contains a good deal of original matter, but generally speaking I have tried to give in a brief and readable form a book which in the main is a careful selection from the works of recognised authorities and from translations of the Scriptures of Hinduism (Dr. J. Muir's *Original Sanskrit Texts* is the translation mainly followed). It is precisely this feature which I hope will give the book value to many of its readers. I acknowledge most gratefully my obligations to the authors whose works are noted on the following pages, and especially to Mr. W. J. Wilkins of the London Missionary Society, to whom I am indebted for the lines on which my book has been largely moulded. Mr. F. Deaville Walker has rendered me invaluable assistance by revising and editing the book, and correcting proof sheets, and the Reverends J. A. Vanes, B.A., and A. S. Geden, M.A., D.D. have given me many helpful suggestions and contributed in no small measure to the reliability of the work. I am deeply indebted to the Rev. H. K. Marsden, M.A. (Secretary for Yorkshire to the British and Foreign Bible Society), who has, with much skill and care, compiled the excellent index which adds greatly to the value of the volume, and to Messrs. Bharat Hitaishi & Co., Photographers, Muttra City, United Provinces, India, for the excellent photographs which illustrate these pages. The photographs not supplied by this firm are comparatively few in number and in every case are separately (and gratefully) acknowledged.

There are one or two other matters to which I wish to refer. For obvious reasons there is little reference in these pages to the obscenities sadly too characteristic of the legends of some of the gods and goddesses. It has been impossible to omit all reference to this feature of Hindu mythology, but it has not been dwelt upon. Possibly the obscenity of the

Hinduism of the Purānas and Tantras is one of the causes which make it so popular with the masses of India to-day. On the other hand it is quite a mistake to imagine, as many do, that Hinduism is full of it. A perusal of these pages will serve to show that just as the philosophy of Hinduism contains many pure and lofty doctrines and ideas, and its social and religious system much that is admirable, so among the gods and goddesses of India there are those worthy of respect if not of honour. The stainless purity of the idyll of Rāma and Sītā is sufficient proof of this assertion.

In an account written by a Christian missionary, readers may be surprised at the comparative absence of comment on some remarkable features of the lives of the gods and goddesses. The fact is that the stories of the Hindu deities need neither denunciation nor condemnation from my pen—they are largely self-condemned. I have honestly striven to be impartial, both in the extracts given and the construction put upon these quotations "naught extenuating and naught set down in malice!" It is worthy of note that the ignorance prevailing on Hindu mythology arises not so much from lack of interest, as from inability, in view of the acknowledged vastness and complexity of the subject, to find the information required. I trust that my gleanings from many sources may be of service and that the perusal of this volume may whet the appetite of those who wish to study further the subject.

E. OSBORN MARTIN.

91 CLARENDON ROAD, LEEDS,
3rd November 1913.

CHIEF BOOKS CONSULTED

		EDITION OF
Religious Thought and Life in India	Sir Monier Williams	1883
Indian Epic Poetry	Sir Monier Williams	1863
Indian Wisdom	Sir Monier Williams (2nd ed.)	1875
Brāhmanism and Hinduism	Sir Monier Williams (3rd ed.)	1887
Essays on the Religions of the Hindus	Prof. H. H. Wilson, F.R.S.	1862
A View of the History, Literature, and Religion of the Hindus	Rev. W. Ward (5th ed.)	1863
Hindu Mythology	W. J. Wilkins (2nd ed.)	1900
The Popular Religion and Folk-Lore of Northern India	W. Crooke, I.C.S., 2 vols (new edition)	1896
The Arsenal	Rev. J. Fr. Stācher	1910
Original Sanskrit Texts	Dr. J. Muir	1870
The Religions of India	Mons. A. Barth (3rd ed.)	1891
The Hindu Pantheon	Edward Moor	1810
The Religions of India	Dr. E. W. Hopkins	1895
History of Ancient Sanskrit Literature	Prof. Max Müller	1859
Chips from a German Workshop (4 vols.)	Prof. Max Müller	1868–1875
Christian Literature Society's Handbooks	Dr. Murdoch	various
Asiatic Studies (2 vols.)	Sir Alfred Lyall, K.C.B.	1897
Hinduism, Ancient and Modern	R. B. Lāla Baij Nāth	1905
Primitive Culture (2 vols.)	Ed. B. Tylor, D.C.L., F.R.S.	1891
A Classical Dictionary of Hindu Mythology	J. Dowson, M.R.A.S.	1888

		EDITION OF
Dictionary of Non-classical Mythology	Marian Edwardes and Lewis Spence	1913
The Epic of Ancient India . .	Romesh Dutt, C.I.E.	1899
The Great Religions of India . .	Dr. J. Murray Mitchell . .	1906
The Light of Asia	Sir Edwin Arnold	1890
The Prem Sāgar	A translation	
Rambles and Recollections (2 vols.)	Maj.-Gen. W. H. Sleeman, K.C.B.	1843
Hindu Mythology	Col. J. Kennedy	1862
The Rāmāyana	Professor Ralph J. H. Griffith, C.I.E.	
Hinduism and Christianity . .	Rev. Dr. J. Robson	1905
A Description of the Character, Manners, and Customs of the People of India	Abbé J. A. Dubois	1862
The Mystics, Ascetics, and Saints of India	Prof. John Campbell Oman .	1903
The Soul of India	Dr. Geo. Howells	1913
A Primer of Hinduism	J. N. Farquhar	1911

CONTENTS

PART I

INTRODUCTORY

PART II

THE NATURE GODS OF THE VEDAS

PART III

THE PURĀNIC GODS

PART IV

INFERIOR GODS AND GODLINGS

ILLUSTRATIONS

PART I

INTRODUCTION

CHAPTER I

THE DEVELOPMENT OF HINDU MYTHOLOGY

"As the web issues from the spider, as little sparks proceed from fire, so from the One Soul proceed all breathing animals, all worlds, all the gods, and all beings."—*Extract from an Upanishad* (translated by Monier Williams).

"I see thee, Mighty Lord of all, revealed in forms of infinite diversity."—*Bhagavad Gītā*.

ONE of the most characteristic traits of childhood is the reality with which everything is clothed. The child invests with living, breathing power all natural phenomena around it. The trees in the garden speak; the wooden doll, repulsively ugly as it may appear to others, has to the child a beautiful form and a distinct personality. Should a table stand in the way and unexpectedly cause pain, the child, once recovered from the feeling of surprise, may beat it in anger. In the darkness of the night a rag doll gives infinite solace and security. In the childhood of a race the same characteristics prevail. The forces and powers of Nature interpret themselves to the opening minds of primitive peoples in a personal light as though each had life and personality.

Nearly four thousand years ago a vigorous and warlike race penetrated through the rocky defiles of the mountains of North-West India into the broad sunny plains of the Punjab.[1] They had no national unity, but came in tribes and clans, and they conquered as they came. Of their

[1] They settled first in the districts watered by the river Sindhu (now called the Indus). The Persians pronounced this word Hindhū, and named their Aryan brethren Hindūs. The Greeks, who probably gained their first ideas of India from the Persians, dropped the hard aspirate and called the Hindus "'Indoí."—Monier Williams, *Hinduism*, p. 1.

previous history very little is known. They were a simple pastoral people, related to the ancient Persians (Iranians) and more remotely to the Greeks and Romans; a primitive race, but possessing already the germs of a high civilisation, gifted, imaginative, and energetic.

These Aryas, or Aryans[1] found the country already occupied by an entirely different people, who were of much darker complexion, and whose habits of life appeared strange and uncouth to them. War speedily ensued, and, with their greater vigour, the immigrants were victorious, and as they conquered so they reduced the original inhabitants to slavery, driving those who would not yield southwards into the wilder parts of the country. The aboriginals were called Dāsyus, *i.e.* slaves, by the invaders, who scoffed at them as "noseless, speechless, and godless," words which simply imply the possession of smaller noses, a different and probably not so polished language, and a religion unlike that of the Aryans.

These early Aryans, like their present-day representatives, the Hindus, were decidedly a religious people. Possessing childlike minds of quick sensibility, it is not difficult to perceive that so long as they remained in the neighbourhood of the giant Himālayas those stupendous mountains exercised a determining influence on them. Everything was wonderful to them, and a feeling of awe and reverence, scarcely distinguishable from worship, was continually called forth. They watched the play of the lightning illuminating the sombre foothills. They saw the white mists rolling along the valleys and blotting out the landscape, the great snowy summits high in the heavens, turning from rose to purple, from purple to dark blue, from blue to grey as the night fell, and in the chilly evening standing forth as spectres, denizens of another world. And thus Nature, so exceedingly vast and beautiful, became greatly adored, and the grandeur and display of its mighty forces were regarded as nothing short of the superhuman, and divine. Their religion was not idolatry in the

[1] Scholars give the meaning of the word Aryan as noble, loyal, or faithful.

sense of image worship. It was nature worship. Their material welfare so depended on the action of the powers of nature, the sky, the air, the sun, that as a matter of course, in the absence of direct revelation, they turned to these with gratitude and love mingled with awe and reverence. But their view of nature was not ours. It was extremely difficult for the Aryan to think of natural objects as other than living. The flowing stream, the rushing wind, the blazing fire; all these appeared instinct with life. In other cases where life was not so obvious, the visible object was believed to be animated by an internal something—call it spirit or god.[1]

As the Aryans advanced into the territories of the aborigines inhabiting the vast plain of Northern India, they adopted not a few of their beliefs and rites, and the corruption of their religion must have proceeded with great rapidity. The aborigines were mainly of Tartar descent, and were devoted to the worship of malignant deities, with rites correspondingly cruel. Some of the Vedic gods were low enough, still they were not demons, but ere long a base demon worship became a part of Hinduism.

Moreover, once settled in their new resting place, simple elemental nature worship no longer satisfied the growing religious cravings of these giant races, awakening to the call of civilisation, and to the consciousness of a new-born national life. A richly peopled mythology arose in India as in Greece. Religious ideas—a sense of dependence on a Higher Power, and a desire to realise His presence—grew with their growth and strengthened with their strength. Soon the Hindu,

[1] Sir W. W. Hunter's dictum on the religious growth of India is that "the Aryans worshipped first as they *feared*, then as they *admired*, and finally as they *reasoned*. The stupendous phenomena of physical nature were the earliest Vedic gods. Then later came the genial household deity Agni, the kindly Sun, the friendly Day, the beauteous Dawn Soma, the intoxicating plant, &c. The Brāhmanic system, with its great Triad and their manifestations covering a whole reasoned scheme of worship, made a successful reply to the demand for orderly system of religious thought."

like the Greek, personified, deified, and worshipped not only the powers exhibited in external nature, but all the internal feelings, passions, moral and intellectual qualities and faculties. Soon he began to regard every object as a visible manifestation of the supreme Providence presiding over the Universe, and every departed hero or benefactor as an incarnation of the same all-wise and omnipresent Ruler. Then, to give expression to the varied attributes and functions of this great Being, thus visibly manifested to the world, both Hindu and Greek[1] peopled their pantheons with numerous divine and semi-divine creations, clothed them with male and female forms, inventing in connection with them various fanciful myths, fables, and allegories, which the undiscriminating multitude accepted as realities without in the least understanding the ideas they symbolised.

The consequence is that although Hindus of all grades always speak of the Veda as the foundation and authoritative support of their religion, they seldom seem to be aware how vast a difference exists between that system as it was in ancient days, and as it is now. There has been a large growth from within and large accretions from without. Modern Hinduism is not a creed, but a vast congeries of conflicting creeds. It has developed into a system of worship of many gods and goddesses, of powers of nature, of men who attained to eminence by their deeds, of ancestors, and of objects both animate and inanimate. Hero-worship came to be one of its chief features. The principal gods and goddesses of the Hindu Pantheon were recruited from deified heroes and heroines. Śiva's conquest of Tripura, Durgā's fight with Mahisha and other demons, Vishnu's exploits in

[1] "Resemblances have been distinctly traced between many of the mythological beings of India and Europe. Indra, who always sends the rain and wields the thunderbolt, and Siva, the god of destruction, resemble Zeus, or Jupiter; Durgā, or Pārvatī, is like to Juno; Krishna to Apollo, Rati to Venus; Lakshmī, or Srī, to Ceres; Varuna to Neptune, Sarasvatī to Minerva, Kārtikeya to Mars, Yama to Pluto, Ganesha to Janus, Kāma to Cupid, and Kailāsa and Meru, the abodes of the gods to Ida and Olympus."—*Indian Epic Poetry*, pp. 47–9.

subduing the Asuras and Rākshasas through various incarnations, and the adventures of Rāma, Krishna, and Hanumān, all point to this conclusion.

With the advent and rapid rise into favour of Buddhism there was brought to pass a great reconstruction of Hinduism. The Brāhman was compelled to set his house in order, to enable him to combat and overcome the new faith.

1. Many of the old gods of Vedic Hinduism now disappeared and a multitude of new ones came in; and they are still continuing to come.[1]

2. New doctrines were introduced—for example, that of *Transmigration*, and no doctrine has impressed the general mind of India more deeply than this. Of great importance, too, is the doctrine of *Bhakti* or "faith, devotion," and we read in the Vishnu Purāna of Prahlāda praying to Vishnu:

> 'In whichever of the thousands of births I may pass, may I, O Lord, always have unshaken devotion to thy lotus feet. That devotion which men of the world have for worldly objects, may I ever have for Thee, always remembering Thee.'

Even Sankara recognised this, for, Pantheist as he was, he says:

> 'Though all difference has ceased to exist, I am thine, O Lord, not Thou mine. The billow is of the sea, not the sea of the billow.'

3. Another novelty is the practice of *pilgrimage*, visiting holy places. Rivers are held in great reverence, and the

[1] *How Gods are made.*—"The fortress of Sanoda in Bundlekhand was built by Raja Chatar Singh about 160 years ago. His son, Rai Singh, soon after the fortress was completed, was killed in an attack upon a town near Chitrakot, a famous place of pilgrimage. He had a temple and a tomb erected over his remains. Some time after someone suffering from a quartan ague went to the tomb one night and said that if Rai Singh would cure his ague for him he would make offerings to him at his tomb for the rest of his life. After that he never had another attack, and was very punctual in his offerings. Others followed his example, until now he is recognised by the people of that part of India as a god."—Sleeman, vol. i. p. 115.

Ganges from the point where it breaks out from the Himālayas to the spot where it mingles with the sea is sacred throughout. Holy places are found all over India, one of the most celebrated of which is Puri in Orissa, where the temple of Jagannāth is. By bathing in a sacred stream all sin is washed away, and much merit is acquired in visiting sacred places and undergoing the toils of a difficult journey to and fro.

4. *Idolatry* itself is a later development. The early Hindus had no image worship and no temples. With the natural objects ever before their eyes—the fire, the stream, the sun—images were not needed. But a love of symbolism was deep in the Aryan mind from the first ; and in later days perhaps the most striking characteristic of Hinduism is idolatry. Idols, idols everywhere ; they are found all over the land in millions. They are of stone, wood, and metal, brass being most frequently used. They are of all sizes, from the gigantic to the most diminutive—each idol is generally bright and glaring, being smeared over with red-ochre, or bright vermilion. Trees and rocks are marked in the same way ; indeed any object may be thus worshipped.

5. *Caste* is another very important innovation. Society is now divided into countless sections separated from each other by iron walls. Caste observances are determined with a view to preserve religious purity. In the late Vedas and in other Hindu books greater and greater prominence came to be given to details of ceremonial and religious service, and now the larger half of a Hindu's duty is contained in obeying fixed restrictions as to eating and drinking, and methods of life. A man now may believe what he pleases, and act as he pleases ; and yet if he keeps caste rules he remains an orthodox Hindu. The laws of caste are often as absurd as they are tyrannical, but by means of them the Brāhman has been able to maintain his pre-eminence for upwards of 2000 years. When the city of Poona was under native government in the days of the Peshwa, no low-caste man was allowed to enter before 9 A.M. or remain in the city after 3 P.M. Why ? Because before nine and after three he cast too long

a shadow; and wherever that shadow fell upon a Brāhman it polluted him, so that he dare not taste food or water till he had bathed and washed the impurity away.

6. One truly remarkable change that has taken place in Hinduism is the comparative cessation of animal sacrifice. In early Hinduism the rite went on steadily increasing for centuries, the victims becoming more numerous and the ritual more complex. The Brāhmanas amaze us by the extent to which the sacrificial system was carried, far exceeding that of any other religion. And yet, except in the worship of the goddess Kālī, and one or two minor deities, animal sacrifice has almost disappeared from Hinduism.

7. Another fearful practice was the burning of widows on their husbands' funeral pyres. There is no authority for this in the Vedas, but probably the rite existed for at least 2000 years, and the number of self-murdered women must have amounted to millions. We know that in Bengal alone, from the time when the battle of Plassey gave Britain the sovereignty of the country to the year 1829 when Satī was finally suppressed, no less than 70,000 widows were burnt to death. The Brāhmans at the time vehemently opposed the suppression of this dreadful custom, but happily the British Government stood firm, and now, except in isolated cases, it has ceased to exist.[1]

[1] The material of this chapter has been largely extracted from Dr. J. Murray Mitchell's *The Great Religions of India*, pp. 42–66.

CHAPTER II

THE SACRED BOOKS OF THE HINDUS

> " The Veda is of patriarchs and men,
> And e'en of gods, a very eye eternal,
> Giving unerring light ; it is beyond
> All finite faculties, nor can be proved
> By force of human argument—this is
> A positive conclusion."
>
> —*Institutes of Manu*, Bk. xii. 94
> (translated by Monier Williams).

IF a Hindu be asked to name his sacred writings, he would probably give them in this order : First in importance the Four Vedas ; the Upanishads ; then the eighteen Purānas ; the two great Epic Poems—the Rāmāyana and the Mahābhārata ; the Institutes of Manu, the great law-giver ; the Tantras ; and to these must be added another class of writings, the Six Darśanas, or philosophical systems.

As this book is limited for reasons of space to a survey of the more important gods and godlings worshipped by the Hindus, it is only necessary for us to concern ourselves in this chapter with a brief characterisation of the books which constitute our sources of information. These, roughly speaking, are the Four Vedas, the Purānas, the Institutes of Manu, the Tantras, and the two Epic Poems. The Hindus believe in two sources of revelation—" Śruti " (*i.e.* " heard "), and " Smriti " (*i.e.* " remembered," or " traditional "). In other words, direct revelation and indirect. In the former class are the Vedas. In the latter class the Code of Manu and the Upanishads[1] are found. " Śruti " scriptures are believed

[1] The Upanishads are also often referred to in Hindu writings as belonging to the " Śruti " class.

to have been uttered by the great Brahma himself (the Supreme Spirit), who breathed forth the mighty word, and a favoured few, men of piety and grace, treasured up and repeated it for the good of races unborn. This class of writings is of full authority and of supreme sanctity. The second or Smriti class is of secondary authority. The holy men, or Rishis, wrote the treatises according to their recollections. No eternal existence is claimed for these writings, and their authority is derived from being a faithful reproduction of the sense of the Śruti.

Before passing on to summarise the scope and contents of each set of writings named, we may quote from Sir Monier Williams a testimony as to the unique charm and value of Hindu thought and literature:

> "I am deeply convinced that the more we learn about the ideas, feelings, drift of thought, religious development, eccentricities, and even errors and superstitions of the natives of India, the less ready shall we be to judge them by our own conventional European standards; the less disposed to regard ourselves as the sole depositaries of all true knowledge, learning, virtue and refinement existing on the earth; the less prone to despise as an inferior race, the men who compiled the Laws of Manu, one of the most remarkable literary productions of the world; who thought out systems of ethics worthy of Christianity; who composed the Rāmāyana and Mahābhārata, poems in some respects out-rivalling the Iliad and the Odyssey; who invented for themselves the science of grammar, arithmetic, astronomy, logic, and who elaborated independently six most subtle systems of philosophy. Above all, the less inclined to stigmatise as 'benighted heathens' the authors of two religions, which, however lamentably antagonistic to Christianity, are at this moment professed by about half the human race."

I. The Four Vedas

The source of the Hindu religion, the basis of the social fabric of Indian life, the highest authority in religious, ceremonial, and social matters, are the Vedas. These are believed to be, not the work of man, but of the Supreme Being himself, and are therefore eternal.

The word Veda comes from the Sanskrit "vid." It is allied to the Latin root "vid" and the English "to wit." It therefore signifies "knowledge," and the Hindu would add "knowledge divinely communicated." These most ancient of Hindu holy books consist of hymns addressed to the various personified powers of Nature, written in the old form of Sanskrit, and, according to the most generally accepted opinion, composed not less than 1000 to 1500 B.C. Some scholars give an even earlier date, as from internal evidence it seems probable that several of the earlier hymns were sung before the Aryan immigration to India. In any case we may take it that these hymns are now 2500 to 3000 years old, are of unquestioned authenticity, and are practically our sole means of studying the development of the early Aryan peoples in religion as in the arts of civilisation. They were orally transmitted from sage and Rishi to their pupils, generation by generation, from a very early date. It is not known when they received written form, but the sage Vyāsa is spoken of as the "arranger" or, as we should say, "editor" of the Vedas.

In general form the Vedas consist of lyric poetry. They contain the songs in which the first Aryan invaders praised their gods, while they were still on the threshold of Northern India, and as they entered the country which they were afterwards to fill with their civilisation.

The Vedas are four in number:

1. The Rig-Veda, or Veda of Praise.

2. The Yajur, or Veda of Sacrifice.

3. The Sāma-Veda, a metrical rearrangement of the hymns of the Rig-Veda.

4. The Atharva-Veda, the Veda of sacred spells.

The Rig-Veda is of primary importance, and the original work contains 1017 hymns, together with 11 of an apocryphal character, in all 1028. It is *the* Veda. So highly is it regarded that the Laws of Manu declare:

> "A Brāhman by retaining the Rig-Veda in his memory incurs no guilt, though he should destroy the three worlds" (xi. 261).

The other three Vedas are considered by scholars to be of later date than the Rig-Veda, and in part dependent upon it; the second and third Vedas consist almost exclusively of hymns derived from the Rig-Veda and arranged for special purposes connected with religious observances.

Each Veda has two main parts: (1) the Mantra, or Sanhita, which is praise or prayer set in verse; and (2) the Brāhmana, or priestly commentary, written in prose. As the Vedic hymns grew ancient, ritual and ceremonial developed in Aryan worship, and theological inquiry arose. Then sprung into existence the Brāhmana, the second portion of the Vedas, which consists of a variety of ritualistic precepts and details of the ceremonial usages of the Brāhman priests. As a further elaboration, attached to each Brāhmana is an *Upanishad* containing secret and mystical doctrine. In this way the simplicity of the Vedic myths gradually became obscured; the deities grew more personal and became invested with fresh attributes, and often changed in character as speculations arose as to the origin of the world and the human race.

The Atharva-Veda is of the utmost interest: the greater part of it is full of charms and spells for the destruction of enemies, and for the restoration to health of friends. It enters into most intimate detail. Instructions are even given as to the most approved method of covering a bald head with hair! It contains 760 hymns, of which only one-sixth are found in the Rig-Veda. Griffith says, "It is the Veda which teaches how to appease the gods, and secure their protecting favour, how to bless friends, and curse and destroy human and ghostly enemies, together with all noxious creatures. It is the Veda of prayers, charms, and spells."

The Rig-Veda carries us back to a society happy in its rude simplicity:

> "Cheerful in spirit ever more, and keen of sight, with scores of children free from sickness and sin, long living may we look upon thee, O Sūrya, uprising day by day."

But the Atharva-Veda draws the dark background to the scene and depicts these same peoples held in the thraldom of demon, ghost, and spirit, and shows us how that the present-day demon and devil worship has a very early origin.

This is a bare outline of the range and scope of the Vedas. They have many defects—there is little love or gratitude expressed in the hymns. The gods and the worshippers are like traders in a bargain. "I give thee this for that." Indra is thus addressed:

"Be thou no trafficker with us; do not give sparingly, nor demand too much" (Rig-Veda, i. 33-3.)

Barth says that with many of the Vedic poets all that is said to their gods amounts to this, "Here is butter; give us cows." Sons, long life, and victory over enemies are other frequent requests. There are, however, scattered prayers for spiritual blessings, especially in hymns to Varuna.

The Rig-Veda, v. 85, contains the following:

"7. If we have sinned against the man who loves us, have ever wronged a brother, friend, or comrade,
The neighbour ever with us, or a stranger, O Varuna, remove from us the trespass.

"8. If we, as gamesters, cheat at play, have cheated, done wrong unwittingly or sinned of purpose,
Cast all these sins away like loosened fetters, and, Varuna, let us be thine own beloved."

Dr. Robson says:

"In the following prayer for forgiveness we find the germ of the tendency, now universal in India, to attribute sin to fate, contrasting strongly with the feeling of responsibility and guilt expressed in the Hebrew Psalms:

"'Absolve us from the sins of our fathers, and from those which we committed with our own bodies.

"'It was not our own will, O Varuna, but some seduction which led us astray—an intoxicating draught, passion, dice, thoughtlessness. The stronger perverts the weaker; even sleep brings unrighteousness.'" (Rig-Veda, vii. 86.)

Nevertheless, with their many blemishes the Vedas show us how strong and all-controlling even in these early times was the religious motive, the reverence for divine things and the belief in immortality. These early poets were intense Nature lovers, and in Nature sought Nature's God. And how pure was the early code of morals! The corruptions which now assail Hindu society were neither found in the Vedas, nor sanctioned by the ancient Rishis.

The hymns are just what we might expect to find, and no one of later generations could possibly have composed them. The marvellous and primitive simplicity of thought, the sentiments so childlike and so fervid—the first sobbing and plaintive cry of the human child to its Great Father, who made it, and to Nature and the elements, the Great Mother, who nourished and sustained it.

There is no attempt at an ordered system of knowledge, nor is there any indication of self-knowledge or self-realisation. Nothing is found in them which would in any way support the gigantic assumption of Brāhmanism. There is no allusion to the great Hindu Triad, or to the transmigration of souls, or to the present distinctions of caste, or to the pantheistic philosophy of the wise or the unwieldy polytheism of the ignorant. No mention of temples, or of a tyrannical and dominant Brāhmanical priesthood, or of child marriage or zenāna seclusion. The blessings asked for are temporal, the worship is domestic, addressed to presences representing the physical forces of Nature, not represented by visible types and therefore not Idol worship. Those that struck the mind most were fire, rain, the wind, the Sun. With them were associated the Dawn, the Storm-gods, the Earth, the waters, the rivers, the sky, the seasons, the moon, and the "manes" (spirits) of ancestors. Sacrifices were offered both by warriors and priests as food to the deities, hymns were sung, and eventually a ritual was established.

But two causes were at work to assist in the debasement of the simple Vedic faith—first was the artifice of the Brāhman priesthood, who sought to secure and to increase their power;

and second, the presence in large numbers of Non-Aryans, with whom the Aryan peoples mingled and who introduced elements into their religion utterly at variance with its early traditions. Thus gradually anthropomorphism and demonolatry came into existence, and the light of early simplicity of faith was obscured, and gross idolatries and grosser practice became prominent.

II. Manu-Sanhita—the Code of Manu

This well-known law-book is the earliest of all the post-Vedic writings, and is chief of the works classified as Smriti. In its present form it belongs to the fifth century B.C. It contains 2685 verses, and is evidently not the work of one man, but the production of many minds. It gives us the observances of a tribe of Brāhmans called Mānavas, who probably belonged to a school of the Yajur (or black) Veda, and lived in North-West India not far from Delhi. It was written in a period later than the Vedas when the Brāhmans had obtained the ascendancy, but its deities are those of the Vedas and not of the Epics and Purānas—so it occupies a middle place between the Vedas and the Purānas.

It is the foundation of Hindu Law—a collection or digest of current laws and creeds rather than a planned systematic code. It is frequently quoted to-day in law courts, and by Hindus in all cases where the customs of Hindu society and the observances of caste are under question. In it the four main castes are clearly defined and their duties and obligations laid down, and the whole system of rules and regulations is instituted by which the Brāhmans sought to perpetuate an organised caste-system in subordination to themselves.

"After eliminating the purely religious and philosophical precepts, the greater number of its rules fall under the following four heads:

"1. Āchāra, 'immemorial practices.' These, in fact, include all the observances of caste, and are regarded as constituting the highest law and highest religion.

STUDYING THE SACRED BOOKS.

Note the sacred marks of Vishnu on the foreheads.

HINDU HOLY MEN.

"2. VYAVAHĀRA, 'practices of law and government,' embracing the procedure of legal tribunals, rules of judicature, and civil and criminal law.

"3. PRĀYAŚ-CHITTA, 'penitential exercises,' rules of expiation, both of the sins of this present life—especially sins against caste—and the effects of offences committed in previous bodies.

"4. KARMA-PHALA, 'consequences of acts,' good or bad, as leading to reward in heaven or punishment in various hells and involving repeated births through numberless existences until the attainment of final beatitude.

"This is one of the most remarkable books that the literature of the whole world can offer. It not only presents a picture of the usages, manners, and intellectual condition of an important part of the Hindu race at a remote period, but some of its moral precepts are worthy of Christianity itself." [1]

III. THE EPIC POEMS AND PURĀNAS

The eighteen Purānas and the two great Epics—the Rāmāyana and Mahābhārata—and the five chief Tantras are the principal sources of our knowledge of the gods of modern India. It must be confessed that to the majority of Hindus "the Veda is a mere name—a name of high authority, often invoked and greatly reverenced—but its language is unintelligible and its gods and rites things of the past. The Purānas and later writings are the great authorities of modern Hinduism ; their mythology and legends fill the popular mind and mould its thoughts. The wonderful tales of the great poems, also, exercise a supreme influence. The heroes of these poems are heroes still ; their exploits, with many exaggerations and embellishments are recounted in prose and verse by hundreds of wandering priests and recited in every temple." [2]

[1] Monier Williams, *Hinduism*, pp. 54–5.

[2] Dowson, *Classical Dictionary*, Introduction xiv.

Little is known as to the date of the Epics beyond that they are later than the Vedas and earlier than the Purānas, A number of scholars place the Rāmāyana at 500 B.C., but some date it earlier, while others say it could not have been composed before 100 B.C.

The Mahābhārata was supposed to be written by Vyāsa a century nearer our own time, but the truth is it is not so much a poem with a single subject as a vast storehouse of Hindu mythology, legendary history, ethics, and philosophy. It is the growth of centuries of Hindu thought. Some parts of it date as early as the fifth century B.C., and others (mainly obvious interpolations in the text) as late as the seventh or eighth century A.D. Altogether it contains 220,000 lines, and fully justifies the saying, "What is not in the Mahābhārata is not in Bhārata (India) so vast it is."

The Rāmāyana (*Rāma* and *ayana* = "the goings or adventures of Rāma") contains only about 50,000 lines, and is largely one continuous narrative written by the sage Vālmīki in pure, flowing style. It is greatly admired, and presents a charming idyll of Hindu life. The mild and gentle Rāma, "husband of one wife," true in thought and noble in action, and Sītā, his faithful wife, pure as the stainless snow, are rightly held in the highest honour.

Unlike the Vedas, the Epics and Purānas may be read by other than Brāhmans. The fourth class of Hindu—the Śūdra—is permitted to hear them read but not to read them. At the end of the first section of the Rāmāyana a promise of great reward is held out to those who read the book:

> "A Brāhmin reading it acquires learning and eloquence;
> A Kshatriya (warrior) reading it will become a monarch;
> A Vaisya will obtain vast commercial profits; and
> A Śūdra *hearing* it read will become great."

And in this poem as well as in the sister poem occur these oft-repeated words:

> "He who reads and repeats this holy life-giving book is liberated from all sins, and exalted with all his posterity to the highest heaven."

The Purānas succeed these two great poems, but at a considerable distance of time. The proof of this is that the Epics treat the deeds and achievements of the heroes described by them as those of men only, but in the Purānas they have had time to assume divinity and the hero has merged into the god. Their composition covers a wide area and dates from A.D. 600 to A.D. 1600. They are the scriptures of modern Hinduism, which assumed their present form slightly earlier than the time of Sankarachārya, the great Saivite reformer, who flourished in the eighth or ninth century. They are not authorities for Hinduism as a whole ; they are special guides for separate and often conflicting branches and sects, written for the evident purpose of promoting either Vishnu or Śiva worship at the expense of the other god. In them the simple primitive fancies suggested by the operations of Nature have become supplanted by the wild imaginings of a more advanced civilisation, and of a more corrupt state of society. They are the stronghold of polytheism, pantheism, and idolatry. Legends about some of the Vedic gods and gods of later times abound. Together with the advocacy of the Purānic gods, each of which is honoured with separate chapters, in which he is supremely praised and lauded above the other gods, the worship of planets is developed, rivers are deified, and many animals and birds receive divine worship as the "Vāhans" or vehicles of the gods and goddesses. Certain trees also are regarded as sacred and receive worship. We may therefore regard the Purānas as giving sanction to the later and more extravagant developments of Hinduism.

"Each Purāna, according to Amara Sinha, a Sanskrit lexicographer, should have six main characteristic topics, viz., the creation, destruction, and renovation of the world, a genealogy of the gods and patriarchs, the reigns of the Manus (rulers over long periods of time), and a history of the Solar and Lunar race of kings. No one Purāna answers these six tests, but the Vishnu Purāna most nearly accords with it." [1]

[1] Stäcker's *Arsenal*, p. 70.

These books, though originally written in Sanskrit, have been translated, in part or the whole, into the various vernaculars and, when the people cannot read, the practice is for their Guru, or the itinerating Brāhman priest, to read a portion of them on his periodic visits. So not only is the knowledge of these books widely disseminated, but by means of them stability and permanence is given to Hindu worship and practice.

IV. The Tantras

This is a series of sixty-four books, only five of which are of importance. The word means "rule" or "ritual," and they were possibly written about the sixth century A.D., or later, in form of a dialogue between Śiva and Pārvatī. Their chief peculiarity is the prominence they give to the female energy of the deity. The god is represented as quiescent, his active nature being personified by his Śakti (or wife). Special prominence is given to the god Śiva to whose gloomy and somewhat repulsive worship is added the bloody and often licentious rites connected with the worship of the Devī, his wife. As Śiva was partly the creator and the bringer of blessings and partly the terrible destroyer, so his wife is partly the mild and benignant Umā or Pārvatī, and partly the ferocious and bloodthirsty Kālī or Durgā. Unfortunately the worship of Kālī and her fiercer manifestations, through motives of fear, very largely prevails over that of the mild and gentle Umā.

The Śaktas (or worshippers of the female energy) are divided into two classes: the Dakshināchāris, or "right hand" worshippers, and the Vāmāchāris, or "left-hand" worshippers. The former class are respectable and reputable in their mode of worship and usually substitute offerings of grain and milk for animal sacrifices. The latter class, which fortunately is not very prevalent, has a partienlarly revolting type of worship, and is a most degraded sect. The female principle is worshipped not only symbolically, but in the person of a living woman. Sexual love and carnal passion is believed to gratify the goddess, and in one of the Tantras we read :

"The only salvation is that which results from liquors, flesh, and co-habitation with women."[1]

The Tantras recommend the use of Mantras or spells which when properly uttered become all-powerful. Modern Theosophists make a good deal of some of the Tantras as books of occult arts.

The following striking passage from Professor Max Müller sums up the relative value of the sacred books of the Hindus :

"A Hindu who believes only in the Veda would be much nearer to Christianity than those who follow the Purānas and the Tantras. From a European point of view there is, no doubt, even in the Veda a great deal that is absurd and childish ; and from a Christian point of view there is but little that we can fully approve. But there is no trace in the Veda of the atrocities of Śiva and Kālī, nor of the licentiousness of Krishna, nor of the miraculous adventure of Vishnu. We find in it no law to sanction the blasphemous pretensions of a priesthood to divine honours, or the degradation of any human being to a state below the animal. There is no text to countenance laws which allow the marriage of children and prohibit the re-marriage of child-widows, and the unhallowed rite of burning the widow with the corpse of her husband is both against the spirit and the letter of the Veda."[2]

[1] Monier Williams, referring to these abuses, writes : "In Śaktism we are confronted with the worst results of the most superstitious ideas that have ever disgraced and degraded the human race."

[2] Max Müller, *Chips*, ii. 313.

PART II

THE VEDIC GODS

CHAPTER I

DYAUS PITAR AND PRITHIVĪ, THE HEAVEN FATHER AND EARTH MOTHER

DYAUS (related to Div = "to shine") is the Greek Zeus, and the Latin Deus. From Deus comes the English word Deity, which suggests a god who is Light. Hence this deity is often invoked as Dyaus Pitar, the Sky, or Heaven Father.

Max Müller says:—

"If I were asked what I consider the most important discovery which has been made in the Nineteenth Century with respect to the ancient history of mankind, I should answer by the following short equation:—Sanscrit, DYAUS-PITAR = Greek, Zeus Pater = Latin, Jupiter = Old Norse, TYR. Think what this formula suggests. It implies not only that our ancestors and the ancestors of Homer and Cicero, in their undivided primitive home, spoke the same language as the people of India—a discovery which, however incredible at first, has long ceased to cause surprise—but it also implies and proves that at one time they all held the same faith and worshipped the same supreme Deity under the same name—a name which meant *Heaven Father.*"

"Thousands of years have passed away since the Aryan nations separated to travel North and South, West and East: they have formed their own languages; they have founded empires and philosophies; they have built temples and razed them to the ground; they have all grown older and it may be wiser and better; but when they search for a name for that which is most exalted and yet most dear to every one of us, when they wish to express both awe and love, the infinite and the finite, they can but do what their old fathers did when gazing up into the eternal sky and feeling the presence of a Being as far and as near as can be; they can but combine the self-same words and utter once more the primeval Aryan prayer, *Heaven Father,* in that form which will endure for ever 'Our Father which art in Heaven.'"

The Heaven Father and the Earth Mother are the most ancient of the Vedic deities, and are revered as the primitive pair from whom the rest of the Vedic gods sprung. They are described in the Vedas as "great, wise, and energetic." They "promote happiness and lavish gifts upon their worshippers." Not only are they the creators, but also the preservers of all their offspring, and are beneficent and kind to all.

Their marriage is a most poetic conception.[1] "The Vedas,"[2] says Huxley, "set before us a world of rich and vigorous life, full of joyous, fighting men

'That ever with a frolic welcome took
The thunder and the sunshine' . . ."

Yet these rough, primitive people pictured the bright, wide-spreading Heaven taking into its strong embrace the rich bountiful Earth which stretched beneath it. The Aitareya Brāhmana says:

"The gods then brought the two, Heaven and Earth together, and when they came together they performed a wedding of the gods."

The Greek similarly addressed the Earth as "the Mother of the gods, wife of the starry heavens."[3]

[1] In the Aitareya Brāhmana, iv. 27, reference is made to the marriage of Heaven and Earth:

"These two worlds (heaven and earth) were once joined, (subsequently) they separated. (After their separation) there fell neither rain, nor was there sunshine.

"The five classes of beings (gods, men, &c.) then did not keep peace with one another. (Thereupon) the gods brought about a reconciliation of both these worlds. Both contracted with one another a marriage according to the rites observed by the gods." It is observed by a recent French author, M. Albert Reville, that "the marriage of Heaven and Earth forms the foundation of a hundred mythologies."

[2] *Evolution and Ethics*, Romanes Lecture, 1894.

[3] In the 41st fragment of Aeschylus (from the "Danaides") Aphrodite is introduced as saying:

"The pure Heaven loves to inflict on the Earth an amorous blow; and desire seizes the earth to obtain the nuptial union. Rain falling

We have considerable reason to believe "that Indra gradually superseded Dyaus in the worship of the Hindus soon after their settlement in India. As the praises of the newer god were sung, the older one was forgotten, and at the present day, whilst Dyaus is almost unknown, Indra is still regarded; but in the Vedas both are called "the god of heaven."[1] The explanation of this change is, as in the case of most of the changes in early Hindu religious ideas, a climatic one. The early Aryans in their common home in Central Asia, where bleak winds howling over cheerless steppes constituted their daily experience, looked to the brilliant radiance of heaven as the holiest and most divine thing in their experience. Then when they settled on the sultry Indian plains where the sun pours down its well-nigh intolerable heat they longed and prayed for the cooling, life-giving showers at Indra's disposal. So Dyaus was quickly forgotten and Indra reigned supreme.

Dyaus, however, for some time continued to be invoked in connection with the worship of the Earth Mother, Prithivī.[2]

The Vishnu Purāna[3] gives us the story of Prithivī's origin: "There was a king named Venā, notorious for his wickedness and general neglect of religious duties. When the Rishis (sages) of that age could bear his impiety no longer, they

---

from the moist Heaven impregnates the Earth, who brings forth for mortals the food of sheep, and the sustenance of Demeter. The verdure of the woods also is perfected by the showers proceeding from this marriage. Of all these things I (Aphrodite) am in part the cause."

[1] Wilkins, *Hindu Mythology*, p. 14.

[2] "At the festivals (I worship) with offerings, and celebrate the praises of Heaven and Earth, the promoters of righteousness, the great, the wise, the energetic, who, having gods for their offspring, thus lavish with the gods the choicest blessings in consequence of our hymn.

"With my invocations I adore the thought of the beneficent Father, and that mighty inherent power of the mother. The prolific Parents have made all creatures, and through their favours (have conferred) wide immortality on their offspring."—*Rig-Veda*, i. 159, 1 and 2.

[3] Wilkins, pp. 14–15.

slew him. But then a worse thing happened: anarchy prevailed and they felt that a bad king was better than no king at all. Upon this they rubbed the thigh of the deceased Venā and there came forth a black dwarf whom they rejected as their king. The right arm of the corpse was then rubbed, and from it came a beautiful shining prince named Prithu, who reigned in his father's place. During his reign there was a terrible famine in the land, and as the Earth would not yield her fruits great distress prevailed. Prithu, moved by the troubles of his people, said: 'I will slay the Earth and make her yield her fruits.' Terrified at this threat, the Earth assumed the form of a cow, and was pursued by Prithu even to the heaven of Brahmā.

"At length, wearied by the chase, she turned to him and said: 'Know you not the sin of killing a female that you thus try to slay me?' The king replied that 'when the happiness of many is secured by the destruction of one malignant being the slaughter of that being is an act of virtue.' 'But,' said the Earth, 'if, in order to promote the welfare of your subjects, you put an end to me, whence, O best of monarchs, will your people derive their support?' The Earth then declared that, at the king's command, she would restore all vegetable products 'as developed from her milk.' 'Do you, therefore, for the benefit of mankind give me a calf so that I may be able to secrete milk. Make also all places level, so that I may cause my milk, the seed of all vegetation, to flow everywhere around.' Prithu acted on this advice. Before his time there was no cultivation, no pasture, no agriculture, no highways for merchants. All civilisation originated in the reign of Prithu. . . . When the ground was made level, the king induced his subjects to take up their abode. . . . He therefore, having made the calf, milked the Earth, and received into his own hand the milk from which proceeded all kinds of corn and vegetables upon which the people now subsist. By granting life to the Earth Prithu became as her father and thence she derived the patronymic, Prithivī."

This legend with variations is found in most of the Purānas. Professor Wilson says: "These are all probably subsequent modifications of the original simple allegory which typifies the Earth as a cow, who yielded to every class of things the milk that they desired, or the object of their wishes."[1]

Prithivī, as a personification of the Earth, also represents Patience. Hindus in their proverbs refer to her as an example of the greatest forbearance. She permits herself to be lacerated with ploughs, to be wounded and bruised, and to suffer every indignity without resentment or murmuring. On the contrary, she actually returns good for evil and confers her richest favours on those who harm her most.

"The worship of the Earth assumes many forms. The pious Hindu does reverence to her when he rises from his bed in the morning and even the indifferently religious man worships her when he begins to plough and sow. In the Punjab when a cow or buffalo is first bought, or when she gives milk after calving, the first five streams of milk drawn from her are allowed to fall on the ground in honour of the goddess, and at every time of milking the first stream is so treated.

"Throughout North India the belief in the sanctity of

[1] *Dyaus Pitar and Prithivī.*—A curious variant of this myth is found among the Khonds of Orissa who give the Earth goddess the most remarkable place in their worship. Their legends say that Boora Pennu or Bella Pennu, the Light-god or Sun-god, created Tari Pennu, the Earth goddess, for his consort and from them were born the other great gods. But strife arose between the mighty parents and the wife tried all ways to thwart the good creation of her husband and to cause all physical and moral ill. This is their explanation of the origin of sin. This evilly-disposed Earth goddess had to be propitiated by hideous human sacrifices known as the Meriah sacrifices, the suppression of which is a matter of recent Indian history. With dances and drunken orgies and a mystery play to explain in dramatic dialogue the purpose of the rite the priest offered Tari Pennu her sacrifice, and prayed for children and cattle and poultry and brazen pots and all wealth; every man and woman wished a wish and they tore the slave-victim piecemeal and spread the morsels over the fields they wished to fertilise. See Macpherson, *India*, ch. vi.

the Earth is universal. The dying man is laid on mother Earth at the moment of dissolution,[1] and so is the mother at the time of parturition. Earth again is regarded as a remedy for disease. It is used frequently as a poultice, and an application for the cure of wounds and sores, and not unnaturally often causes great mischief and irritation."[2]

At the side of a Mission Compound in North India is a tank which during half the year is dried up. The women of a neighbouring Chamār village, before any wedding, go in procession to the dry tank to fetch from it the sacred earth used to make the marriage altar and fireplace on which the wedding feast is cooked. The ground close to which the earth is taken away is smeared with vermilion, and marigold flowers are scattered here and there, while pūjā (worship) is offered before the soil is removed. The earth is always given by the digger to a maiden, usually the prospective bride herself, and married women are not allowed to touch it. The maiden receives it into her sāri (dress) and heads the procession on its return to the village. This rite is performed with secrecy, and usually at nightfall, and must surely be a relic of ancient earth-worship.

[1] "'till like ripe fruit thou drop
Into thy mother's lap."
—MILTON, *Paradise Lost*, ix. 273.

[2] W. Crooke, *Popular Religion and Folk-Lore in Northern India*, i. 13.

CHAPTER II

AGNI, THE FIRE GOD

> " Great Agni, though thine essence be but one,
> Thy forms are three ; as fire thou blazest here,
> As lightning flashest in the atmosphere,
> In heaven thou flamest as the golden sun."
>
> —DR. MUIR, *O.S.T.*, p. 221.

WITH the exception of Indra more hymns are addressed to Agni (Latin *Ignis*, " fire ") in the Vedas than to any other deity. Several reasons may be adduced for this. Fire is very necessary for human existence. It enables food to be cooked. By its agency work can be carried on at night, and the demons that people the darkness lose their terrors. Then, to the ancients, as also to the primitive peoples in India to-day, there was always something very mysterious in the origin of fire. In some magic way the god was called into existence by friction out of two pieces of wood. He was even ready to leap forth out of the hard rock. Little wonder that a vast mythology sprang up regarding this marvellous deity.

Before very long, fire was identified by the Vedic poets as light and heat. Then the presence of Agni was discerned not only in the warmth of the fire on the hearth and altar, but in the Dawn, in the Sun, and in that bright world that lies beyond the Sun. So Agni appears in three phases: in heaven as the Sun, in mid-air as lightning, and on earth as ordinary fire.

" In old Vedic hymns there is an interesting reference to Agni. He is spoken of as dwelling between two pieces of wood. It is noticed as a remarkable fact that a living being should spring out of dry, dead wood. Stranger even than this. The child, Agni, as soon as he is born, begins to consume the wood, his parents, that gave him birth. Wonderful indeed is his growth, seeing he is born, says the Vedic poet, 'of a mother who cannot nourish him, but whom, as he grows, he destroys!' "[1]

So in a comparatively short time Agni rose into great prominence. The gods themselves owed to Agni their splendour, and the gift of immortality was his; his divine spark was latent in all things and could vivify the dead. He was celebrated as an immortal who made his abode with mortal men, their domestic priest who rose before dawn, and, as soon as the fire was kindled on the hearth in the dim morning light, the whole family gathered round it, regarding it with love and awe; at once as a friend and a priest—a visible god deigning to sit as guest in the very dwellings of men, the witness of their actions, their counsellor and director. He was the first to kindle the sacrificial fire, and as the fire spread upwards it was held to convey the oblation and sacrifices of mortals to the gods, and Agni was considered the mediator between men and gods. As evening drew on, and the darkness deepened, Agni was the only divinity left on earth to dispel the terrors of the night. When his gracious beams shone forth the hearts of men took courage again, for what power had the demons over them when Agni was present to succour and save? No wonder indeed that the very first hymn in the Rig-Veda—one of the earliest poems extant in any language—is addressed to Agni. The hymn is translated by Griffith as follows:

" I laud Agni, the greatest high priest, god, and minister of sacrifice,
The herald, lavishest of wealth,
Worthy is Agni to be praised by living as by ancient seers,
He shall bring hitherward the gods.
Through Agni man obtaineth wealth, yea, plenty, waxing day by day
Most rich in heroes, glorious.
Agni, the flawless sacrifice, which thou encompassest about
Verily goeth to the gods.
May Agni, sapient-minded priest, truthful, most gloriously great
The god, come hither with the gods.

[1] Wilkins, *Hindu Mythology*, pp. 23–7.

AGNI, THE FIRE GOD.

NARAYAN (VISHNU), THE SUN GOD,
being worshipped by DHROO (KASYAPA), the
Pole Star.

Whatever blessing, Agni, thou wilt grant thy worshippers,
That Agni, is thy true gift.
To thee, dispeller of the night, O Agni, day by day with prayer
Bringing thee reverence we come:
Ruler of sacrifices, guard of Law Eternal, Radiant One,
Increasing in thine own abode,
Be to us easy of approach, even as a father to his son,
Agni, be with us for our weal."

The presence of Agni to this day is invoked on all solemn occasions by the Hindus. The bride still circumambulates the sacred fire, the dead are still consigned to that dread element. At solemn sacrifices, clarified butter is the offering made to Agni. As the flame mounts higher and higher when fed by the butter the gods are said to have devoured the gift and thereby signified their pleasure and satisfaction at the burnt offering. Somewhat facetiously the gods are said to have two mouths: the Brāhman (type of a devouring nature) and Agni!

In later days Agni has lost the pre-eminence he enjoyed in the Vedas, where he is the son of the Heavens and the Earth, and Indra's twin brother.

In the Mahābhārata the reason given is that he has exhausted his vigour by devouring too many oblations. He was said to be desirous of recruiting his shattered health by devouring the whole Khāndava forest. This, Indra for a long time prevented him from doing, but by the help of Krishna he succeeded in his object.

In India there may yet be found the so-called Fire priests (Agnihotri) who perform according to the Vedic rite the sacrifices entitling worshippers to heavenly life. The sacred fire-drill for churning the new fire by friction of wood (arani) is used so that Agni still is new born of twirling fire sticks and receives the melted butter of sacrifice.

Agni is represented as a corpulent man, red in colour, with two faces, and eyes, eyebrows, and hair of a reddish tawny hue. He has three legs and seven arms. He rides a ram and has that animal emblazoned on his banner. From his mouths forked tongues or flames issue, by means of which he licks up the butter used in sacrifices. These characteristics have each and all their special significance. The two faces represent the two fires, solar and terrestrial, or creative heat and destructive fire. The three legs probably refer to the three sacred fires of the Brāhmans—the nuptial, the ceremonial or funeral, and the sacrificial; or they may denote his power over the three portions of the universe—the celestial, terrestrial, and infernal regions, which is manifested by the three forms he takes, sun, lightning, and sacrificial fire. His seven arms, like the seven heads of Sūrya's horse, are originally derived from the prismatic divisibility of a ray of light, or may denote the universal power of the all-pervading nature of fire.

Whatever may be the explanation of the mysterious import of the numbers, three and seven, it is interesting to find that these are the favourite numbers amongst Hindu, Jewish, Muhammadan, and Christian peoples, the Buddhist alone stands out for the number eight.

> " Fire ! Seven are thy fuels ; seven thy tongues ;
> Seven thy holy sages ; seven thy beloved abodes
> Seven ways do sacrificers worship thee ; thy
> Sources are seven. Be content with this
> Clarified butter : may this oblation be efficacious."
>
> —*The Brāhman Prayer to Agni.*

CHAPTER III

SŪRYA, OR SAVITRI, THE SUN GOD

" Fountain of living Light;
But far more glorious He, who said serene,
BE! and THOU WAST—Himself unform'd, unchang'd, unseen."
—SIR W. JONES, *Hymn to Sūrya.*

THIS deity rejoices in several names, but these are the two names interchangeably given to him in the Vedas. Some think Sūrya is used when the sun is visible, and Savitri when invisible to his worshippers;[1] but from the character ascribed to Savitri in the Vedas, it seems more natural to regard him as the sun shining in his strength, and Sūrya as the rising and setting sun. Savitri is described as "golden-eyed, golden-handed, and golden-tongued. He rides the heavens in a chariot drawn by seven ruddy, white-footed mares. As the Vivifier and Quickener he raises his long arms of gold in the morning, rouses all beings from their slumber, infuses energy into them, and buries them in sleep in the evening."[2]

Sūrya is one of the three supreme deities of the Vedas, and with Agni and Vāyu he constitutes the earliest Hindu Triad. His ancient title is Prajāpati, " Lord of Creatures," because he was regarded as the great source of light and

[1] The following curious passage occurs in the Aitareya Brāhmana, iii. 44:

" The Sun neither ever sets or rises. When people think he sets, he (only) turns himself round, after reaching the end of the day, and makes night below and day above. Then when people think he rises in the morning he (only) turns himself round after reaching the end of the night, and makes day below and night above. In truth, he never sets. The man who knows this, that the sun never sets, enjoys union and sameness of nature with him and abides in the same sphere."

[2] Wilkins, *Hindu Mythology*, p. 33.

warmth, and therefore lord of life itself. His ancestry is distinguished and worthy of so great a deity. He is called the son of Dyaus Pitar, the Heaven Father. Ushas (Aurora) was his daughter. The two Asvins, his charioteers and physicians to the gods, ever young and handsome, were his twin sons by Sanjnā, who fled from him in the form of a mare. In their three-wheeled chariot they make the circuit of the world every day.

Sir Monier Williams has translated one of the Vedic hymns to the Sun: [1]

"Behold the rays of Dawn, like heralds, lead on high
The Sun, that men may see the great all-knowing God.
The Stars shrink off like thieves, in company with Night,
Before the all-seeing eye, whose beams reveal his presence,
Gleaming like brilliant flames, to nation after nation. . . .
Sūrya, with flaming locks, clear-sighted god of day.
The seven ruddy mares bear on thy rushing car.
With these thy self-yoked steeds, seven daughters of thy chariot,
Onward thou dost advance. To thy refulgent orb
Beyond this lower gloom, and upward to the light
Would we ascend, O Sun, thou god among the gods."

Sūrya's wife was Sanjnā, daughter of Visvakarma (Tvashtri), the Hindu Vulcan. She bore him three children, of whom one was Yama, Judge and Regent of the Dead. But after living with him for some years she was so utterly oppressed by his brightness and glory that she was compelled to leave him. She returned to her father's house, but left Chhāyā (the Shade) in her place, who bore him two sons, the morning and the evening twilight. Her father was angry with her for forsaking her husband, but, as he considered her complaint reasonable, he put the luminary on his lathe and cut away one-eighth of his effulgence, trimming him in every part except his feet. The fragments that were cut off fell blazing to the earth, and out of them Visvakarma shaped the wonder-working Discus of Vishnu, the trident of Śiva, the

[1] *Indian Wisdom*, p. 19.

lance of Kārtikeya (the god of war), and the weapons of Kuvera (the god of riches). Then Sanjnā consented to return to her too glorious husband.

Max Müller shows us very clearly the processes by which the Sun has gradually developed into a supreme being; still after all the centuries worshipped as one of the great gods of the Hindus:

"The first step leads us from the mere light of the sun to that light which in the morning wakes man from sleep, and seems to give new life, not only to man, but to the whole of nature. He who wakes us in the morning, who recalls the whole of nature to new life, is soon called 'the giver of daily life.'

"Secondly, by another and bolder step, the giver of daily light and life becomes the giver of light and life in general. He who brings light and life to-day, is the same who brought life and light in the first of days. As light is the beginning of the day, so light was the beginning of creation, and the sun, from being a mere light bringer or life giver, becomes a creator, then soon also a ruler of the world.

"Thirdly, as driving away the dreaded darkness of the night and likewise as fertilising the earth, the sun is conceived as a defender and kind protector of all living things.

"Fourthly, as the sun sees everything and knows everything, he is asked to forget and forgive what he alone knows."[1]

"Passing on to medieval times it is clear that, in the days of Sankara, there were a large number of persons who adored the Sun as their exclusive divinity. These were divided into six sects as follows:

"1. Worshippers of the rising Sun as identified with Brahmā.

"2. Worshippers of the meridian Sun as identified with Śiva.

"3. Worshippers of the setting Sun as identified with Vishnu.

"4. Worshippers of the Sun in all three phases as identified with the Tri-mūrti. (See p. 82.)

[1] *Hibbert Lectures*, pp. 265, 266.

"5. Worshippers of the Sun regarded as a material being in the form of a man with golden beard and golden hair. Zealous members of this sect refused to eat anything in the morning till they had seen the Sun rise.

"6. Worshippers of an image of the Sun formed in the mind. These continually meditated on the Sun and were in the habit of branding representations of his disk on their foreheads, arms, and breasts."[1]

"The Emperor Akbār endeavoured, Muhammadan though he was, to introduce a special form of Sun worship into his dominions. He ordered his subjects to adore the Sun four times a day; morning, noon, evening, and midnight. His majesty had one thousand and one Sanskrit names of the Sun collected, and read them daily, devoutly turning to the Sun. He then caught hold of both his ears by their upper parts and turning himself quickly round used to strike the lower ends (the lobes) with his fists. He ordered his band to play at midnight, and was weighed against gold at his solar anniversary."[2]

To this deity worship has been rendered for many centuries and is continued up to the present day. There are now few temples and images to the Sun; but every devout Hindu, on rising in the morning, stands on one leg, and with face turned eastward, addresses him with the Gāyatrī, the most sacred text in the Vedas:

"May we attain the excellent glory of the divine Vivifier; so may he enlighten, or stimulate our understanding."

It is a text which when recited conveys incalculable benefits to the user. The Skanda Purāna says:

"Nothing in the Vedas is superior to the Gāyatrī. No invocation is equal to it as no city is equal to Kāsi (Benares). The Gāyatrī is the mother of the Vedas, and of the Brāhmans. By repeating it a

---

[1] Monier Williams, *Religious Thought and Life in India*, p. 342.

[2] Blockman's translation of the *Ain-i-Akbari*, p. 266.

man is saved. What is there, indeed, that cannot be effected by the Gāyatrī? For the Gāyatrī is Vishnu, Brahmā, and Śiva and the three Vedas."

After this eulogy can we be surprised at the continuance of Sun worship?

"Nowadays the Sun has largely become a village godling under the name of Sūraj Nārāyan, or 'Nārāyan (or Vishnu) occupying the Sun.' In the chilly winter mornings, as you wake in camp, you can often hear the coolies yawning and muttering Sūraj Nārāyan as the first gleam of light spreads over the eastern sky. One of the marks of Nārāyan worship is that many villagers in North India do not eat salt on Sundays (which corresponds, curiously enough, with our own day of rest) and will not sell their milk for making butter on that day, but prefer to use it in making rice cakes to give to the Brāhmans. It is the custom to walk "with the Sun" in circumambulating a shrine or temple. When the bride and bridegroom circle the sacred fire in the marriage ceremony they follow the course of the Sun. The Hindu bride is brought out to salute the rising Sun on the morning after she has begun to live with her husband. 'Happy truly is the bride on whom the Sun shines.' The cattle when treading out the corn follow the path of the sun.

"There is a special sect of Sun Worshippers called the Nīmbārak. They are Vaishnavas and, as their name implies, they worship 'the Sun in the Nīm tree.' The story runs that their founder invited a Bairāgi (a wandering ascetic) to dine with him. He prepared the dinner, but unfortunately delayed to call his guest until the Sun had well nigh set. Now the holy man was forbidden by the rules of his order to eat except during the daytime, and was afraid he would be compelled to refuse the dinner; but at the solicitation of his host, Sūraj Nārāyan, the Sun god, descended on the Nīm tree under which the feast was spread and continued beaming upon them till the feast was over." [1]

The Sun is believed to have descended from his chariot

[1] Crooke, *Popular Religion and Folk-Lore*, i. 5–12.

in human form and to have left traces on earth of his descent. The Ajodhya royal family of ancient times claimed the Sun as their progenitor. Rāma, the great hero-god, was Sun-descended. To-day the reigning family of the Udaipur Rājputs, a very ancient royal race, claim direct descent from the Sun. Consequently at Udaipur his worship has special prominence. The city bears many marks of the belief in this legend. The chief gate, the chief apartment of the palace, and the royal parasol, all bear the image of the Sun god.

VARUNA, THE OMNISCIENT GOD OF THE UNIVERSE, being reverenced by ŚIVA, PĀRVATĪ, BRAHMĀ, &c.

CHAPTER IV

VARUNA, THE OMNISCIENT GOD OF THE UNIVERSE

"Light-giving Varuna! Thy piercing glance doth scan
In quick succession all this stirring active world,
And penetrateth, too, the broad ethereal space,
Measuring our days and nights and spying out all creatures."

—*From the Rig-Veda* (translated by Monier Williams).

"VARUNA," says Max Müller, "is one of the most interesting creations of the Hindu mind, because, though we can still perceive the physical background from which he rises, the vast, starry, brilliant expanse above, his features more than those of any other Vedic god have been completely transfigured, and he stands before us as a god who watches over the world, punishes the evil-doer, and even forgives the sins of those who implore his pardon."

In the Rig-Veda an exceedingly high position is ascribed to Varuna. He is chief of the Ādityas, "inviolable, imperishable, eternal beings," sons of Aditi, an abstract, mysterious creation representing Infinity, who, as Muir says, "may best be regarded as a personification of universal, all-embracing Nature or Being." This great mother goddess had twelve sons, of whom the chief were Varuna, Mitra, Daksha, Indra, Savitri, and Sūrya. The name Varuna is derived from the Sanskrit *var* "to cover." He is, therefore, the god of the heavens covering all things. The same word in Greek is οὐρανός = "heaven," and he is clearly one of the earliest Aryan gods, worshipped by Greek and Aryan alike before the separation took place. At this early period he was the supreme deity. A mysterious presence, a mysterious power, and a mysterious knowledge were all ascribed to him. "He it is who makes the Sun to shine in the heavens; the winds that blow are but his breath; he has hollowed out the channels of the rivers which flow at his command, and he has made the depths of the sea. His ordinances are fixed and unassailable; through their operation the moon walks in brightness, and the stars which appear in the nightly sky vanish in daylight. The birds flying in the air, the rivers in their sleepless flow, cannot attain a knowledge of his power and wrath. But he knows the flight of the birds in the sky, the course of the far travelling wind, the paths of ships on the ocean, and beholds all the secret things that have been, or shall be, done. He witnesses men's truth and falsehood."[1]

In truth, omniscience is his outstanding attribute. The Sun and the thousand stars are his eyes searching out all that passes on earth, from which even darkness cannot hide. When two are in company he is the third. He is the god of the serene distant heaven, yet he is not far from any one of us.

> "His spies descending from the skies glide all this world around;
> Their thousand eyes, all scanning, sweep to earth's remotest bound.
> Whate'er exists in heaven and earth, whate'er beyond the skies,
> Before the eye of Varuna the thing unfolded lies.
> The secret winkings all he counts of every mortal's eyes
> And wields this universal frame as gamester throws his dice!"[2]

Still higher attributes than those in the translation of the Vedic hymn just quoted are ascribed to him in the Vedas. Indeed the attributes and functions ascribed to Varuna impart to his character an unparalleled moral grandeur and a sanctity far surpassing that attributed to any other Vedic deity. The early Aryan pleads with him:

> "Be gracious, O mighty God, be gracious. I have sinned through want of power; be gracious.
>
> "Seeking to perceive that sin, O Varuna, I inquire; I resort to the wise to ask. The sages all tell me the same; it is Varuna who is angry with thee. What great sin is it, Varuna, for which thou

[1] Muir, *O.S.T.*, V. 58. [2] *Ibid.*, V. 64.

seekest to slay thy worshipper and friend? Tell me, O unassailable and self-dependent god; and, freed from sin, I shall speedily come to thee for adoration. Release us from the sins of our fathers, and from those which we have committed in our own persons.

"It was not our will, Varuna, but some seduction which led us astray—wine, anger, dice, or thoughtlessness. The stronger perverts the weaker. Even sleep occasions sin."[1]

"In the Yajur-Veda the following is narrated of Varuna. He is found instructing Bhrigu, one of the Divine Rishis, as to the nature of Brahma, the Supreme Spirit, 'whence,' he says, 'all beings are produced; by which they live when born, towards which they tend, and unto which they pass.'

"Bhrigu, after meditating in devout contemplation, recognised food (or body or matter) to be Brahma: 'for all things are indeed produced from food; when born they live by food; towards food they tend; they pass into food.'

"Unsatisfied, however, after further meditation he discovered breath to be Brahma: 'for all things are indeed produced from breath; when born they live by breath; towards breath they tend; they pass into breath.'

"Again he sought Brahma in deep meditation, and discovered intellect to be Brahma: 'for all things are produced by thought,' &c., &c. This he understood, but coming to Varuna said, 'Venerable Father, make known to me Brahma.' Varuna replied, 'Inquire by devout contemplation; profound meditation is Brahma.'

"He thought deeply and then he knew 'ānanda' (or felicity) to be Brahma: 'for all things are indeed produced from desire; when born they live by joy; they tend towards happiness; they pass into felicity."[2]

Such is the science taught by Varuna of the origin of things.

"Varuna appears to have retained his supremacy as god of the illimitable universe as long as the Aryans were only in the Northern Panjāb; but by and by they spread to the

[1] Rig-Veda, vii. 86, 3–6.

[2] Moor's *Hindu Pantheon*, p. 275.

territory watered by the Jumna and Ganges, and he was superseded by the tumultuous Indra, the god of cloud and storm. The awful purity of the visible heaven, or of the invisible being presiding over it (for the Hindu made no distinction between the two) became oppressive, and they were not unwilling to forget him so fierce was his heat. But it was a deplorable fall when men began to say, 'The haughty Indra takes precedence of all the gods.'"[1]

In the Purānas a sad change comes over the scene. Varuna, from being one of the highest of the Vedic gods, becomes a mere god of the ocean, a second-rate Neptune. He carries about with him a kind of waterproof umbrella formed of the hood of a cobra and called "Ābhoga."[2] His moral character suffers a corresponding declension. Instead of hating sin, it is narrated of him in the Mahābhārata that he carried off the wife of the sage Utathya, and as Varuna would not restore her, Utathya drank up all the sea and then Varuna yielded. He also joined with Sūrya, the Sun god, in an intrigue with the courtesan Urvasī, by which means an eminent ascetic was born called Agastya.

It seems possible from the following legend found in the Rig-Veda[3] that human sacrifices may at one time have been offered to Varuna. A certain being, named Harischandra, had no son. On the advice of Nārada, the sage, he went to Varuna and said:

> "Let but a son be born, O King! to me,
> And I will sacrifice that son to thee."

Varuna granted the request. When the boy grew up, his father told him of the vow he had made, but unfortunately

[1] Murray Mitchell, *Great Religions of India*, p. 48.

[2] Professor Roth ventures a reason for this change: "When, on the one hand, the conception of Varuna as the all-embracing heaven had been established, and, on the other hand, the observation of the rivers flowing towards the ends of the earth and to the sea, had led to the conjecture that there existed an ocean enclosing the earth in its bosom, then the way was thoroughly prepared for connecting Varuna with the ocean."

[3] Monier Williams, *Indian Wisdom*, p. 29.

the son was not willing to be sacrificed, and ran away from home. Varuna, being displeased at the non-fulfilment of the king's vow, afflicted him with dropsy. For six years the boy wandered in the jungle; at length, happening to meet a poor Brāhman with his three sons, the prince proposed to purchase one of them to offer as a substitute for himself. The father would not give up his first-born, and the mother clung to the youngest, so the middle one was taken. When the boy was bound and ready to be sacrificed, he asked permission to recite some texts in praise of the gods. The deities that he lauded were so pleased that they interceded with Varuna to spare his life. Varuna granted their request and Harischandra recovered from the dropsy.

"Varuna is represented as a white man sitting on a fabulous marine monster with the head and front legs of an antelope and the body and tail of a fish. In his right hand he carries a noose. He is occasionally worshipped in seasons of drought, and by fishermen as they cast their nets, but nowadays no images of him are made." [1]

The Vedic deity Mitra is commonly associated with Varuna, and possesses similar attributes. There is a distinction between the two. Mitra is more generally represented as a god typifying the light of the day, whereas Varuna represented the starry expanse of the night. Hymns are frequently addressed to both interchangeably, and the same terms are employed to Mitra as to Varuna.

[1] Wilkins, *Hindu Mythology*, p. 43.

CHAPTER V

INDRA, THE RAIN GOD

"Mounted on the Sun's bright beam—
Darter of the swift blue bolt—
Sprinkler of genial dews and fruitful rains
Over hills and thirsty plains."

—*Vedic Hymn to Indra.*

PROMINENT amongst the deities of the Vedas, and most popular with the Aryan peoples is Indra. "In Sanskrit," says Max Müller, "the drops of rain are called *indu,* and he who sends them is called Ind-ra, the 'rainer,' the 'irrigator.'" In Roman mythology the corresponding deity is Jupiter Pluvius. "Indra is king of the stormy heavens, the god of thunder and of nature's elements, with inferior genii at his command; he governs the Eastern quarter of the world, and also presides over the celestial bands stationed on the Golden Mount Meru[1] where he solaces the gods with nectar and heavenly music. He resides in the celestial city of Amrāvati, where his palace is situated. There are to be found the Apsaras, the celestial dancing girls, and in the palace gardens grow the all-yielding trees, Pariyataka Kalpa-druma, and three others equally bountiful. The possession of even one of these trees would qualify its owner for the title which Indra bears of 'Lord of Wealth.' His consort is Indrānī, and he rides the elephant Airāvata, who was produced at the churning of the ocean, and is driven by Mātali."[2]

How can we explain the premier position of this deity? The climatic conditions under which the Aryan peoples lived

[1] A mythical mountain, probably situated in the Himālayas.
[2] Moor's *Hindu Pantheon,* p. 259.

are solely accountable for it. "In the Gangetic plain there are three great seasons—the cold, the hot, and the rainy. Towards the end of the hot season all nature languishes, the sun pours down its terrible heat, the water courses dry up, great rivers become mere trickling streams, all around are thousands of acres of sun-baked earth with scarcely a vestige of verdure for the starving cattle. The suffering people look up to the sky and see there the clouds, laden with life-giving waters, floating in from the ocean; but they move on impelled by demons who wish to chain them in the recesses of the mountains. The people call on Indra to avert widespread calamity and break the power of the cloud-compelling demons. They pour out to him large libations of the liquor which both he and they love so well—the Soma juice. The flash of the lightning is seen. It is Indra hurling his bolts against the demon Vritra. The thunder roars—Ah! that is the demon, struck, and howling as he flies away. Then the blessed waters rush down to earth, they change the desert into a garden, and man and beast, tree and flower rejoice in Indra's praise."[1] It is not surprising that in the Rig-Veda, amongst a large number of hymns to Indra the following hymn is found descriptive of his triumph over the demon of drought:

"Thou art our guardian, advocate, and friend,
A brother, father, mother—all combined.
Most fatherly of fathers, we are thine,
And thou art ours. Oh! let thy pitying soul
Turn to us in compassion when we praise thee,
And slay us not for one sin or for many.
Deliver us to-day, to-morrow, every day.
Vainly the demon dares thy might, in vain
Strives to deprive us of thy watery treasures.
Earth quakes beneath the crashing of thy bolts.
Pierced, shattered lies the foe—his cities crushed,
His armies overthrown, his fortresses
Shivered to fragments; then the pent up waters,
Released from long imprisonment, descend

---

[1] *Great Religions of India*, p. 44.

> In torrents to the earth, and swollen rivers
> Foaming and roaring to their western home,
> Proclaim the triumph of the Thunderer."[1]

The following Vedic references to Indra are also noteworthy:

"Now will I sing the feats of Indra, which he of the thunderbolt did of old. He smote Ahi (the cloud dragon) then he poured forth the waters, he divided the rivers of the mountains. He smote Ahi by the mountain where Tvashtri forged for him the glorious bolt."[2]

"Whet, O strong Indra, the heavy strong red weapon against the enemies."[3]

> "May the axe (the thunderbolt) appear with the light;
> May the red one blaze forth bright with splendour!"[4]

In the Vedas Indra holds high rank as the Son of the Heaven Father (Dyaus Pitar) and the Earth Mother (Prithivī). He is the twin brother of Agni, the god of fire. But the gods of the Hindus are like beings who reign for a time and then give place to successors. No sooner was Indra born than he manifested his ambition for supremacy. He called for his weapons and asked the Earth, his mother, "Who are renowned as fierce warriors?" Immediately after reaching manhood came the first struggle for supremacy in the Hindu Pantheon, a struggle destined to have many successors, and his father and mother, the bright blue heavens and the wide-spreading earth, were obliged to yield to his might.

"The divine Dyaus bowed before Indra, before Indra the great Earth bowed with her wide spaces."

His sovereignty, however, did not endure for long. In the Brāhmanic days he sinks to the rank of a secondary god, inferior to the great Hindu Triad, and liable at the end of every hundred divine years to be superseded by some other god or man who by his merit should raise himself to the

[1] Translated by Monier Williams.
[2] Rig-Veda, i. 32, 1. [3] *Ibid.*, iii, 34–9. [4] *Ibid.*, iv. 20.

INDRA AND HIS CONSORT INDRĀNĪ,
represented as worshipping ŚIVA, and his consort PĀRVATĪ,
with GANESHA in her arms

necessary status. The sacrifice of one hundred horses is sufficient for the purpose.[1] This inferiority is well represented by the accompanying illustration in which Indra and Indrānī are seen riding the white elephant, and worshipping Śiva, Pārvatī, and Ganesha mounted on the sacred bull Nandi, whose head takes the place of the head of the elephant. Indra is thus relegated to an inferior position to that of Śiva. This is characteristic of the whole process whereby the Vedic deities are degraded by the Brāhman authors of the Purānas to a lower level than their own greater gods.

This god is represented by a fair man riding a white elephant, Airāvata, whose trunk is said to be the water-spout. He has four arms. In one hand he holds the weapon Vajra, the terrible thunderbolt, in the others are seen a conch shell, bow and arrows, a hook and a net. He is still worshipped in some parts of India, especially in seasons of drought. His moral character is of the lowest. He is greatly addicted to drinking the intoxicating Soma juice. "Thy intoxication," it is said, "O, Indra, is most intense." "Impetuous as a bull," he rushes to the place "where liquor flows," and drinks it "like a thirsty stag."

> "Thou Indra, oft of old hast quaffed
> With keen delight our Soma draught;
> All gods the luscious Soma love
> But thou all other gods above."

The mighty Indra was thought to be especially fond of Soma juice, as the following extracts from the Rig-Veda will show.

> "I declare the mighty deeds of this mighty one; the true acts of this true one. At the Trikadruka festival Indra drank of the Soma, and in its exhilaration he slew Ahi (the demon). He propped up the vast sky in empty space. . . . Indra has done these things in the exhilaration of the Soma. He hath meted with his measures the eastern (regions) like a house; with his thunderbolt, he has opened up the sources of the rivers," &c.[2]

---

[1] See Wilkins, *Hindu Mythology*, p. 58.

[2] Rig-Veda, ii. 15, 1.

"1. I have verily resolved to bestow cows and horses: I have quaffed the Soma.

2. The draughts which I have drunk, impel me like violent blasts: I have quaffed the Soma.

3. The draughts which I have drunk impel me as fleet horses a chariot: I have quaffed the Soma.

4. The hymn (of my worshipper) has hastened to me, as a cow to her beloved calf: I have quaffed the Soma.

5. I turn the hymn round about in my heart as a carpenter a beam: I have quaffed the Soma.

6. The five tribes of men appear to me not even as a mote: I have quaffed the Soma.

7. The two worlds do not equal even one half of me: I have quaffed the Soma.

8. I surpass in greatness the heaven and this vast earth: I have quaffed the Soma.

9. Come, let me plant this earth either here or there: I have quaffed the Soma.

10. Let me smite the earth rapidly hither or thither: I have quaffed the Soma.

11. One half of me is in the sky, and I have drawn the other down: I have quaffed the Soma.

12. I am majestic; elevated to the heavens: I have quaffed the Soma.

13. I go prepared as a minister, a bearer of oblations to the gods: I have quaffed the Soma." [1]

From drunkenness he makes the easy descent to immorality and seduces the wife of his spiritual teacher, Gautama, and his profligacy has passed into a proverb. He is also represented as being exceedingly jealous of worship paid to other gods.

"Indra had in his heaven many Apsaras of surprising beauty. These he used to tempt ascetics who, by reason of their austerities, were endangering the dominion of the gods. One such ascetic, Visvāmitra, who for thousands of years had been engaged in the most rigid mortifications, was subjugated by the charms of the damsel, Menakā. 'What!' exclaimed at length, the reflecting sage, 'my wisdom, my austerities, my firm resolutions, all destroyed at once by a

[1] Rig-Veda, x. 119, 1–13.

woman? Seduced by the crime in which Indra delights I am stripped of the advantages arising from my penances!'"[1]

On one occasion Indra assumed the form of a shepherd boy so that he might more easily steal some pomegranate blossoms from a garden to deck the dark tresses of his consort Indrānī. The sequel is told in Sir William Jones' charming hymn to him:

"The reckless peasant, who these glowing flowers,
Hopeful of rubied fruit has fostered long,
Seized, and with cordage strong,
Shackled the god who gave him showers.
Straight from the seven winds immortal genii flew—
Varuna green, whom foamy waves obey;
Bright Vahni, flaming with the lamp of day;
Kuvera, sought by all, enjoyed by few;
Marut, who bids the wingéd breezes play;
Stern Yama, ruthless judge! and Isa cold;
With Narrit, mildly bold:
They, with the ruddy flash that points his thunder,
Rend his vain bands asunder.
Th' exulting god resumes his thousand eyes,
Four arms divine, and robes of changing dyes."

These "robes of changing dyes" are of course the clouds, and the "thousand eyes" were the marks of the displeasure of the gods for his intrigue with Gautama's wife.

The following is characteristic of the stories told of this god and his doings:

On a certain occasion many of the gods were invited to an entertainment in Indra's palace. To complete their happiness, several of the Apsaras, beautiful nymphs, danced before them. Gandharvasenu, son of Indra, was so fascinated with the charms of one of them and behaved so indelicately that his father commanded him to descend to earth in the form of an ass. All the assembled gods beseeched him to modify this sentence, and ultimately Indra agreed that his son should be an ass by day, but a man by night. With this he dismissed him to wander about the earth. One day a Brāhman

[1] Moor's *Hindu Pantheon*, p. 265.

came to bathe at a pond near which the ass was wandering. The animal spoke to him and told him he was Indra's son, and asked him to speak to King Dharu to give him his daughter in marriage. The Brāhman consented, and next day the king went with his counsellors and held a conversation with the ass, who related his story and the cause of his degradation. The king refused consent to the marriage unless the ass would perform some miracle to prove his descent. To this he agreed, and the following night he built a fort of iron, forty miles square and six high. Then the king was forced to yield, and appointed the day of marriage. The day came, and with splendid show, dancing, and music the bride, adorned with jewels and the richest attire, was led into the iron fort to be married to the ass. The bridegroom on seeing her could not refrain from giving voice. The guests on hearing the ass bray were filled with grief and astonishment. Some hid their faces with sorrow, some because of laughter. Others, more bold, went to the king and said: "O King, is this the son of Indra? O Monarch! you have found an excellent bridegroom. Don't delay the wedding! we never saw so glorious a match. We have heard of a camel being married to an ass, when the ass, looking on the camel said, 'Bless me! what a fine form!' and the camel, hearing the voice of the ass, said 'Dear me! what a sweet voice!' In that wedding the bride and the bridegroom were equal, but that your daughter should have such a bridegroom is truly wonderful!" Then the Brāhmans said, "O King! at some weddings, as a sign of joy, the sacred conch shell is blown, but thou hast no need of that" (alluding to the braying of the ass). The women then cried out, "O King! what is this! To give so angelic a damsel in marriage to an ass!"—the king felt ashamed and hung his head. At length Gandharvasenu reminded the king of his promise, and urged upon him that the body is merely a garment, that wise men never estimate the worth of a person by the clothes he wears, and, moreover, he was in this shape from the curse of his father, and during the night he would assume the form of a man. The king then withdrew his objection and the marriage was celebrated. By the time the guests were dismissed the night drew on, and a handsome man, suitably dressed, presented himself to the king. The king brought the bride in great state to the palace and gave her to her husband. The next day he gave jewels, horses, camels, and servants to her and dismissed the guests with suitable presents. Dharu, however, could not but feel anxious that his son-in-law should finally throw off his ass-body. After a thousand contrivances he said to himself, "Gandharvasenu is the son of Indra, therefore he can never die; at night he casts off his ass's body, which lies like a dead body. I will burn it and so keep him always in the form of a man." This he did and the curse was removed.

CHAPTER VI

SOMA, THE INDIAN BACCHUS

(AFTERWARDS IDENTIFIED WITH THE MOON)

"Thou nectar-beaming Moon,
Regent of dewy night—
Wilt thou desert so soon
Thy night flowers pale, whom liquid odour steeps,
And Oshadhi's translucent beam,
Gleaming in darkest glade?

. . . .

He fades, he disappears;
E'en Kasyapa's [1] gay daughters twinkling die,
And silence lulls the sky,
Till chatacs twitter from the moving brake,
And sandal-breathing gales on beds of ether wake."

—*Extract from Sir Wm. Jones' Hymn.*

THIS god is by far the most extraordinary Vedic creation. It well-nigh eclipses the fantasies of some of the later conceptions of deity found among the village godlings. A little plant, a creeper, almost destitute of leaves, whose pure white juice had a mild acrid taste, grew on the hills of the Panjāb, in the Bolan Pass, and in a few other northern situations. Some adventurous Aryans, wearied with their pilgrimage, found this plant produced a liquid which had remarkable powers. It dispelled weariness and depression of spirit and filled them with a strange gladness and exhilaration: [2] they felt

[1] The Pole Star.

[2] The close agreement of Hindu and classical mythology has often been noted in these pages. This is further illustrated by the following quotation from the *Bacchae* of Euripides, &c., p. 272, translated by Dr. Muir, which expresses the adoration of the Greeks for Dionysius, the Grecian Soma:

"I cannot express how great this young god, whom thou ridiculest, "the god within their veins" on quaffing the slightest drop. Professor Whitney explains how it came to be worshipped :[1] "The simple-minded Aryan people, whose religion was a worship of the wonderful powers and phenomena of nature, had no sooner perceived that this liquid had the power to elevate the spirits and produce a temporary frenzy, under the influence of which the individual was prompted to and capable of deeds beyond his natural powers, than they found in it something divine : it was to their apprehension a god, endowing those into whom it entered with godlike powers : the plant which afforded it became to them the king of plants ; the process of preparing it was a holy sacrifice and the instruments used in its manufacture were therefore sacred." Listen to their ancient drinking song :

> "We've quaffed the Soma bright
> And are immortal grown ;
> We've entered into light,
> And all the gods have known.
> What mortal now can harm,
> Or foeman vex us more ?
> Through thee, beyond alarm,
> Immortal God, we soar."[2]

---

is destined to become in Greece. For, young man, there are two things which are foremost among men, the Goddess Demeter, who is the Earth—call her by whichever name thou pleasest—who nourishes mortals with dry food. But he, the Son of Semele, took the contrary course. He discovered and introduced among men the liquid draught of the grape which puts an end to the sorrows of wretched mortals—when they are filled with the stream from the vine—and induces sleep and oblivion of the evils endured by day. Nor is there any other remedy for our distresses. He, born a god, is poured out in libations to gods, so that through him men receive good. . . . And this god is a prophet. For Bacchic excitement and raving have in them great prophetic power. When this god enters in force into the body, he causes men to rave and foretell the future. And he also partakes of the character of Ares (Mars). For panic (sometimes) terrifies a force of armed men drawn up in battle array, before the actual clashing of hosts. This madness too is derived from Dionysius."

[1] Some scholars dispute this account of the origin of Soma worship.

[2] Muir, *O.S.T.*, V. 130.

Henceforth the plant became to them a god; and Soma, the invisible spirit that animated the wondrous fermented juice, had divine attributes ascribed to him, and divine honours paid to him. He is addressed as a god in the highest strains of veneration. All powers belong to him, and all blessings are his to bestow. He clothes the naked, heals the sick, gives sight to the blind, and power to the impotent. He is able also to confer immortality on gods and men. Future happiness is asked from him:

"Place me, O Pavamāna, in that everlasting and imperishable world where there is eternal light and glory."[1]

In fact there is no limit to the honour paid to this most popular deity. The whole of the Ninth Book of the Rig-Veda, containing no less than 114 hymns, is devoted to his praise, and constant references are made to him in many other hymns beside.

Of Soma's origin we have this account in the Vedas. Soma dwelt amongst the Gandharvas, the choristers of Indra's heaven, and the gods, knowing his heavenly virtues, wished to obtain him. Gāyatrī, Brahmā's wife, in the form of a bird tried first to bring him away, but was prevented by his guardians, the Gandharvas; then Vāch (the goddess of speech) said: "The Gandharvas are fond of women; let me go, and I will obtain him for you." The gods said "How can we spare you?" She replied, "Let me obtain the god; and I will return to you, whenever you may want me." The Gandharvas could not resist her seductions and allowed her to bring Soma away and present him to the gods.

"When Soma was first brought to the notice of the gods a dispute arose as to who should have the first draught. At length, it was agreed to decide it by a race. Vāyu (the wind) first reached the goal, Indra being second. Indra tried hard to win, and when near the winning post proposed that they should reach it together, Vāyu taking two-thirds of the drink. "Not so," said Vāyu, "I will be the sole winner." Then

[1] Rig-Veda, ix. 113–7.

Indra said, "Let us come in together, and give me one-fourth of the draught divine." Vāyu consented to this, and so the juice was shared between them.[1]

Nowadays the Hindus are a temperate race and Soma, in his Vedic character, has ceased to be worshipped. The name, however, is still given to the Moon, together with that of Chandra.[2] In the later Vedas the word Soma is used interchangeably—either as the god of the intoxicating liquor or as the moon ruling over the night. This may be accounted for by the subtly beguiling character of the Queen of the Night. A Vedic quotation supports this view:

> "The sun has the nature of Agni, the moon of Soma."

Nectar too, was supposed to exist in the bright spots of the moon, and Vishnu's fabled man-bird Garuda was sent to get it, so that the gods might quaff the subtle liquor.

It is related that this god was blest with thirty-three wives—all daughters of Prajāpati. He found the same difficulty that many a much-married Oriental monarch has to-day. He could not hold the balance fairly, and alas! showed distinct preference for Rohinī. Thereupon the remaining thirty-two returned to their fathers full of loud complaints against their treatment. Soma begged that they might come back to him, and they consented to do so provided in future they all shared equally in his favours. He eagerly promised to do this, but once again the superior charms of Rohinī overcame his resolve. Then Soma as a punishment was smitten with the curse of consumption, and Hindus say that this accounts for the waxing and waning of the moon.

Another curious explanation of the changes in the moon is current in the Bombay Presidency. One day Ganesha fell off his steed, the rat. The moon could not help laughing at the strange sight. To punish him, the angry god vowed that no one should ever see the moon again. The moon

[1] Muir, *O.S.T.*, V. 144.

[2] Atharva-Veda, xi. 6–7. "May the god Soma free me, he whom they call the moon."

prayed for forgiveness and so the curse was modified, and it was agreed to confine his punishment to certain seasons.

Soma is charged with carrying off Tārā, the wife of Vrihaspati, the preceptor to the gods. Her husband punished the wife by turning her into a stone, and the Moon by throwing his shoe at him. This left a black mark on his surface, which is the explanation of the spots on the moon. Other Hindus say that a hare lives in the moon and children often say that an old woman sits there working her spinning wheel.

Soma is represented as a white man, drawn in a chariot of three wheels by ten horses. With his right hand he gives a blessing, but in the other he holds a club. Which thing is surely an allegory. The only worship paid to him to-day is rendered in conjunction with the sun and the planets.

Śiva bears a half moon on his forehead, and this is the explanation:

" The god Soma, or Chandra, was traversing the earth in company with his favourite consort Rohinī and they unwarily entered the forest of Gaurī, Śiva's wife. There, it is said, some men, having surprised the god caressing his wife, were punished by a change of sex, and the forest retained the power of effecting a like change on all males who should enter it. Chandra instantly became a female and was so afflicted and ashamed at the change that he hastened far to the west, sending Rohinī to take his seat in the sky. He concealed himself in a mountain, afterwards named Soma-giri, where he performed a most rigorous penance. Darkness then covered the face of the world night by night, the fruits of the earth were destroyed, and the universe was in such dismay that the gods with Brahmā at their head, implored Śiva's assistance, who no sooner placed Chandra on his forehead than he assumed his real sex, and hence Śiva acquired the title of Chandra Sekhara (*i.e.* "he who has the moon for a crest.") The explanation given of this fable is that the Moon, when in the mansion, or sphere of Rohinī, or the Pleiades, seems to vanish behind the southern mountains."[1]

[1] Moor, *Hindu Pantheon*, p. 290.

Mr. Crooke, in his book *Popular Religion and Folk-Lore of Northern India,* has an interesting note on the moon :

" The moon has several special functions in relation to disease. Roots and simples collected by moonlight are more efficacious. This is quite Shakesperian, for Jessica says :

> ' In such a night Medea gathered the enchanted herbs
> That did renew old Aeson.'

And Laertes speaks of the poison ' collected from all simples that have virtue under the moon.' Also very common is the belief that any disease contracted by a man under the waning moon tends to diminish. Patients are often told to look at the moon reflected in butter or milk or water, and the cure will be effected. This is mostly done in the case of leprosy and similar diseases.

" In spite of all these advantages there is very little special worship of the Moon. When an image is erected to him it is usually associated with that of the Sun god. Moon worship is most popular in Bengal and Behar."

CHAPTER VII

YAMA, JUDGE AND REGENT OF THE DEAD

> "The good which thou on earth hast wrought,
> Each sacrifice, each pious deed,
> Shall there receive its ample meed;
> No worthy act shall be forgot.
>
> "In those fair realms of cloudless day,
> Where Yama every joy supplies,
> And every longing satisfies,
> Thy bliss shall never know decay."
>
> —DR. MUIR, *O.S.T.*, p. 327.

THE first mortals born into this world were the children of the Sun god, and were known as Yama, the Hindu Pluto, and Yamunā (Yamī), his sister (the River Jumna). As Yama was the earliest born so he was the first to depart this life,[1] and as he discovered the way to the other world it is only to be expected that the Vedas should invest him with the dread office of conducting the dead to the home which he has made secure for them. From this function it is only a step to his next office. He becomes President of the Dead. The whole pageantry of Justice is his when he holds Court and presides as Judge. As record-keeper he has Chitra-Gupta, who reads out of his great register, called Agra-Sandhānī, the tale of the

[1] Max Müller suggests the origin of the Hindu god of the Dead may be inferred from his being called the son of the Sun—Vivasvat. The sun, conceived as setting or dying every day, was the first who had trodden the path of life from East to West—the first mortal—the first to show us the way when our course is run and our sun sets in the far West. Thither the fathers (Pitris) followed Yama; there they sit with him rejoicing, and thither we too shall go when his messengers (day and night) have found us out. . . . Yama is said to have crossed the rapid waters, to have shown the way to many, to have first known the path on which our fathers crossed over.

man's life. After which Yama gives sentence according to the balance of good or evil recorded, and the soul of the deceased either ascends to Swarga, the abode of the blessed, or is sent to one of the twenty-one hells of Hinduism (Naraka) according to his degree of guilt, or is immediately born again to work out its fate on earth in another form.

In the hour of death Hindus sometimes imagine they see Yama's messengers in fearful shape, coming to take them away. At death all souls go direct to Yama. The journey takes four hours and forty minutes to accomplish, and so a dead body must not be burned until that time has elapsed. Immediate judgment takes place on the arrival at Yama's abode of the dead man's soul or spirit. The way there is fraught with danger. There are two insatiable dogs, called Karbura (spotted) and Syāma (black), with four eyes, gnashing teeth, and wide nostrils which guard the road, and which the departed one is advised to hurry past with all possible speed. These dogs are said to wander among men as Yama's messengers, no doubt for the purpose of summoning them into their master's presence in his city of Yamapura where the soul repairs on quitting its tenement of clay. Yama, in addition to the record-keeper, has two chief attendants, Chanda and Kāla-Purusha, who execute his commands. His messengers or orderlies—Yama Dūtas—bring in the souls of the dead, and the door of the judgment-hall is kept by his porter, Vaidhyata.

What then becomes of the dead after judgment? The following is an account of the future of a *good* Hindu. "Leaving behind on earth all that is evil and imperfect, and proceeding by the paths which the fathers trod, invested with lustre like that of the gods, he soars to Swarga, the first heaven—the realm of eternal light—in a car or on wings, and recovers there his ancient body in a complete and glorified form, meets with his forefathers who are living in festivity with Yama, and obtains from him a delectable abode, and enters upon a more perfect life, which is passed in the presence of the gods, and employed in the fulfilment of their pleasure."[1]

[1] Muir, *O.S.T.*, p. 302.

In this future world husband meets again with wife, children with parents, sister with brother. They enjoy all the pleasures of earthly existence freed from its infirmities, pains, and sorrows. In these the gods also participate, and all together live in a state of blessedness.

The Rig-Veda contains the following hymn:

"To Yama, mighty king, be gifts and homage paid,
He was the first of men that died, the first to brave
Death's rapid rushing stream, the first to point the road
To heaven, and welcome others to that bright abode.
No power can rob us of the home thus won by thee—
O King, we come; the born must die, must tread the path
That thou hast trod—the path by which each race of men,
In long succession, and our fathers, too, have passed.
Open thy arms, O earth, receive the dead
With gentle pressure and with loving welcome.
Enshroud him tenderly, e'en as a mother
Folds her soft vestment round the child she loves.
Soul of the dead! depart; fear not to take the road—
The ancient road—by which their ancestors have gone;
Ascend to meet the god—to meet thy happy fathers,
Who dwell in bliss with him. Fear not to pass the guards,
The four-eyed brindled dogs—that watch for the departed.
Return unto thy home, O Soul! Thy sin and shame
Leave thou behind on earth; assume a shining form—
Thy ancient shape—refined and from all taint set free." [1]

The following is a list of the five chief Heavens of the Hindus to which the soul of the departed may be admitted according to his sectarian leanings in his earthly life.

1. "*Swarga* is Indra's heaven. Indra there is attended by troops of Apsaras (dancing girls) and Gandharvas (heavenly musicians).
2. "*Kailāsa* in the Himālayas is the heaven of Śiva, where he dwells with his wife Pārvatī and his sons Ganesha and Kārtikeya, and from which he controls the troops of evil spirits.

[1] Rig-Veda, x., translated by Monier Williams.

3. " *Vaikuntha* is Vishnu's abode situated on Mount Meru and is made entirely of gold. It contains pools of water on which float blue, red, and white lotuses. Vishnu sits on a throne glorious as the mid-day sun; on his right is Lakshmī like a blaze of lightning. He is called the holy being (unfortunately his holiness does not shine in his incarnations as Krishna, &c.).
4. " *Go-loka* is Krishna's heaven when he lives in the cow-world (Go-loka). He is splendidly adorned with gems and holds a flute in his hand. His companions are the Gopis and Gopas, the cow-herdesses and cow-herds.
5. " *Brahmā-loka* Brahmā's heaven need not concern us as he is little worshipped to-day."[1]

The fate of the *wicked* after judgment is also clearly set forth in the Hindu Scriptures, and Yama is not only Judge but is ruler over the many hells where the wicked suffer. He is Regent of the " South " quarter, the abode of the damned. In the Vishnu Purāna we read "there are many dreadful hells which are the awful provinces of Yama, terrible with instruments of torture and fire." There is no doubt that the Hindu emphatically believes in the torments of the lost in Hell. In the Rig-Veda only one hell is mentioned. It is a dark place, but not a place of torture. We read " knowing, he beholds all creatures; he hurls the hated and irreligious into the abyss" (ix. 73). But in the Brāhmanas hell has become a place of torture. In Manu's Code twenty-one hells are enumerated, called Darkness, Frightful, Burning, Place of Spikes, Frying Pan, Thorny Tree, Sword-leaved Wood, Place of Iron Fetters, &c. &c. A liar is condemned to go to the Raurava (dreadful) hell. He who kills a cow or strangles a man goes to the Rodha hell (hell of obstruction). A horse-stealer falls into the " red-hot iron " hell. The vile wretch who eats his meal before offering food to the gods, to his ancestors (the Pitris) or to his guests, falls into a hell

[1] Stācker's *Arsenal*, p. 210.

where, instead of food, saliva is given to him. He who cuts down trees goes to the hell of the sword-leaved wood, &c. You will see in this enumeration that the punishment is strictly made to fit the crime !

" In the Bhavishya Purāna the following legend of Yama's marriage is found. He was exceedingly pleased with a girl named Vijaya, a Brāhman's daughter. When first she saw him she was greatly alarmed, alike at his appearance and on learning who he was. At length he allayed her fears and she consented to marry him. On her arrival at Yama's abode her husband cautioned her and assured her that all would be well if she never visited the southern portion of his kingdom. After a while curiosity overpowered her, and, thinking that a rival wife lived in the south, she visited the forbidden region. There she saw the torments of the wicked, and alas ! amongst these she recognised her own mother. Greatly distressed she applied to Yama to release her mother, but Yama declared that this was impossible unless some one then living on earth would perform a certain sacrifice, and transfer the merit of the act to the poor woman then suffering. After some difficulty a woman was found willing to perform the sacrifice, and Vijaya obtained her mother's release."[1]

From the following exquisite idyll of wifely devotion told in the Mahābhārata we learn that the dread King of Death is sometimes propitious to prayer, and permits those who have entered his abode to return to earth.

" Sāvitrī, the lovely daughter of King Aswapati, fell in love with Satyavān, the son of a hermit, but is warned by a seer to overcome her affection, as Satyavān is a doomed man and has only a year to live. She replied:

" Whether his years be few or many, be he gifted with all grace
Or graceless, him my heart hath chosen, and it chooseth not again."

They were married, and the bride strove to forget the terrible warning; but, as the last day of the year approached,

[1] Wilkins, *Hindu Mythology*, p. 84.

VISVAKARMA, THE HINDU VULCAN.

(See p. 70.)

YAMA, THE JUDGE OF THE DEAD, on his buffalo, seeking to deprive SIVA of a worshipper, who is seen to the extreme left grasping the Linga Stone, from out of which SIVA rises accompanied by PĀRVATĪ and GANESHA.

her anxiety became irrepressible. She exhausted herself in prayers and penances, appeals and entreaties, hoping to stay the hand of the destroyer, yet all the while her husband is unconscious of his fate and she dared not reveal it to him. At last the dreaded day dawned, and Satyavān set out to cut wood in the forest. His wife asked leave to accompany him, and walked behind him, smiling, but with heavy heart. Satyavān soon made the wood resound with the strokes of his hatchet, when suddenly a thrill of agony shot through his temples, and, feeling himself falling, he called on his wife to support him:

> "Then she received her fainting husband in her arms, and sat herself
> On the cold ground, and gently laid his drooping head upon her lap;
> Sorrowing, she called to mind the sage's prophecy, and reckoned up
> The days and hours. All in an instant she beheld an awful shape
> Standing before her, dressed in blood-red garments, with a glittering crown
> Upon his head; his form, though glowing like the Sun, was yet obscure,
> And eyes he had like flames, a noose depended from his hand and he
> Was terrible to look upon, as by her husband's side he stood
> And gazed upon him with a fiery glance. Shuddering she started up
> And laid her dying Satyavān upon the ground, and with her hands
> Joined reverently, she thus with beating heart addressed the shape:
> 'Surely thou art a god, such form as thine must more than mortal be!
> Tell me, thou god-like being, who thou art, and wherefore art thou here?'"

The Shape replied that he was Yama, King of Death, and that he had come to bind and take away her husband's spirit:

> "Then from her husband's body forced he out, and firmly with a cord
> Bound and detained the spirit, like in size and length to a man's thumb.
> Forthwith the body, reft of vital being and deprived of breath,
> Lost all its grace and beauty, and became ghastly and motionless."

After binding the spirit Yama returned to his home in the South, but the faithful wife followed him closely. She persisted in following, although Yama told her to go home and prepare her husband's funeral rites. At length, pleased with her devotion, he granted her any boon she pleased except the life of her husband. She asked that her husband's father who is blind may recover his sight. Yama consented and bade her now be satisfied and return home. Still she persisted in following, and two other boons were granted in the same way. At last, overcome by her unwearying devotion and constancy, Yama gave Sāvitrī a boon without exception. She exclaimed:

"'Nought, mighty king, this time hast thou excepted: let my husband live,
Without him I desire not happiness, nor even heaven itself;
Without him I must die.' 'So be it, faithful wife,' replied the King of Death:
'Thus I release him,' and with that he loosed the cord that bound his soul."[1]

[1] Monier Williams, *Indian Epic Poetry*, pp. 37–8.

CHAPTER VIII

MINOR VEDIC DEITIES

I. USHAS—THE DAWN GODDESS

"Do thou, O Dawn,
Like one who clears away a debt, chase off
This black yet palpable obscurity,
Which came to fold us in its close embrace."
—MONIER WILLIAMS.

WITHOUT doubt the most poetic conception of the Vedas, and greatly admired and loved is the Dawn goddess, Ushas. She is daughter of the Sky, wife of the Sun, and has Night for her sister. The Asvins, the charioteers of the Sun, are her friends. Again, Agni the Fire-god is her lover. Bright glorious immortal goddess! She is ever young, being born every day. And, alas! all too brief a life is hers, for she perishes in the fierce embrace of her husband the Sun, who daily pursues her until at last she turns shuddering to meet her fate,[1] and yet she is old, for she lives on through unnumbered years. With her far-streaming radiance returning from the land of

[1] There is a parallel in Greek mythology to the death of the Dawn maiden in the arms of her too glorious lover the Sun. Daphne is young and beautiful—Apollo loves her—she flies before him and dies as he embraces her with his brilliant rays. The Vedic poet (Rig-Veda, x. 189) employs similar imagery:

"The Dawn comes near to him,
She expires as soon as he begins to breathe.
The mighty one irradiates the sky."

Thus even so modern a poet as Swift commemorates the daily tragedy —the Dawn rushing and trembling through the sky, and fading away at the sudden approach of the bright Sun—when he says:

"She blushes and with haste retires
When Sol pursues her with his fires."

darkness and mystery, seated in a shining chariot, she drives back the terrors of night and illumines the world, revealing its treasures to all. Through her the sleepers awake, the young birds flutter from their nests, and men resume their myriad tasks:

> " Hail, ruddy Ushas, golden goddess, borne
> Upon thy shining car, thou comest like
> A lovely maiden by her mother decked,
> Disclosing coyly all thy hidden grace
> To our admiring eyes ; or, like a wife
> Unveiling to her lord, with conscious pride,
> Beauties which, as he gazes lovingly,
> Seem fresher, fairer, each succeeding morn.
> Through years and years thou hast lived on, and yet
> Thou'rt ever young. Thou art the breath and life
> Of all, that breathes and lives, awaking day by day
> Myriads of prostrate sleepers, as from death,
> Causing the birds to flutter in their nests
> And rousing men to ply with busy feet
> Their daily duties and appointed tasks,
> Toiling for wealth, or pleasure, or renown."[1]

II. The Asvins, Charioteers of the Sun

These twin deities are charioteers of the Sun and are represented as ever young and handsome, bright and full of glory. They ride upon horses and are the harbingers of Ushas, the Dawn. " They are the earliest bringers of light in the morning sky, who in the clouds hasten onwards before the Dawn and prepare the way for her " (Roth). Their whip is said to distil the honey on the dew. They succour the distressed. They reveal to the gods the places where the Soma plant of magical properties grows. It is the opinion of Yāska, commentator on the Vedas, that " they represent the transition from darkness to light when the intermingling of both produces that inseparable duality expressed by the twin nature of these deities."

[1] Hymn from the Rig-Veda, paraphrased by Monier Williams.

Another office they hold is that of physicians to Swarga, the heaven of the gods. Strange that the gods in heaven need a physician! They did not, however, limit their healing activities to heaven; they delighted in wandering about the world performing cures.

The following legend is told of a cure they effected on Chyavāna, who was a shrivelled up old man abandoned by his family. The sons of a Rishi (Brāhman sage) discovering him prone upon the road, pelted him with stones, thinking him dead. The Rishi was greatly grieved at their conduct, and, taking his daughter, he apologised for what his sons had done, and gave her to the decrepit old man as a peace-offering. She thereupon became his wife. The Asvins, on seeing the beautiful girl, coveted her and said, "Who is this shrivelled old man near whom you are lying? Leave him and follow us." She replied that whilst he lived she would not leave the man to whom her father had given her. Then they came to her a second time. Acting on her husband's suggestion, she said, "You speak contemptuously of my husband, whilst you are incomplete and imperfect yourselves." They pressed her to explain herself, and on condition that they would make her husband young again, she consented to tell them in what respect they lacked. They told her to take her husband to a certain pool, and declared that after bathing there he would come forth as a youth renewed in strength. She then told the Asvins that they were imperfect because they had not been invited to join the other gods in a great sacrifice that was about to be celebrated. The Asvins proceeded to the place of sacrifice and asked to be allowed to join in the sacrifice; the gods forbade them because, as physicians, they wandered about among men performing cures, and were therefore unclean. They pleaded that their work was necessary and eventually were purified and allowed to join the sacrifice.[1]

[1] Muir, *O.S.T.*, p. 250.

III. Visvakarma (Tvashtri), the Hindu Vulcan

The great Architect of the Universe and Mechanic to the gods is Visvakarma, the Hindu Vulcan. He fashioned the celestial weapons, forged the thunder bolt of Indra, and the iron-axe of Agni. In two hymns in the Rig-Veda he is described as "the one all-seeing god, who, when producing heaven and earth, blows them forth (or shapes them) with his arms and wings; the father, generator, disposer, who knows all worlds, gives the gods their names, and is beyond the comprehension of mortals." In the Mahābhārata, consequent on the development made by the Hindus in the arts of civilisation, Visvakarma is described as "the lord of the arts, executor of a thousand handicrafts, the carpenter of the gods, the fashioner of all ornaments, the most eminent of artisans on whose craft men subsist and whom, as a great and immortal god, they continually worship."

No images of this god are now made, but each artisan worships his tools, and one day in the year (in August) is specially set apart for this purpose. The writer has frequently seen carpenters at the beginning of their day's work chip a few pieces of wood from a larger piece, and, placing the chippings together with their tools in front of them, invoke their aid before beginning the day's tasks. In the same way in India to-day the cultivator worships his plough, the student his books, and the clerk his pen, the potter his wheel, the black-smith his hammer and bellows, and the weaver his shuttle, putting it for this purpose into the hole he has dug in the ground under his loom. Soldiers and warlike tribes worship their weapons, the Rājput his sword; and when a man of lower caste marries a Rājput girl of high caste, as in the case of the Māhārājah Holkar, the bride is married to the bridegroom's sword with his handkerchief bound round it.

All Hindu workmen regard their tools as the cause of their prosperity and happiness and worship them as such.

Habakkuk's remark concerning a different race is true of the artisan of to-day in India :

"They sacrifice unto their net, and burn incense unto their drag ; because by them their portion is fat and their meat plenteous."

This strange custom was known to the Aryans of Vedic times ; and in the Atharva-Veda, the *kettle,* which was the vessel used for boiling milk and other liquids of sacrificial purposes, is thus adored :

"As Sakra (or mighty) he measures the threefold paths. Meting out the worlds, whatever has been or shall be, he performs the functions of the gods. Being born as Indra among men, the kindled and glowing kettle works. That which neither the lord of the sacrifice nor the sacrifice rules, which neither the giver nor the receiver rules, which is all-conquering, all-supporting, and all-working, declare to us the kettle, what quadruped is it?"[1]

The Aryas also worshipped the *sacrificial ladles* under the following names which they used in worship and to which they ascribed divine powers :

"The Jehu has established the sky, the Upabhrit, the atmosphere, and the Dhruva the stable earth."[2]

Other objects are considered divine, as for instance the post yūpa, to which animals were tied in sacrifice. A hymn is also addressed to weapons of war. The Dhenki, a wooden pounder used for pounding bricks into dust for making mortar, and for husking grain, is worshipped as the Vāhan or vehicle of Nārada, one of the Divine Rishis. The Kusa grass, which provided seats for the gods, is said to support heaven and earth, and as for the frogs, a hymn in their honour concludes with this curious bit of biology :

"The frogs who gave us cows in hundreds, lengthen our lives in this most fertilising season."

---

[1] Atharva-Veda, iv. 11, 2.
[2] Atharva-Veda, xviii. 4–5.

IV. The Maruts, or Storm Gods

The Maruts, as storm gods, the sons of Rudra,[1] the wild boar of the sky, hold a very prominent place in the Vedas. They are represented as being companions of Indra, whose rain-giving exploits they copy. They are said in the Rig-Veda to be 180 in number, but in the Purānas as only 49. They ride on the wings of the wind, roaring like lions, and rule the fierce storms which blow so strongly that they are beyond the control of any one god, no matter how powerful he be. They are, in colour of a reddish sunny hue, gleaming like flames, their chariots yoked with ruddy horses, their spears of lightning, so sweep they over the world.

V. Ka, the Interrogative Pronoun

The Athenians, who erected their altar to the "Unknown god," have a Vedic parallel in Ka ? or Who ?—the interrogative pronoun, which was exalted into a deity and worshipped as a god. Max Müller,[2] quoting several Brāhmanas, says, "Whenever the interrogative verses occur, the author states that Ka is Prajāpati, or the lord of creatures. Nor did they stop here. Some of the hymns in which the interrogative pronoun occurred were called Kadvat, *i.e.* having kad or quid. But soon a new adjective was formed, and not only the hymns, but the sacrifices also, offered to the god, were called Kāya, or 'Who-ish.' . . . After this, we can hardly wonder that in the later Sanskrit literature of the Purānas, Ka appears as a recognised god, with a genealogy of his own, perhaps even a wife ; and that in the laws of Manu one of the recognised forms of marriage generally known by the name of the Prajāpati marriage, occurs under the monstrous title of Kāya."

. . . .

[1] See lengthy description under Śiva, p. 167.

[2] See Dowson's *Classical Dictionary* under Ka.

Altogether there is mention in the Vedas of "thrice eleven shining ones."

"Ye gods, who are eleven in the sky, who are eleven on earth, and who in your glory are eleven dwellers in the (atmospheric) waters, do ye welcome this our offering."

But in the Rig-Veda the gods are mentioned as being much more numerous:

"Three hundred, three thousand, thirty and nine gods have worshipped Agni" (iii. 9-9).

At the same time it must be remembered that some of the old poets declare that one god is identical with others; the formula used frequently in the Hymns is "the gods are only a single being under different names." In the Atharva-Veda (xiii. 3-13) we read:

"In the evening Agni becomes Varuna; he becomes Mitra when rising in the morning; having become Sāvitrī (Sūrya) he passes through the sky; having become Indra he warms the heaven in the middle."

From these quotations it is evident that with the many lapses into polytheism found in the Vedas the old singers treasured the memory of pre-Vedic times when the Indo-Aryan worship was monotheistic. Max Müller sums up the position when he says:

"There is a monotheism which precedes the polytheism of the Veda, and even in the invocation of their innumerable gods, the remembrance of a God, one and infinite, breaks through the mist of an idolatrous phraseology, like the blue sky that is hidden by passing clouds."

PART III

THE PURĀNIC DEITIES

THE GODS OF MODERN HINDUISM

CHAPTER I

BRAHMA, THE SUPREME SPIRIT, AND THE HINDU TRIAD

"There is one only Being who exists
Unmoved, yet moving swifter than the mind;
Who far outstrips the senses, though as gods
They strive to reach him; who himself at rest
Transcends the fleetest flight of other beings;
Who, like the air, supports all vital action.
He, the All-pervading, Self-existent,
Is brilliant, without body, sinewless,
Invulnerable, pure, and undefiled
By taint of sin.
He moves, yet moves not, he is far yet near;
He is within this universe. Whoe'er beholds
All living creatures as in him and him—
The Universal Spirit—as in all,
Henceforth regards no creature with contempt."

—*Extract from an Upanishad* (translated by Monier Williams).

I. Brahma, the Supreme Spirit

If you were to accuse a well-educated Hindu of idolatry, after seeing him worship at a shrine, he would probably be very indignant and would reply with hauteur: "I worship no idol. I bow before the great eternal Spirit, who is the source and spring of all things. Idols are only symbols and aids to worship. Ignorant village folk may imagine that these are real gods, but we who are educated know that these are mere representations of deity. God himself is eternal and invisible."

Similarly a Brāhman was once asked to give an explanation of the fact that even Indians of cultivated intellect who assert the unity of God appear to Europeans to be worshippers of many gods. His reply was:

"All orthodox Hindus believe in one Universal Spirit, who becomes Supreme Lord over all—(PARAMESVARA). At the same time they believe that this one God has taken various forms, all of which may be worshipped; just as gold is one everywhere though it may take different forms and names in different places and countries. Every man chooses his favourite god, or divine object, to which he pays especial homage. . . . Different places have also their favourite presiding deities. Benares is specially watched over by a form of Śiva; Muttra by Krishna, &c. We may propitiate every one of these gods with ceremonies and sacrifices, but the Supreme Being present in them is the real object of all our offerings and religious services. At the end of each we say: 'By this act may the Supreme Lord be gratified!' Hence, though to you we appear Polytheists, we are really Monotheists. Nor are we Pantheists in your sense of the term. Only our deepest thinkers look beyond the personal God to the impersonal Spirit which underlies everything. We educated Brāhmans are practically Theists."[1]

The Supreme Spirit Brahm, or Brahma, must not be confounded with Brahmā the Creator, and the first member of the Hindu Trinity. Brahma, the eternal Being, is described as Nirguna, or destitute of qualities, and the word is neuter gender from the root *brih* = "to expand." It is the great soul of the Universe, self-existent, absolute, and eternal, and is called Brahma because IT[2] expanded Itself through all space and is in all nature, animate and inanimate, in the highest god as in the meanest creature. IT is pure essence, limitless being, incorporeal, invisible and all-pervading in its manifestations.[3]

[1] Monier Williams, *Religious Thought and Life in India*, p. 50.

[2] Strictly speaking Brahma should be rendered by "IT," since it is neuter gender.

[3] "The Deity, they tell us, pervades all, earth and the expanse of sea, and the deep vault of heaven; from Him, flocks, herds, men wild beasts of every sort, each creature at its birth draws the bright

"Hence all visible forms on earth, say the Brāhmans, are emanations from the one eternal Entity, like drops from an ocean, like sparks from fire. Stones, mountains, rivers, plants, trees, and animals—all these are traceable upwards as progressive steps in the infinite evolution of Brahma's being. The highest earthly emanation is man, and the emanation of men is in classes, and is also traceable upwards according to a graduated scale, the highest class being that of the Brāhmans."[1]

This Supreme Soul receives no direct worship. "Of Him, whose glory is so great there is no image" (Veda) Throughout the length and breadth of the land no temple is reared to IT's honour. Yet Brahma is the object of intense though abstract devotion. Every devout Hindu through a painful cycle of deaths and rebirths [2] hopes eventually to gain

---

thread of life; further, to Him all things return, are restored and reduced—death has no place among them. But they fly up alive into the ranks of the stars and take their seats aloft in the sky."—Virgil, *Georgics*, iv. 221 (John Conington's translation).

How wonderfully the true import of Virgil's lines is taken up by our English poet:

> "I have felt
> A presence that disturbs me with the joy
> Of elevated thoughts; a sense sublime
> Of something far more deeply interfused,
> Whose dwelling is the light of setting suns,
> And the round ocean, and the living air,
> And the blue sky, and in the mind of man;
> A motion and a spirit, that impels
> All thinking things, all objects of all Thought,
> And rolls through all things."

[1] Monier Williams, *Religious Thought and Life in India*, p. 43.

[2] *Transmigration.*—To the Hindu the soul is like a solitary pilgrim tarrying in the caravanserai of the body, and, because it is bound in the chains of deeds and eating the fruits of past actions, it promotes or degrades itself along well-nigh infinite series of embodiments. The range of possible soul-migration is 8,400,000, and stretches downward from gods and saints through Brāhmans, nymphs, kings, counsellors, to actors, drunkards, birds, dancers, cheats, elephants, horses, Śūdras, barbarians, wild beasts, snakes, worms, insects, and inert things.

The doctrine of *Retribution* (Karma) is seen in the laws of Manu absorption into the Universal Spirit. To this end he practises self-abnegation and countless austerities. He longs to be free from passion, from birth, from pain, yea,—from existence itself. This is a fundamental doctrine of Brāhmanism, the religion of the post-Vedic days, and an underlying motif of Hinduism to-day.

To sum up. There is One Eternal Spirit, Brahma, and emanations of this Spirit dwelling in created things: men, animals, birds, insects, &c., in decreasing intensity as we reach the lower forms of creation. In the higher forms, *i.e.* human, these spirit-emanations partake of the passions and pains incident to residence in matter. They are purified from this stain by austerities and numerous transmigrations and at length reobtain absorption into the divine nature, and in such reunion gain their final beatitude.

The dogma which expresses the doctrine of the Universal Spirit is this " Ekam eva advitīyam "—" There is but one Being, no second "—which means that nothing really exists except the One Universal Spirit. It is addressed by the mysterious syllable OM (A.U.M.) which is found at the beginning of prayers and religious exercises, and is so sacred that none should hear it pronounced.

Naturally the question springs up: " Why with this high doctrine of one Eternal Spirit, Brahma, have we the idolatry and polytheism of modern Hinduism? " The answer can be given from the Hindu Scriptures themselves. First from the Atharva-Veda:

(xi. and xii.): " In whatsoever disposition of mind a man accomplishes such and such an act he shall reap the fruit in a body endowed with such and such a quality." It is the necessary counterpart of Transmigration. The punishments are weighed out with a startling appropriateness of penalty. The stealer of food becomes dyspeptic, the scandalmonger has foul breath in a future existence. The murderer of a Brāhman passes into a wild beast or a pariah, the cruel become bloodthirsty beasts, stealers of grain and meat turn into rats and vultures, the thief who took dyed garments, kitchen herbs, or perfumes shall become accordingly a red partridge, a peacock, or a musk-rat.—Tylor's *Prim. Culture*, ii. p. 10.

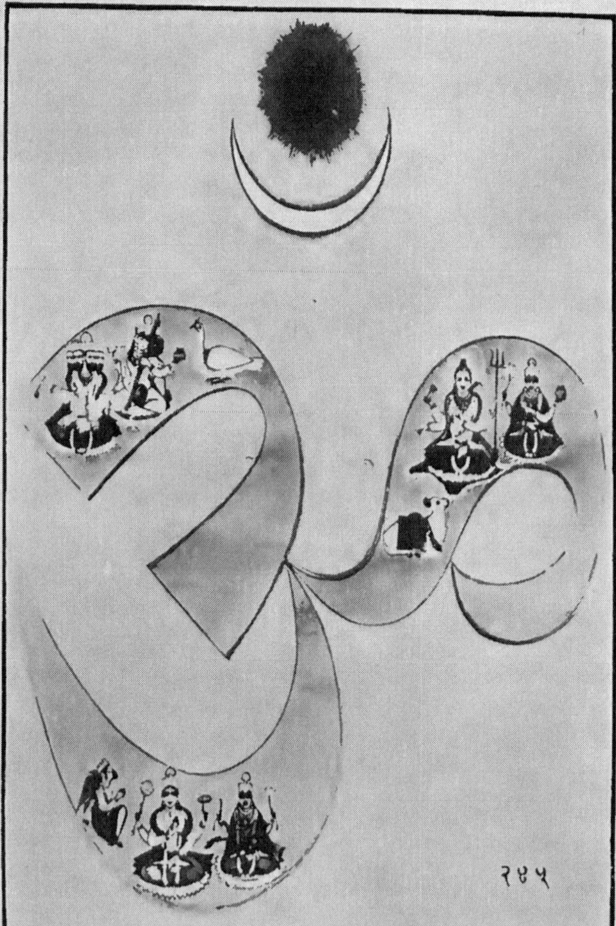

THE MYSTERIOUS SYLLABLE OM
The members of the Hindu Triad are seen in each section.
(1) BRAHMĀ, with SARASVATĪ and his goose.
(2) ŚIVA, with PĀRVATĪ and his bull NANDI.
(3) VISHNU, with LAKSHMĪ, and GARUDA.

A BUDDHIST REPRESENTATION OF THE HINDU TRIAD (Trimūrti.)

ŚIVA AS COMPRISING THE HINDU TRIAD.

"All gods are in Brahma as cows in a cow-house. In the beginning Brahma was this (universe). He created gods. Having created gods, he placed them in these worlds, viz. Agni in this world, Indra-Vāyu in the atmosphere, and Sūrya (Mitra) in the sky (A.U.M.). These gods were originally mortal; but when pervaded by Brahma they became immortal." [1]

Then in the Vishnu Purāna the subject is further elaborated:

"There are two states of this Brahma—one *with* and the other *without* shape; one perishable, one imperishable. These are inherent in all beings. The imperishable is the Supreme Being, the perishable is in all the world. The blaze of fire burning in one spot diffuses light and heat around; so the world is nothing more than the manifested energy of the Supreme Brahma; and inasmuch as light and heat are stronger or feebler as we are near the fire or far off from it, so the energy of the Supreme is more or less intense in the beings that are more or less remote from it. Brahmā, Śiva, and Vishnu are the most powerful energies of God; next to them are the inferior deities; then the attendant spirits; then man, then animals, birds, insects, and vegetables; each becoming more and more feeble as they are farther removed from their primitive source." [2]

High and lofty as the doctrine of the unity of the Supreme Spirit is, it proved unsatisfactory to the common people. The Aryans soon began to worship local deities found amongst the people they conquered, and these deities began to influence their lives. Rather than lose their hold of the people the priests adopted these new deities and found a parentage for them from amongst the old Vedic gods. So by easily discerned stages the present developments of Hindu mythology were reached. The rage for personification appears to have been unbounded. There are said to be at present 330,000,000 gods and godlings among the Hindus, while the population of India in the recent census was slightly smaller, being 315,000,000. Monier Williams truly says: "There is not an object in heaven or earth which a Hindu is not prepared to worship—sun, moon, and stars; rocks, stocks, and stones; trees, shrubs, and grass; sea, pools, and rivers; his own implements of trade; the animals he finds most useful, the

[1] Muir, *O.S.T.*, pp. 3–7.

[2] Wilkins, p. 95.

noxious reptiles he fears, men remarkable for any extraordinary qualities—for great valour, sanctity, virtue, or even vice; good and evil demons, ghosts, and goblins, the spirits of departed ancestors; an infinite number of semi-human and semi-divine existences, inhabitants of the seven upper and the seven lower worlds—each and all come in for a share of divine honours or a tribute of more or less adoration."

II. The Hindu Triad

> " Lord of the triple qualities, the cause
> Of man's existence, bondage, and release."
>
> —*Upanishad.*

The Trimūrti, *i.e.* " triple form," denotes the great Hindu Trinity—Brahmā, Śiva, and Vishnu, the august representatives of the creative, destructive, and preservative energies or principles. *Brahmā* is the embodiment of the Rajo-guna the quality of passion, or desire, by which the world was called into being; *Śiva* is the embodied Tamo-guna, the attribute of darkness, or wrath, and the destructive fire by which the world is consumed; and *Vishnu* is the embodied Sattva-guna, or property of mercy and goodness, by which the world is preserved. To put the same truth in another way we find that dominated by activity the Supreme Being is Brahmā, by goodness he is Vishnu, and by darkness Śiva. These three are the supreme deities of the Purānas and of modern Hinduism.

According to the theory of Brāhmanism, from the Supreme Spirit, Brahma, when overspread by Māyā, or the illusory creative force, proceeded the primeval male god, Brahmā, who in turn created the three worlds and all living things. But the act of creation necessarily involves the other two acts of preservation and dissolution. Hence the association with Brahmā of Vishnu, the Preserver, and Rudra-Śiva, the Dissolver and Reproducer. These three gods, concerned in the threefold operation of integration, maintenance, and dissolution, form the primary group of deities around which the entire system of modern Hinduism, with its diversified and countless ramifications of deity, grows.

These are typified by the three letters composing the mystic and profoundly significant syllable OM (or A.U.M.), to which reference has already been made. This syllable, said also to typify the three Vedas, has been handed down from Vedic times when there were three principal objects in nature, Earth, Water, and Sun, or Fire; and three worlds, Earth, Air, and Sky; and three forms of matter, Solid, Liquid, and Gaseous; and the three Vedic gods, Fire, Wind, and Sun—Agni, Indra-Vāyu, and Sūrya.[1]

One great authority [2] confirms the opinion often expressed that the Trimūrti, the triple divinity of the Hindus, was originally no more than a personification of the Sun in his triple capacity of *producing* forms by his genial heat, *preserving* them by his light, and *destroying* them by the concentrated force of his igneous matter. At night, therefore, when setting in the West the Sun is Vishnu, the preserver, Brahmā when rising in the morning, and Śiva at noon.

The true theory of Brāhmanism teaches that no one of the three persons in the Triad ought to take precedence over the other two—they should each be equal, so that each may represent the Supreme Lord and take the place of the other. The greatest of Indian poets, Kāli-dāsa, sings:

> "In those Three Persons the one God was shown
> Each first in place, each last—not one alone;
> Of Brahmā, Vishnu, Śiva, each may be
> First, second, third, among the blessed Three."

This co-equality, however, was soon overthrown and is not found in later mythology. Brahmā, the act of creation having ceased, becomes less and less worshipped, while the other two rise greatly in honour and importance. The story told in the chapter on Vishnu well illustrates this.

[1] Monier Williams, *Religious Thought and Life in India*, p. 45.
[2] Moor, *Hindu Pantheon*, pp. 278–9.

"These three gods differ from and are superior to all the other divine and human organisms in that they are not subject to the law of transmigration. They are beings who have obtained the highest condition possible, short of absorption into Brahma.

"The difference between the Hindu and Christian idea of the Trinity lies in this fact. Brahmā, Vishnu, and Śiva have only derived or secondary existences, and the Supreme Being may be worshipped through the worship of these three, or of any one of the three, supposed for the time to be superior to the others. It is even possible for the members of this trinity themselves to worship the One Spirit through the worship of the other, each being in turn regarded as inferior.

"Then, in the next place, homage may be paid to the Universal Spirit by and through the worship of the inferior gods, goddesses, departed ancestors, living Brāhmans, heroes, animals, and plants." [1]

Thus the contrast is very great between the pure doctrine of Christianity of three persons eternally existing in One God and a derived and subordinated Trinity which quickly degenerates into Polytheism.

[1] See Monier Williams, *Religious Thought and Life in India*, pp. 46 and 50.

CHAPTER II

BRAHMĀ, THE CREATOR, AND SARASVATĪ, GODDESS OF LEARNING

I. Brahmā, the Creator

" Hail, primal blossom ! Empyreal gem !
Say what four-formed godhead came,
With graceful stole and beamy diadem,
Forth from thy verdant stem ?
Full-gifted Brahmā."

—Sir Wm. Jones, *Ode to the Lotus.*

Brahmā is the first of the three great Hindu gods, the personified emanations of the Supreme Spirit, Brahma. He is called the Creator, the framer of the Universe. Like Jupiter he is " the father of gods and men," and in the Vedas his style and title is Prajāpati, " Lord of Creatures." From him all created things proceeded, as in him all things pre-existed. As the oak exists in the acorn, or, as the Hindu would express it, " the fruit is in the seed," so all material forms existed in Brahmā awaiting development and expansion.

" Grain with grain, successive harvests dwell,
And boundless forests slumber in a shell."

—Darwin.

The following remarkable passage from the Rig-Veda (x. 129, 1–6), describes the creation of the Universe :

" There was then (in the beginning) neither nonentity nor entity ; there was no atmosphere, nor sky above. What enveloped (all) ? Where, in the receptacle of what (was it contained) ? Was it water, the profound abyss ? Death was not there, nor immortality ; there was no distinction of day or night. That One breathed calmly, self-supported ; there was nothing different from, or above, it. In the beginning darkness existed, enveloped in darkness. All this was undistinguishable water. That One which lay void, and wrapped in nothingness, was developed by the power of fervour. *Desire* first arose in IT, which was the primal germ of the mind; (and which) sages, searching with their intellect, have discovered in their heart to be the bond which connects entity with nonentity. The ray (or cord) which stretched across these (worlds), was it below or was it above? There were there impregnating powers and mighty forces, a self-supporting principle beneath and energy above. Who knows, who here can declare, whence has sprung this creation?"

The explanation which Max Müller gives[1] of this remarkable account of creation is this: "The One which in the beginning breathed calmly, self-sustained, is developed by the power of its inherent heat (Professor Roth understands the word to mean 'by rigorous and intense abstraction'). This development gave occasion to *desire* (Kāma) which immediately took possession of the One, and is the first germ of mind, the earliest link between nonentity and entity." The Vedic poet goes on to speak of impregnating powers and mighty forces, of receptive capacities and active energies, but confesses himself unable to declare how the universe was produced.

There are so many accounts of the Creation in Hindu writings that it is quite impossible to reconcile or harmonise them. The sage, Manu, gives the following, which shows the tangle of ideas in which Hinduism lives:

"This universe was enveloped in darkness, unperceived, undistinguishable, undiscoverable, unknowable, as it were entirely sunk in sleep. Then the irresistible, self-existent Lord, undiscerned, causing this universe with the five elements and all other things to become discernible, was manifested, dispelling the gloom. He who is beyond the cognisance of the senses, subtle, undiscernible, and eternal, who is the essence of all beings, and inconceivable, himself shone forth. He, *desiring*, seeking to produce various creatures from his own body, first created the waters, and deposited in them a seed. This (seed) became a golden egg, resplendent as the sun, in which he himself was born as Brahmā, the progenitor of all the world. . . . That lord having continued a year in the egg, divided it into two

[1] See *Anc. Sanskrit Lit.*, p. 561.

parts by his mere thought. With these two shells, he formed the heavens and the earth, and in the middle he placed the sky, the eight regions, and the eternal abode of the waters."[1]

The Vishnu Purāna describes the wonderful egg thus :

"Its womb, vast as the mountain Meru, was composed of mountains, and the mighty oceans were the waters which filled its cavity. In that egg were the continents, seas, and mountains ; the Planets, and divisions of the universe ; the gods, the demons, and mankind. This egg, after the Creator had inhabited for a thousand years (one 'divine' year), burst open, and Brahmā, issuing forth by meditation, commenced the work of creation."[2]

In the Mahābhārata and some other Purānas, Brahmā is said to have issued, not from an egg, but from the lotus that sprang from the navel of Vishnu.

Still another account is given in the Rāmāyana (ii. 110–12) of the creation of the world. Vasishtha says :

"Lord of the world, understand from me this (account of) the origin of the worlds. All was water only in which the earth was formed. Thence arose Brahmā, the self-existent, with the deities. He then, becoming a boar, raised up the earth (on his mighty tusks) and created the whole world with the saints (Rishis) his sons."

Ward gives a more detailed account of the order of Creation: "Brahmā first produced the waters, then the earth, next from his own mind he caused a number of Brāhman sages (the Divine Rishis, see p. 300) and four females to be born. Then from his arms sprung the warriors (Kshatriya), and from his thighs the merchants and traders (Vaisya caste), while from his feet sprung the Śūdras, or menials. In this way the whole social order of Hinduism arose and the caste system with its infinite variety of sub-castes had its origin. Also, it is said that the sun sprung from Brahmā's eye, the moon from his mind, and he called into being all the different forms of animal and vegetable life, as they are now seen, by germs produced from his body."

[1] Muir, *O.S.T.*, vol. iv. p. 31.

[2] Wilkins, *Hindu Mythology*, p. 100.

"Brahmā is represented in pictures as a red man with four heads, though in the Purānas, it is said, he originally had five. He is dressed in white garments and rides upon a goose. In one hand he carries a staff, and in the other a dish for receiving alms."[1]

The following legend is given to explain the origin of Brahmā's five faces. According to the Matsya Purāna: "Brahmā assumed a mortal form and one half of his body springing forth, without its suffering any diminution whatever, he framed out of it the beauteous Satarūpā. She was so lovely that he became fascinated by her charms; but as she was born from his body Brahmā considered her to be his daughter and was ashamed of his emotion. During this conflict between desire and shame he remained motionless with his eyes fixed upon her. Satarūpā, understanding the situation and anxious to avoid his looks, stepped aside. Brahmā, unable to move, but still desirous to see her, caused a face to spring out in the direction to which she moved. She shifted her place four times and as many faces, corresponding to the four corners of the world, grew out of his head."[2] The four Vedas are said to have issued one out of each mouth.

The loss of the fifth head is described in the Mahābhārata: One day Brahmā was asked by the Sages (Divine Rishis) in the presence of Vishnu who was greatest, Brahmā, Śiva, or Vishnu. Brahmā declared that he was; whereupon a dispute arose between Brahmā and Vishnu. At length they agreed to refer the matter to the authority of the Vedas. The sacred books declared that this honour belonged to Śiva. The other two protested: "How can the lord of goblins, the delighter in graveyards, the naked devotee covered with ashes, haggard in appearance, wearing twisted locks ornamented by snakes, be supreme?" Even as they said this Śiva sprang into their midst in human form, vast and terrible. On seeing him the fifth head of Brahmā glowed with

[1] Wilkins, *Hindu Mythology*, p. 100.
[2] Moor, *Hindu Pantheon*, p. 704.

anger, and said: "I know thee well, O Chandra Sekhara, for from my forehead didst thou spring, and because thou didst weep I called thee Rudra. Hasten then to seek the refuge of my feet, and I will protect thee, O my son!" At these proud words Śiva was incensed, and from his anger sprang a most terrible form (Bhairava) who instantly cut off the head of Brahmā with the thumb of his left hand![1] What a scene is this for the wonder of the world! The great Creator's head cut off by the thumb nail of Bhairava's left hand!

Brahmā, notwithstanding his venerable appearance, his majestic task, and his lordly name, has an unenviable moral record. He, the Creator of the three worlds, committed incest with his own daughter, and for this horrible crime was punished by the rest of the gods by having his worship restricted. We find drunkenness also laid to his charge, and in the Skanda Purāna[2] is an indelicate legend in which the charge of falsehood is proved against him, and this fact also is given as a reason why his worship has almost ceased:

> "Since thou hast childishly and with weak understanding asserted a falsehood, let no one henceforth perform worship to thee."

To-day he is scarcely worshipped at all in India. Only two temples exist, one at Lake Pushkara in Rājputāna, and the other near Idar, close to Mount Abu. It is true that Brāhmans, in spite of this prohibition, repeat in their morning and evening worship an incantation containing a description of Brahmā, and at noon present to him sometimes a single flower and at other times offerings of clarified butter.

But other gods with an equally evil record continue to be worshipped. The true reason that Brahmā receives scant recognition nowadays is that his work was one single act of creation, and once accomplished, it has lost its interest for the Hindu race.

Brahmā's life, in Hindu mythology, is said to consist of

[1] Wilkins, *Hindu Mythology*, p. 102.
[2] Kennedy, *Hindu Mythology*, p. 271.

a hundred of his own years, and a year consists of days each of which (known as a Kalpa—a period of time) is equal to 4,320,000 of our years, followed by a night of equal duration. At the close of each Kalpa the universe is destroyed and has to be recreated after Brahmā has rested through his prolonged night.

II. Sarasvatī, Goddess of Learning

"We thirst, Vāgdevi,[1] for thy balmy lore,
Drawn from that rubied cave
Where meek-eyed pilgrims hail the triple wave."[2]
—Sir W. Jones, *Hymn to Sarasvatī.*

All Hindu goddesses are represented as the subordinate powers or energies of their husbands. So Sarasvatī, whose husband was Brahmā, the Creator, is renowned as the goddess of wisdom, possessing qualities of Invention and Imagination which may be fairly termed creative. She is called "the Mother of the Vedas," and is honoured as the inventor of the Devanāgari character and of the Sanskrit language. She is the patroness of fine arts, especially of music and rhetoric, and so is styled Vāgdevi which means "goddess of speech."

Sarasvatī means literally "the watery one." It is the ancient name of a stream in the Panjāb on whose banks in early times solemn sacrifices to the gods were performed.[3] The flow of its purifying waters was compared aptly enough

[1] Vāch, Brāhmani, Savitrī are all names for Sarasvatī.

[2] This alludes to the celebrated place of pilgrimage near Allāhabād where the Ganges, Jumna, and the mythical Sarasvatī meet.

[3] As a river goddess Sarasvatī was to the early Hindus what the Ganges is to their descendants:

The Rig-Veda, x. 17–20, after mentioning Sarasvatī, says: "May they (the waters) who purify with butter, purify us with butter; for their goddesses bear away defilement; I come out of them pure and cleansed." And again:

"Ye, opulent waters, command riches; ye possess excellent power and immortality; ye are the mistresses of wealth and progeny; may Sarasvatī bestow this vitality on her worshipper."—*Rig-Veda*, vi. 52–6.

to the roll of eloquent speech, and the music and rhythm of the repetition of sacred texts and prayers. Hence Sarasvatī takes her place as the inspirer of speech, the patroness of science and literature.

In later mythology Sarasvatī became under different names the spouse of Brahmā:

> "A voice derived from Brahmā entered into the ears of them all; the celestial Sarasvatī was then produced from the heavens." [1]

"This goddess is regularly worshipped by the student classes all over India, and her image, mounted on her favourite peacock, playing a musical instrument, while in her duplicate hands she clasps a book and holds out a flower to her husband, is found over the principal entrances and gateways of many Hindu Schools and Colleges. Her worship is specially celebrated on the fifth day of Māgh (January) either before her image, or before a pen, or an inkstand, or book, which articles are supposed to form a proper substitute for the goddess. The image, or its substitute, is placed on the table either to the west or south of the house. And after the officiating Brāhman has read the formulas and presented the offerings each worshipper, whose name has been included, takes flowers in his hands, and repeating a prayer for her favour, presents them to the goddess. After which follow the customary gifts to the Brāhmans and feasting. On the day following no Hindu will take up a book or will write, although they carry on their ordinary secular business. They eat only once in the day and avoid fish." [2]

The last watch of the night is peculiarly sacred to Sarasvatī. In Manu's Institutes we read:

> "Let the housekeeper awake in the time sacred to Brahmī (feminine of Brahmā) goddess of speech, reflect on virtue and virtuous employments, and on the whole meaning and very essence of the Vedas." (Ch. iv., v. 92.)

---

[1] *Mahābhārata, Sāntiparva,* v. 6811.

[2] Ward, *Hindoos,* p. 107.

Brahmā, in addition to the learned and beautiful Sarasvatī, had a second wife in the milkmaid Gāyatrī. An interesting story is told in the Skanda Purāna of their rivalry and subsequent reconciliation. Śiva addresses his wife Devī (Pārvatī):

" Listen, O Devī, and I will tell you how Sarasvatī forsook Brahmā, and he in consequence, espoused Gāyatrī. The Vedas have declared the great advantages which are derived from sacrifice, by which the gods are delighted and bestow rain upon the earth. . . . For this purpose Brahmā, Sarasvatī, the gods, and the holy sages repaired to Pushkara; but when all preparations were made, with all our rites and ceremonies for performing the sacrifices, Sarasvatī, detained by some household affairs, was not in attendance. A priest accordingly went to call her; but she replied, 'I have not yet completed my dress, nor arranged several affairs. Lakshmī, Gangā, Indrānī, and the wives of other gods and holy sages have not yet arrived, how therefore can I enter the assembly alone?'

"The priest returned, and addressed Brahmā: 'Sarasvatī is engaged and will not come; but without a wife what advantage can be derived from these rites?' The god was incensed at her conduct and commanded Indra: 'Hasten, and in obedience to my order bring a wife from wherever you can find one.' Indra passed hastily out and saw a milkmaid, young, beautiful, and of a smiling countenance, carrying a jar of butter. He seized her and brought her in to the assembly, when Brahmā spoke thus: 'O gods and holy sages, if it seem good unto you I will espouse this Gāyatrī.' Whereupon he was united to Gāyatrī, who was led into the bower of the bride and adorned with the costliest ornaments.

"At this time Sarasvatī, accompanied by the wives of Vishnu, Rudra, and the other gods, came to the place of sacrifice. Seeing the milkmaid seated in the bride's bower and the priests engaged in the performance of the sacrifice, she cried out: 'O Brahmā, hast thou conceived the sinful intention to reject me who am thy wedded wife ? Hast thou no sense of shame, that thus, influenced by love, thou committest so shameful an act ? Thou art called the great father of gods and holy sages, and yet thou hast publicly acted in such a manner as to excite the derision of the three worlds. But how can I show my face ; or deserted by my husband, call myself a wife ? ' Brahmā replied: 'The priests informed me that the time for the sacrifice was fast passing away, and that it could not be performed unless my wife were present . . . and Indra having brought Gāyatrī, Vishnu and Rudra gave her in marriage to me. Forgive me therefore this one act and I will never again offend thee ! '

"On hearing these words, Sarasvatī exclaimed: 'By the powers, which I have obtained by the performance of sacrifices, may Brahmā never be worshipped in temple, or sacred place, except one day in the year. And Indra, since thou has brought this milkmaid to Brahmā, thou shalt be bound in chains and confined in a strange country.' Addressing Vishnu, she said: 'Since thou gavest her in marriage to Brahmā thou shalt be born amongst men, and long shalt thou wander the humble keeper of cattle!' To the priests and Brāhmans: 'Henceforth shall ye perform sacrifices solely from the desire of obtaining gifts: from covetousness shall ye attend the holy places.' Having pronounced these curses Sarasvatī left the assembly, but Vishnu and Lakshmī, at Brahmā's request, followed her and induced her to return, while Gāyatrī modified the curses which had been pronounced, and promised all kinds of blessings, including final absorption into him, to all worshippers of Brahmā.

"When Sarasvatī returned, Brahmā asked her what she wished him to do with Gāyatrī, and Gāyatrī threw herself at Sarasvatī's feet. She raised her up and said: 'A wife ought to obey the wishes and orders of her husband ; for that wife who reproaches her husband and who is complaining and quarrelsome shall most assuredly when she dies go to hell. Therefore let us both be attached to Brahmā.' 'So be it,' said Gāyatrī, 'thy orders will I always obey, and esteem thy friendship precious as my life. Thy daughter am I, O goddess! Deign to protect me!'"[1]

And so the reconciliation was complete, but the curses pronounced by Sarasvatī in her anger are wonderfully fulfilled in the popular Hinduism of to-day.

[1] Wilkins, *Hindu Mythology*, pp. 111–13.

CHAPTER III

VISHNU, THE PRESERVER, AND LAKSHMĪ, GODDESS OF FORTUNE

I. Vishnu, the Preserver

> "Hail, self-existent, in celestial speech,
> Nārāyan: from thy watery cradle nam'd."
>
> —Sir W. Jones.

As all Hindus may be grouped into three great classes, the Vaishnavas (followers of Vishnu), the Śaivas (followers of Śiva), and the Śāktas (worshippers of the female counterpart or energy of the gods), it will easily be seen how important a place is occupied by this god in the Hindu Pantheon. Vishnu, in his various Avatāras (incarnations) is probably worshipped by more Hindus than any other deity. His followers also are mostly found amongst the sturdy warlike races of the North, whereas those of Śiva are mainly found amongst the milder Southern peoples. Śakti worship is practically confined to parts of Bengal and Orissa.

Vishnu is called the second person in the Hindu Triad. This does not imply any inferiority to Brahmā. As will be seen later, Vishnu claims pre-eminence. His special work is that of the preservation of the world as Brahmā's is that of its creation. "The Supreme Spirit," we read,[1] "in order to create this world, produced from his right side Brahmā, then, to preserve the world, from his left side Vishnu; and to destroy the world he produced from his middle, Śiva."

"Of the three persons of the Hindu Triad Vishnu is the most human, as he is also the most humane in his character,

[1] Padma Purāna, see Wilkins, *Hindu Mythology*, p. 116.

attributes, and sympathies. So, therefore, he has become the most popular. He has four arms, symbolical of the power he exerts in the deliverance of his worshippers (a duplication of limbs is the Hindu method of expressing additional power). Portions or the whole of his divine nature have descended in earthly incarnations to deliver the earth in times of danger and emergency. They are believed to be still descending in good men and living teachers." [1]

The character of Vishnu is faithfully portrayed in the caste marks of the Vaishnavas. Their distinguishing mark is a V-shaped sign on their foreheads with the point downwards. This identifies Vishnu with "Water," as the property of water is to descend. Nor is the angle with the apex pointing upwards a less appropriate symbol for Śiva. It is the symbol both of life-giving and of destructive force as typified in "Fire." In this connection it is worth noticing that the Vaishnavas frequently call Vishnu Nārāyan. The explanation of this is given in the Institutes of Manu (ch. i., v. 10), "The waters are called Nāra, because they were the first production of Nāra, or the Spirit of God; and since they were his first "ayana," or place of motion, he is called Nārāyāna, or "moving on the waters." [2] Light is also connected with Vishnu as light is said to be produced from water.

Whether, in fact, Vishnu be connected with light, with heat, with air, or with water, it is evident that his function is that of a Divine Pervader (Sanskrit root, *viś* = to pervade), infusing his essence for special purposes into created things, animate and inanimate; for example, into stones, such as the black Shālagrāma; into rivers, such as the Ganges; into trees and plants, such as the Tulasī; into animals such as a fish, a tortoise, a boar, and lastly into men.[3]

The superiority of Vishnu over the two other great deities is seen in two legends, the first of which is taken from the Bhāgavata Purāna.

[1] Monier Williams, *Religious Thought and Life in India*, p. 46.
[2] Moor's *Hindu Pantheon*, p. 74.
[3] Monier Williams, *Religious Thought and Life in India*, p. 346.

SAVITRĪ (SARASVATĪ, Goddess of Learning) seated on a goose, the bird sacred to BRAHMA (The Creator), with open book and scroll in her hands.

GAYATRĪ, BRAHMA'S SECOND WIFE, with five heads.

A VAISHNAVA PRIEST, showing full caste marks.

HARI-HARA.
The form of VISHNU in the guise of MOHINĪ, united to ŚIVA (see p. 196).

"A dispute once arose amongst the holy sages when they were performing a sacrifice on the banks of the Sarasvatī as to which of the three gods was greatest. They sent Bhrigu son of Brahmā to ascertain the point. He first went to the heaven of Brahmā, and, desirous of discovering the truth, entered his court without paying the usual honours. Brahmā was incensed by this disrespect, and was about to destroy him when he recollected that Bhrigu was his son, and assuaged his anger. Bhrigu then proceeded to Kailāsa, the abode of Śiva, and Śiva hastened to embrace him as brother, but he turned away from the proffered embrace. Enraged at his conduct, the god seized his trident and prepared to kill him, but Pārvatī fell at Śiva's feet and pleaded for his life. He next went to Vishnu's heaven and kicked the god's breast as he lay in slumber. The lord, rising from his couch, bowed respectfully to Bhrigu and addressed him: 'Welcome to thee, O Brāhman! Be seated and deign to excuse the fault I have committed by not performing the duties requisite on the arrival of a guest, and the hurt which thy tender foot must have received!' He then rubbed the foot of Bhrigu with his own hands, and added: 'To-day I am a highly honoured vessel, since thou, O Lord! hast imprinted on my breast the dust of thy sin-dispelling foot.' Bhrigu was so overcome with this reply to his incivility that with tears in his eyes he hastened back to the sages, and they at once voted that Vishnu was the greatest of the gods because he was exempt from impatience and passion."[1]

Also, it is related in the Skanda Purāna that when the whole earth was covered with water, and Vishnu lay extended asleep on the bosom of Sesha, the thousand-headed serpent, a lotus arose from his navel and its ascending flower soon reached the surface of the flood, and that Brahmā sprang from that flower. Brahmā, looking round without seeing any creature on the boundless expanse, imagined himself to be the first born, and entitled to rank above all other beings; he nevertheless resolved first to investigate the deep, and

[1] Kennedy, *Hindu Mythology*, p. 240.

ascertain whether any being existed in it who could controvert his claim to pre-eminence. He glided therefore down the stalk of the lotus, and, finding Vishnu asleep, asked loudly who he was? "I am the first born," answered Vishnu, and when Brahmā denied this a spirited quarrel arose between them. This lasted till Śiva pressed between the two combatants, saying wrathfully: "It is I who am truly the first-born; but I will resign my pretensions to either of you who shall be able to reach and behold the summit of my head, or the soles of my feet." Brahmā instantly ascended; but, having fatigued himself to no purpose in the regions of immensity, yet loth to abandon his claim, lied and said he had seen the crown of Śiva's head. For this double sin of pride and falsehood Śiva ordained that no sacred rites or worship should be performed to Brahmā. Vishnu afterwards returned and acknowledged that he had not been able to see the feet of Mahādeva (Śiva), who then told him that he was the first born among the gods and should be raised above all. In this way Vishnu's primogeniture and moral superiority was established.[1]

Vishnu is the only one of the three great gods worshipped under the same name by the Vedic Hindus and by modern Hinduism. In the Rig-Veda Vishnu is conceived as the sun in its three stages—rise, zenith, and setting. The Vedic poets conceive him as striding through the heavens in three steps. This is Vishnu's great deed, and constitutes his peculiar glory. Concerning these steps it is said that two of them, "the rising" and "setting" are near the habitation of men. The third step none can attain; not even the eagle in its flight. He took these steps for the preservation and benefit of mortals, so that the world might live in happiness under them. The zenith, or middle station, is fitly called Vishnu's place.[2]

[1] Moor, *Hindu Pantheon*, p. 18.

[2] *Vishnu as the Sun God.* "May the gods preserve us from the place from which Vishnu strode through the seven regions of the earth. Vishnu strode over this (universe); in three places he planted his

VISHNU reclining on the thousand-headed SESHA, while LAKSHMĪ shampoos his feet, and BRAHMĀ, the Creator, springs on a lotus from his navel.

THE BIRTH OF LAKSHMĪ.
(See pp. 104-105.)

The trait which differentiates Vishnu from other deities is in the Avatāras or Incarnations (properly speaking "descents") which he assumes. In his various forms (as Rāma, Krishna, &c.) Vishnu pervades the thought, and stirs the life of millions of the human race. The explanation given for these Avatārs is that they took place in the carrying out of Vishnu's supreme work in the preservation of the human race. Whenever any great calamity overtook the sons of men or the wickedness of the Asuras (demons) proved an insuperable obstacle to their progress and happiness, Vishnu, the preserver, laying aside his invisibility, came to earth in some form to rescue man, and when his special work was done, returned again to the skies.

Kennedy says[1] regarding these Incarnations, "Some of these are of an entirely cosmical character; others, however, are probably based on historical events, the leading personage of which was gradually endowed with divine attributes, till he was regarded as an incarnation of the deity himself."

---

step. . . . Sages constantly behold that highest position of Vishnu" (*i.e.* the sun's zenith).—*Rig-Veda*, i. pp. 16–22.

"I declare the valorous deeds of Vishnu, who measured the mundane regions, who established the upper world, striding thrice, the wide-stepping. Therefore is Vishnu celebrated for his prowess, terrible like a wild beast, destructive, abiding in the mountains (or clouds); he within whose three vast spaces all the worlds abide. Whose three stations, replenished with honey, imperishable, gladden us spontaneously; who alone sustained the triple universe, the earth and the sky, and the firmament. May I attain to that beloved heaven of his, where men devoted to the gods rejoice; for (them) there is a spring of honey in the highest abode of the wide-stepping Vishnu."—*Rig-Veda*, i. 154.

"Thou who, with thy body, growest beyond our measure, (men) do not attain to thy greatness; we know both thy two regions of the earth; thou, divine Vishnu, knowest the remotest (region). No one, O divine Vishnu, who is being born or who has been born, knows the furthest limit of thy greatness. Thou didst prop up the lofty and vast sky; thou didst uphold the eastern pinnacle of the earth (*cf.* Isaiah xl. 22, xlv. 12, 18). . . . Vishnu thou didst prop asunder these two worlds; thou didst envelope the earth on every side with beams of light."—*Rig-Veda*, vii. 99, v. 1 and 2.

[1] *Hindu Mythology*, p. 244.

This may be taken as the best explanation of these appearances and one in full agreement with the growth and evolution of mythological thought. We notice also an evolution in these incarnations from the lower forms of life, *i.e.* the fish, the tortoise, and the boar, through the form of half animal and half man—the Man Lion—to the dwarf incarnation, or smallest type of manhood, and then to the highest forms of heroes, and men endowed with semi-divine attributes. Some authorities think that many of these stories were originally written as fables, but the marvellous credulity of modern Hindus has converted them from fables into facts and magnified the events into miracles.

Vishnu disputes with Yama his supreme power over the dead. It is recorded that a certain man named Ajamīla was notoriously wicked. He killed cows and Brāhmans, drank spirits, and lived in the practice of evil all his days. After his death messengers of Yama came to seize him and were about to drag him away to punishment when Vishnu's messengers rescued him. As Yama's records were full of this man's iniquities he hastened to Vishnu's heaven and demanded an explanation. Vishnu told him that the reason was that on the point of death he had repeated his name. This was sufficient, and that no matter how evil a man's life may have been if he died with the name of Vishnu or the name of one of his incarnations on his lips, he would most certainly be saved.

Most Hindus believe this. They have only to gasp out the name of " Rāma " or " Krishna," " Nārāyan " or " Hari " —all names sacred to Vishnu—at the last hour and they are certain of a full salvation. As the dead body of a Hindu wrapped in swathes of white cotton is laid on bamboo poles and taken down to the Burning Ghāt, the mourners cry " Rāma, Rāma, Satya Nāma "—" Rāma, Rāma, the True name." That name in itself, representing an incarnation of Vishnu, has power to swing back the portals of Death, to defeat the emissaries of Yama, and to secure certain admittance to heaven.

"It is a matter of common belief that Vishnu sleeps for four months every year, from the eleventh of the bright half of the month Āsark (June–July) till the corresponding time of the month Kārttik (October–November). During these four months, while the god sleeps, demons are abroad, consequently an unusual number of protective festivals are held in this period. On the day the god retires to rest women mark the house with lines of cow-dung as a safeguard; they fast during the day and eat sweetmeats at night. During this time it is considered unlucky to marry, to repair the thatch of a hut, and make string beds. The day of his rising from sleep marks the commencement of the sugar-cane harvest, when the sugar-cane mill is marked with red paint, and lamps are lighted upon it. On a wooden board about 1½ feet long two figures of Vishnu and Lakshmī, his wife, are drawn with lines of butter and cow-dung. On the board are placed offerings of cotton, lentils, water-nuts, and sweets; and a fire sacrifice is offered and five sugar-canes are placed near the board and tied together at the top. The Shālagrāma, or stone emblematical of Vishnu, is lifted up, and all sing a rude melody calling on the god to wake and join the assembly.

"The words of the incantation used to awaken the sleeping deity are these:

'The clouds are dispersed, the full moon will soon appear in perfect brightness. I come in hope of acquiring purity, to offer to thee the fresh fruits of the season. Awake from thy long slumber; awake, Lord of the worlds, awake!'

"After the ceremony has been duly performed the officiating Brāhman declares that the auspicious moment has arrived. The god is awake and the harvest may commence. The whole village is then a scene of mirth and revelry, and dancing and singing go on while the fresh fruits of the harvest are being brought in."[1]

Vishnu is usually represented as a black man with four

[1] Crooke, *Popular Religion and Folk-Lore in Northern India*, ii. 299.

arms; in one hand he holds a club; in another a shell; in the third a discus, a kind of quoit, the instrument with which he slew his enemies; and in the fourth a lotus. He reclines on a snake, his dwelling-place is in the water, and he rides on the mythical bird, Garuda.

The means by which the favour of this god is to be obtained are explained in the Vishnu Purāna. "The supreme Vishnu is propitiated by a man who observes the institutions of caste, order, and purificatory practices; no other path is the way to please him. He who offers sacrifices, sacrifices to him; he who murmurs prayer prays to him; he who injures living creatures injures him: for Hari (Vishnu) is all things. Kesava (another name, meaning 'he who has excellent hair') is more pleased with him who does good to others; who never utters abuse, calumny, or untruth; who never covets another's wife, or another's wealth, and who bears ill-will towards none; who never beats or slays any animate or inanimate thing; who is ever diligent in the service of the gods, of the Brāhmans, and of his spiritual preceptor (Guru); who is ever desirous of the welfare of all creatures, of his children, and of his own soul; in whose pure heart no pleasure is derived from the imperfections of love and hatred. The man who conforms to the duties enjoined by scriptural authority for every caste and condition of life is he who best worships Vishnu; there is no other mode."[1]

In the Bhāgavata Purāna this high teaching is further emphasized: "The favour of Vishnu is to be obtained by pure unselfish love in the hearts of his worshippers, and not by high birth, vast learning, boundless wealth, or any other worldly things. Therefore, ye men, offer supreme love unto Hari. I tell you that the highest attainments of man consist of two things: supreme love and devotion unto the Lord, and regarding him with the greatest reverence as manifested in all created things. This 'love' or 'devotion' is defined as full and undivided attachment towards God. The attachment that a miser has for his gold, a mother for her

[1] Wilkins, *Hindu Mythology*, p. 124.

new-born babe, and a lover for his mistress. The means by which this deep affection may be attained are specified as (1) devotion to one's Guru or religious teacher; (2) companionship with 'God-devoted men' and men full of universal sympathy; (3) surrendering to the Lord all actions and acquirements—this being the 'door to non-attachment'; (4) loving Vishnu, and dwelling beneath his lotus feet with a purified mind; (5) loving all things because in them the deity exists; (6) exercising constant control over the six internal foes of a godly life, viz. lust, anger, greed, worldly-mindedness, pride, and envy."

II. Lakshmī, Goddess of Fortune

"Then, seated on a lotus,
Beauty's bright goddess, peerless Srī, arose
Out of the waves."

—Monier Williams, *Indian Wisdom*, p. 499.

A more general name for Lakshmī is Srī; she is the Śakti or active energy of Vishnu, a goddess of exceptional charm and beauty and of spotless character. No god appears in so many different forms or incarnations as Vishnu; and, Lakshmī, accommodating her husband, is likewise found in many guises. When Vishnu was born as a dwarf, the son of Aditi, Lakshmī appeared from the lotus as Padmā; when he was born as Rāma, she was Sītā; when Krishna, she was Rukminī. If he takes a celestial form she appears as divine; if a mortal, she becomes mortal too, transforming her own person agreeably to whatever character it pleases Vishnu to assume.[1]

Lakshmī is regarded throughout India as the goddess of Beauty, Prosperity, Fortune. When a man grows rich it is said that Lakshmī has come to dwell with him, and when he sinks into adversity he is spoken of as "forsaken by Lakshmī." She reigns in the hearts of all Hindus as Fortune's queen, and although she has no temples she is assiduously courted and is

[1] *Vishnu Purāna*, p. 80; quoted by Wilkins, p. 128.

more invoked for increase of prosperity than Kuvera, the god of wealth, himself.

The account of her birth, as given in the Rāmāyana, is the one commonly received. She rose like Aphrodite, radiant and glorious, from the sea—only it was the Hindu sea of milk! She was one of the most precious of the inestimable articles produced by the churning of the ocean by the gods and demons.[1] The reason for Lakshmī's birth is given in the Vishnu Purāna. The story runs as follows: "One day a saint named Durvaras, a portion of Śiva, was travelling, when he met a celestial nymph with a sweet-smelling garland, which, at his request, she gave to him. He grew excited by the scent and began to dance. Meeting Indra, seated on his elephant, to please the mighty god he presented him with the garland. The god placed it round the elephant's neck and the elephant in turn grew excited, seized the garland with his trunk, and threw it on the ground. Whereupon the saint was displeased that his gift was slighted, and cursed Indra in his anger, so that from that time his power began to wane. As the effects of this terrible curse were experienced by the gods, they sought help from Brahmā, who could not help them, but conducted them to Vishnu. Vishnu told them to seek help from the demons, and that if the gods and demons unitedly stirred the ocean a Being would be born who would lift the curse from Indra. On Lakshmī's appearance the sages were enraptured, the heavenly choristers sang her praises, and the celestial nymphs danced before her. Mā Gangā and the other sacred rivers followed her, and the heavenly elephants poured the pure river waters upon her. The sea of milk presented her with a wreath of unfading flowers and the artist of the gods decorated her with lovely ornaments. Thus bathed, attired, and adorned she cast herself on the breast of Vishnu, and then presented to the gods the divine cup of nectar, which, having quaffed, they went forth to the conflict and were successful in removing the curse from Indra."[2]

[1] See *Kūrma Avatara*, p. 111.

[2] Wilkins, *Hindu Mythology*, pp. 130–2.

"When many a year had fled,
Up floated, on her lotus bed,
A maiden fair, and tender eyed
In the young flush of beauty's pride.
She shone with pearl and golden sheen,
And seals of glory stamped her queen.
On each round arm glowed many a gem,
On her smooth brows a diadem.
Rolling in waves beneath her crown,
The glory of her hair rolled down
Pearls on her neck of price untold,
The lady shone like burnished gold.
Queen of the gods, she leapt to land,
A lotus in her perfect hand,
And fondly of the lotus sprung,
To lotus-bearing Vishnu clung,
Her, gods above and men below
As Beauty's Queen and Fortune know."[1]

It is said that even the gods were envious of Lakshmī's graces and gifts and desired to appropriate them. In the Satapatha Brāhmana, xi. 4, 3, we read:

"Beholding her there standing resplendent and trembling the gods were covetous of her and proposed to Prajāpati that they should be allowed to kill her and appropriate her gifts. He replied that she was a female and that males did not generally kill females. They should therefore take from her her gifts without depriving her of life. In consequence Agni took from her food; Soma, kingly authority; Varuna, imperial authority; Mitra, martial energy; Indra, force; Brihaspati, priestly glory; Sāvitrī, dominion; Pūshan, splendour; Sarasvatī, nourishment."

As Lakshmī is the goddess of fortune the epithet "fickle" is sometimes given to her. But there is no sound reason why Lakshmī should be so stigmatised. She is always seen with her lord, the model of constancy and wifely devotion. When Vishnu is reclining in profound peace on the thousand-headed serpent, Sesha the type of infinity—Lakshmī is found shampooing his feet. When her lord is incarnated as Rāma,

[1] Griffith, *Rāmāyana*, i. 204.

Lakshmī springs of her own will from the furrow as Sītā, the most faithful of wives. In the Vishnu Purāna we read:

> "Srī, the bride of Vishnu, the mother of the world, is eternal, imperishable. As he is 'all-pervading,' so she is omnipresent. Vishnu is meaning, she is speech; he is polity, she prudence. He understanding, and she intellect. He righteousness, and she devotion. In a word Vishnu is all that is called male and Lakshmī all that is termed female; there is nothing else than they."[1]

The son of Vishnu and Lakshmī is Kāmadeva, the god of Love.

The Dīwāli, or "Feast of Lamps," which is performed on the last day of the dark fortnight in the month of Kārttik (October-November), is quite a feature in most North Indian towns. Every house burns a lamp or shows a light outside, and often lights are placed on wells and in the fields to guard the crops from demons. This festival is a very popular one and is chiefly observed in honour of Lakshmī. The people believe that the goddess of wealth and good-luck can be propitiated by gambling. Consequently much gambling takes place at this festival.

In Bengal, immediately following the Durgā Pūjā, the festival of Lakshmī is held. In every Hindu house a basket, which serves as a representation of wealth and prosperity, is set up and worshipped. This basket, or corn measure, is filled with rice, encircled with a garland of flowers, and then covered with a piece of cloth. The householders sit up all night with the basket in front of them and wait for Lakshmī to come, and any negligence of watching is believed to bring misfortune on the family. Also at this time no alms must be given away, nor any money lost or wasted, lest the goddess, who is guardian of wealth and prosperity, should be angry.[2]

[1] *Vishnu Purāna*, p. 59; Wilkins, p. 128.

[2] *Calcutta Review*, vol. xviii. p. 60.

CHAPTER IV

THE TEN INCARNATIONS, OR AVATĀRAS OF VISHNU

"From the unreal lead me to the real,
From darkness lead me to light,
From death lead me to Immortality."
—*Prayer in an Upanishad.*

As already explained in the chapter on Vishnu, whenever any great calamity threatened the life of gods and men, or any evil shook the world, Vishnu the Preserver came to earth in some form, animal or human, to right the wrong. There is no definite information as to the exact number of these incarnations. Some of the Hindu Scriptures give ten, some mention twenty-four, and some declare them innumerable. Ten, however, is the most commonly accepted number, and these are the most important ones. Of these ten, nine have already been accomplished and one, the Kalki, is still to come.

This is the way a Hindu states the doctrine of the Avatāras: "As He (the Supreme Spirit) is an ocean of boundless grace, kindness, love, and generosity, He assumed various similar forms without putting away His own essential God-like nature, and time after time incarnated Himself in the several worlds, granting to his worshippers rewards according to their desires, namely,—religion, riches, earthly love and salvation; and descending, not only with the purpose of relieving the burden of earth, but also to be accessible to men even such as we are, so revealing Himself in the world as to be visible to the sight of all, and doing such marvellous works as to ravish the hearts and eyes of all beings high and low." [1]

[1] Rāmānuja, a philosopher of the Bhagavad Gītā School, quoted in *Edinburgh Conference Report*, iv. p. 179.

There is an element of truth in the doctrine of the Avatāras. The Rev. T. E. Slater says: "The doctrine responds to a deep heart-cry of the people for a religion of faith in a personal God, for a God sympathising with humanity and meeting it in its need. It expresses the desire for a divine deliverer amid the evils and miseries of life. The belief that the gods can, and do, come down to men in their extremity contains a promise of redemption, but while the Hindu, in conceiving of God condescending to man, and assuming a human form, so far resembles the Christian, the conception itself is very different from the Christian."

The pity of it is that in these conceptions the unreal and fabulous have distorted and misplaced the real and true. "The shape and operations of these divine and semi-divine beings are generally suggestive of the monstrous, the frightful, the hideous, and the incredible; the deeds of its heroes, who are themselves half gods, transport the imagination into the region of the wildest chimera; and the whole pantheon presents itself, teeming with grotesque and unwieldy symbols, with horrible creations, half animals, half gods, with man-eating ogres, many-headed giants, and disgusting demons" (Monier Williams).

The conception of an Avatāra or "God in the flesh," undoubtedly marks a great development in the religious ideas of the Hindus. There must be some deep truth underlying the conception that God should descend from heaven and assume the form of a creature for the purpose of saving the world. Of the nine manifestations recorded—the earlier ones are animals or partly so, the later heroes, the fish succeeding the tortoise, the man-lion the bear. Then the dwarf, then the full-grown heroes—Paraśurāma, Rām Chandra, Krishna, and Buddha. With regard to the animal Avatāras we can do nothing but speculate about their meanings, but with regard to the latter manifestations we may observe that as they are all incarnations of Vishnu they are therefore creations of a period when the worship of that god was paramount. In the story of Paraśurāma we for the first time reach actuality. We recognise this story as the outcome of the fierce struggle and ultimate victory of the Priest over the Warrior class; and in Rām Chandra, Krishna, and Buddha we admit real persons, who have undergone a double transformation, first into legendary heroes, and afterwards into powerful gods. Here we arrive at something which resembles history, our feet seem to touch solid ground. We have no hesitation in believing it possible that these heroes existed in the flesh at some remote period of Indian history.

The Ten Incarnations, or Avatāras, of Vishnu, are:

I. The Fish Incarnation, or Matsya Avatāra

In Hindu writings mention is frequently made of a great flood that in the early ages devastated the world. This bears a striking resemblance to the flood described in the Book of Genesis. In order to preserve the human race from absolute extinction in the flood Vishnu appeared in the form of a great fish and rescued Manu, the progenitor of the new human race, from destruction. Manu, like Noah, by his piety in an age of universal depravity, won the favour of the Supreme Being. The story is found in verse: [1]

> "There lived in ancient time a holy man
> Called Manu, who, by penances and prayers,
> Had won the favour of the Lord of Heaven.
> One day they brought him water for ablution;
> Then, as they washed his hands, a little fish
> Appeared, and spoke in human accents thus:
> 'Take care of me, and I will be thy Saviour!'
> 'From what wilt thou preserve me?' Manu asked.
> The fish replied: 'A flood will sweep away
> All creatures; I will rescue thee from that.'
> 'But how shall I preserve thee?' Manu said.
> The fish rejoined, 'so long as we are small,
> We are in constant danger of destruction,
> For fish eat fish; so keep me in a jar,
> When I outgrow the jar, then dig a trench,

[1] Monier Williams, *Indian Wisdom*, p. 24.

And place me there; when I outgrow the trench,
Then take me to the ocean—I shall then
Be out of reach of danger.' Having thus
Instructed Manu, straightway rapidly
The fish grew larger; then he spoke again:
'In such and such a year the flood will come;
Therefore construct a ship, and pay me homage.
When the flood rises, enter thou the ship,
And I will rescue thee.' So Manu did
As he was ordered, and preserved the fish,
Then carried it in safety to the ocean;
And in the very year the fish enjoined
He built a ship, and paid the fish respect,
And there took refuge when the flood arose.
Soon near him swam the fish, and to its horn
Manu made fast the cable of his vessel.
Thus drawn along the waters, Manu passed
Beyond the northern mountain. Then the fish
Addressing Manu, said, 'I have preserved thee,
Quickly attach the ship to yonder tree;
But lest the waters sink from under thee,
As fast as they subside, so fast shalt thou
Descend the mountain gently after them.'
Thus he descended from the northern mountain.
The flood had swept away all living creatures:
Manu alone was left."

This account differs slightly from others. In the Purānas we find that, in addition to Manu, the Seven Divine Rishis,[1] the mind-born sons of Brahmā, and their wives were also preserved by the Fish from extinction. By them the world was afterwards repopulated. Again it is said that the purpose of the Fish Incarnation was to rescue the Four Holy Vedas. After the earth had been submerged in the waters these sacred books remained immersed and the world was in danger of perishing for lack of knowledge. Vishnu then took the form of a fish and descended into the waters and brought to light again the holy books.

[1] See chapter on *Divine Rishis*, Pt. IV, ch. xi.

THE TEN AVATARAS OF VISHNU.

(1) FISH (Matsya). (2) TORTOISE (Kūrma). (3) BOAR (Varāha). (4) MAN-LION (Nrisinha). (5) DWARF (Vāmana). (6) PARAŚURAMA (with Axe). (7) RĀM CHANDRA. (8) KRISHNA. (9) BUDDHA. (10) KALKI.

II The Tortoise Incarnation, or Kūrma Avatāra

In Hindu mythology a never-ending warfare is waged between gods and demons. The demons (Asuras), by practising severe austerities, often obtained boons which gave them ascendancy over the gods. This incarnation was on one such occasion. The demon forces were triumphant and the gods implored Vishnu to help them to regain their lost power. Vishnu replied:

> " Your strength shall be restored, ye gods ;
> Only accomplish what I now command.
> Unite yourselves in peaceful combination
> With these your foes ; collect all plants and herbs
> Of diverse kinds from every quarter ; cast them
> Into the sea of milk ; take Mandara,
> The mountain, for a churning stick, and Vāsuki,
> The serpent, for a rope ; together churn
> The ocean to produce the beverage—
> Source of all strength and immortality." [1]

This immortal beverage was the water of life, Amrita, which with several other priceless things had been lost in the deluge. The churning began, and Vishnu himself, in the form of a tortoise, descending to the bottom of the sea, allowed his broad back to serve as a pivot on which the mountain swung as it was whirled round by the gods and demons. Once having quaffed the nectar the host of heaven with strength renewed

> " Struck down their foes who fell
> Headlong through space to lowest depths of hell."

The list [2] of the priceless and typical things rescued at the Churning of the Ocean is:

1. The Amrita, or nectar, conferring immortality.
2. Dhanvantari, physician of the gods, who holds the cup containing the Amrita.

---

[1] Monier Williams, *Indian Wisdom.*
[2] Monier Williams, *Hinduism*, p. 105.

3. Lakshmī, or Srī, goddess of beauty and fortune.
4. Sura, goddess of wine.
5. Chandra, the Moon.
6. Rambha, a nymph, prototype of a lovely amiable woman.
7. Uccaihstravas, a wonderful horse, prototype of race of horses.
8. Kaustubha, a wonderful jewel.
9. Pārijāta, a tree yielding all desires.
10. Surabhi, the cow of plenty.
11. Airāvata, a wonderful elephant prototype of the elephant race.
12. Sankha, a shell, supposed when blown as a horn to ensure victory.
13. Dhanus, an unerring bow.
14. Visha, poison.

III. The Boar Incarnation, or Varāha Avatāra

There are conflicting accounts of this incarnation. In the Brāhmanas it is said that Brahmā the Creator, as Prajāpati, took the form of a boar for the purpose of raising the earth out of the boundless flood, but the more modern books and present popular belief unite in ascribing this deed to Vishnu. Here again we return to the time of the Flood. The earth, we read, was submerged under the waters by a demon named Hiranyāksha and the final extinction of all life was imminent when Vishnu infused part of his essence into the form of a huge boar who dived into the abyss of waters and after a struggle lasting a thousand years slew the demon and rescued the earth. As is to be expected, an allegorical interpretation of this miracle is given in the Purānas. The elevation of the earth on the tusks of a huge boar is regarded as the extrication of the world from the deluge of sin by the power of the Supreme Being.

IV. The Man-Lion Incarnation, or Nrisinha Avatāra

A demon named Hiranya-Kasipu, brother to Hiranyāksha, had obtained a boon from Brahmā that he should not be slain by any gods, men, or animals. This immunity from danger so increased his pride that he usurped universal dominion. The demon's son, Prahlāda, was an ardent worshipper of Vishnu, and by doing so he incensed greatly his father, who hated Vishnu for having slain his brother in a previous incarnation, and, moreover, disputed Vishnu's claim to the lordship of the three worlds in this one. In the Bhagavad Gītā we are told that Prahlāda, arguing with his father, said that Vishnu was in him, in his father, indeed everywhere. Hiranya-Kasipu replied: "Why, if Vishnu is everywhere, is he not in this pillar?" So saying he struck it violently with his hand. Immediately Vishnu took the form of a being half lion and half man (as by this combination of man and animal the letter of Brahmā's promise was kept), and coming forth from the midst of the pillar, laid hold of the demon by his thighs and tore him asunder with his teeth.

V. The Dwarf Incarnation, or Vāmana Avatāra

The origin of this incarnation is in the three strides of Vishnu, who, as the sun god, is called in the Vedas "the wide-stepping one," explained in the previous chapter.[1] Bali, king of the demons, was the grandson of Prahlāda. He, by reason of his devotions and austerities, had acquired dominion over the three worlds—the heaven, the earth, and the lower regions, and had laid siege to and captured Indra's capital city, Amrāvati. To remove this insult to the gods and to recover their lost estate Vishnu appears in the form of a Brāhman dwarf. This apparently contemptible little being asked the tyrant Bali for the grant of as much land as he could cover in three strides. No sooner was his request granted than, miraculously expanding, the dwarf became a giant and with one step he strode over the heavens, and with the second covered the earth, but then relenting he left the

[1] See p. 98.

dominion of the lower regions to Bali and the demon hosts.[1] Another legend, narrated by Wilkins, declares that after his conquest Vishnu gave Bali the choice of going to heaven, taking with him five ignorant people, or of going to hell with five wise. He chose the latter, for as he said, "There is no pleasure anywhere in the company of the ignorant; whilst a bad place with good company is enjoyable."

VI. Rāma-with-the-Axe (Paraśurāma) Avatāra

The incarnation of Rāma with Axe[2] was undertaken for the sole purpose of exterminating the Kshatriya, or warrior, caste. Between the two great castes, the Brāhman and Kshatriya, there was a prolonged struggle in early days for pre-eminence. Over and over again the warrior or kingly caste tried to assert its authority over the priestly. But eventually success lay with the Brāhmans, and for over 2000 years now they have been the dominant caste.

Paraśurāma, an incarnation of Vishnu, was of Brāhman

[1] "The Dwarf: 'Wherefore I ask from thee, the chief of the bountiful, a small portion of ground, three paces, lord of the Daityas, measured by my steps. I desire nothing more from thee, the generous lord of the world. A wise man incurs no sin when he asks only as much as he needs. He who is not contented with three paces of ground will not be satiated even with a continent, he will desire the gift of the seven continents. Wherefore I desire from thee, who art the chief of the bountiful, only three paces of ground. With so much as suffices for my maintenance I am complete.' Being thus addressed Bali said, smiling: 'Take what thou desirest.'

"That dwarfish body of the infinite Hari (Vishnu) consisting of the three qualities increased miraculously (v. 33). He traversed the earth of Bali with one pace; and (filled) the air with his body and the points of the compass with his arms. His second pace, as he strode (occupied) the heaven; and not the minutest fraction of it remained for his third pace. The foot of the wide-striding deity rose upwards and upwards," &c.—Bhāgavata Purāna, viii., sections 19, v. 16, and 20, v. 21.

[2] So called because he always carries an axe, said to have been given him by Śiva. Paraśurāma is to be distinguished by this sign from Balarāma, Krishna's brother, and Rām Chandra, another incarnation of Vishnu.

parentage, and the son of a devout Rishi, Jamadagni. It happened that one day, during the absence of the sage, a mighty monarch of the Kshatriya caste, Karttavīrya by name, who was endowed with a thousand arms, and possessed a wonderful golden chariot which went wherever he willed it to go, visited the hermitage and was hospitably entertained by the Rishi's wife. The king not only failed to make any return for the hospitality, but on his departure carried off the calf of the wonderful Cow of Plenty owned by the Rishi (see p. 221). Paraśurāma was so enraged at the indignity offered to his father that he pursued the king and killed him in battle. Then the king's sons retaliated, and in Rāma's absence from home attacked the hermitage and killed his aged and helpless father. Paraśurāma then vowed vengeance against the whole Kshatriya race, and seven times over cleared the world of every male member of that caste, filling with their blood five large lakes. After taking this terrible revenge he retired in peace to the Mahendra mountain.

VII. The Rām Chandra Avatāra

This incarnation is one of the most important, and throughout North India is a most popular object of worship. One of the most beautiful poems in the world's literature—the " Rāmāyana "—enshrines the legend of the bravery, the sufferings, and the devotion of the " moon-faced " Rāma, and the equally matchless purity and grace of his wife Sītā. Volumes might be written about this hero-god, but the merest outline of his doings will be presented in the succeeding chapter.[1]

VIII. The Krishna Avatāra

This also is so important an incarnation of Vishnu that a separate chapter will be devoted to it.[2] Krishna disputes with Rām Chandra the honour of popular pre-eminence in North India. His worship is immensely popular, and his

[1] See Part III, chap. v.

[2] See Part III, chap. vi.

votaries regard him not as a mere incarnation of Vishnu but as the Supreme Being himself.

IX. The Buddha Avatāra

"The Buddha incarnation was originally foreign to the cycle of the Avatāras of Vishnu, and therefore is only briefly alluded to in some of the Purānas. Where this is done the intention must have been to effect a compromise between Brāhmanism and Buddhism by trying to represent the latter religion as not irreconcilably antagonistic to the former." [1] The meagre mention of Buddha in Hindu writings need occasion no surprise if we remember that the Brāhmans, in their antagonism to Buddhism, teach that Vishnu became incarnated as Buddha for the purpose of inculcating error! The Bhāgavata Purāna says, "By his words, as Buddha, Vishnu deludes the heretics." What a dreadful conception is this. The incarnate Deity teaching damnable error. Yet this was the means devised by the Brāhmans to prevent the people becoming Buddhists. To account for this hatred it must be remembered that at one time throughout Northern India Buddhism supplanted Hinduism as the predominant faith. After some centuries of supremacy the inherent weaknesses of Buddhism, its divisions, its monasticism, and its inertia caused its decay. To-day scarcely a Buddhist remains on the vast Gangetic plain where Buddha lived and wrought righteousness. Hinduism, all accommodating, appropriated Buddha,[2] and found a niche for him in the Pantheon of Brāhmanism as an incarnation of Vishnu. Buddhism nevertheless, though conquered and submerged, has left an indelible mark upon its conquerors. To-day to Hindu and Buddhist alike all things tend towards the life contemplative rather than the life active. "Action," as Amiel says, is "coarsened thought." Passivity is, therefore, preferred by the Eastern. Life is weariness and vexation of spirit, and death is an object of desire rather than a dread. The bourne

[1] Goldstücker, article in *Chambers's Encyclopædia*.

[2] The life story of Buddha is given in Part III, chap. vii.

BUDDHA AS AN AVATĀRA OF VISHNU.

A very rare example of BUDDHA as worshipped in a Hindu Temple, with typical Hindu guardian godlings on either side.

of all life's struggle is to be absorbed in the Universal Soul, to be again what one was before birth, unseparated, non-differentiated from the Supreme.

X. The Kalki Avatāra[1]

Unlike all the others, this incarnation is not yet accomplished. As the Jews still wait for the promised Messiah who is to inaugurate a reign of righteousness, so it is the pious hope and expectation of the Hindus that Vishnu will again visit the scene of his past exploits, to usher in a reign of universal prosperity and peace.

In striking agreement with the Christian prophecy of the second coming of Christ in the Book of Revelation, this descent will not come to pass until the end of the Kali Yuga, or Fourth Era, which began when Krishna reascended into heaven, from which time the world has become wholly corrupt. When evil reigns supreme Kalki is to be revealed in the sky,[2] riding a white horse, with drawn sword, blazing like a comet, for the final destruction of the wicked, and the restoration of a new era of purity, righteousness, and peace, similar to the first period, the Krita-Yuga, or Golden Age. Some of the depressed classes in India comfort themselves, contrary to the prophecy quoted, by the expectation that Kalki will appear as their future deliverer and the restorer of their lost social position. How remarkable it is that a belief in a coming Redeemer seems to exist in all religions. The Jew, Christian, and Hindu, the Buddhist, who looks forward to a future Buddha, and the Muhammadan, who awaits the coming Mahdi, all unite in this great hope of the future.

[1] This incarnation is called the Nishkalank, "spotless," or "sinless" one.

[2] It is also said that Vishnu, as Kalki, will be re-born in the family of Vishnuyasas, a devout Brāhman of Sambhal village, when he will be endowed with eight superhuman faculties, by means of which he will destroy all the Mlechchhas (pariahs and outcasts and low caste peoples), thieves and robbers, and all whose minds are devoted to iniquity. These Mlechchhas now number upwards of 50 millions of people.

CHAPTER V

RĀMA AND SĪTĀ, THE HINDU IDYLL

" Her presence is ambrosia to my sight ;
Her contact fragrant sandal ; her fond arms,
Twined round my neck, are a far richer clasp
Than costliest gems, and in my house she reigns
The guardian goddess of my fame and fortune.
Oh ! I could never bear again to lose her."

—*Rāma's description of his love for Sītā* (translated and set in verse by Prof. H. H. WILSON).

THE fame of Ajodhya, second only to Benares in sanctity, rests securely in its association with the wondrously beautiful idyll of the loves of Rāma and Sītā, the gem of Hindu literature. The legend is told in the Sanskrit Epic of the Rāmāyana (*c.* 1000 B.C.), and in Ajodhya are laid all the early and later scenes of the story. Here is the birthplace of Rāma ; here, too, the young bridegroom brought home the peerless Sītā, endowed with youth, beauty, sweetness, goodness, and prudence, dear as his own soul. Here also, the long conflict over, Rāma returns to reign in triumph on the throne of his fathers. If the description of the city given in the Epic is true the place must have been splendid indeed in those early days. A city of broad streets and famous temples, green groves and palace gardens, pools of limpid water, banners waving in the scented air ; Brāhmans chanting Vedic hymns ; musicians playing and singing lyrics in honour of King Dasaratha, the Mahārājah who dwelt in his palace in the midst of the city.

The character of this potentate, the father of Rāma, as given in the Rāmāyana, is an exceedingly pleasant one. He is learned and accomplished. He knew the sacred Vedas and

Vedāngas, *i.e.* helps to the study of the Vedas. These are six in number, and in the light of our modern knowledge it is interesting to learn that they were helps to ritual, pronunciation, metre, grammar, the explanation of the meaning of words, and astronomy.

Only one misfortune hindered his perfect felicity. The king was childless, and for a Hindu to be without a son to perform his funeral rites is a calamity indeed. The people of Ajodhya loved their king and wished for the dynasty to be maintained. The king determined to make the great horse sacrifice to the gods, and for a year the votive horse was allowed to wander at will and was after that time slain.

Now the gods, also, were in trouble. They were constantly at war with the Rākshasas, a race of savage demons whose leader was Rāvana, the king of Lankā (Ceylon). So when the sacrifice was made by Dasaratha, king of Ajodhya, for the gift of a son, Vishnu appeared before the gods and asked what request they had to make :

> " King Dasaratha, thus cried they,
> Fervent in penance many a day,
> The sacrificial steed has slain,
> Longing for sons, but all in vain.
> Now at the cry of us forlorn,
> Incarnate as his seed be born.
> Three queens has he ; each lovely dame
> Like Beauty, Modesty, and Fame.
> Divide thyself in four, and be
> His offspring by these noble three ;
> Man's nature take, and slay in fight
> Rāvan, who laughs at heavenly might ;
> This common scourge, this rankling thorn
> Whom the three worlds too long have borne." [1]

Vishnu agreed to the god's request, and sent a messenger with a golden vase of nectar, which he gave to the king and instructed him to give the liquid to his queens to drink. Queen Kausalya drank half the nectar, and so became the

[1] Griffith, *Rāmāyana*, i. 84.

mother of Rāma. The other half he divided between his other two wives, and they were blessed with progeny. Kaikeyī bore Bhārata, and Sumitra, Lakshman and Satrughna. Rāma and Lakshman had from the first the strongest affection for each other, and when they grew up became inseparable.

Now King Janaka of Mithalā had a most beautiful daughter. Her origin was as wondrous as her beauty. One day as he was ploughing an infant sprang from the ground over which his plough had just gone, and he named her Sītā (*i.e.* a furrow). On account of her magic birth Sītā is said to be another form of Lakshmī, born again so that she might revenge herself and accomplish the death of Rāvana, who had insulted her grievously in a former birth.[1]

[1] *Birth of Sītā.*—The story of the birth of Sītā is also related in the *Rāmāyana,* Uttara Kānda, section xvii, p. 1.

"Rāvana, in the course of his wanderings through the world, comes to the forest on the Himālaya, where he sees a damsel of brilliant beauty, but in ascetic garb, of whom he straightway becomes enamoured. He tells her that such an austere life is unsuited to her youth and attractions, and asks who she is, and why she is leading an ascetic existence. She answers that she is called Vedavatī, the daughter of the sage Kusadhvaja, sprung from him during his constant study of the Vedas. The gods wished that she should choose a husband, but her father would give her to no one else than to Vishnu, the lord of the world, whom he desired for his son-in-law. This resolution provoked Samblni, king of the Daityas, who slew her father, Kusadhvaja, while sleeping, on which her mother, after embracing his body, entered into the fire. Vedavatī then proceeds: 'In order that I may fulfil this desire of my father in respect of Nārāyana (Vishnu) I wed him with my heart. Having entered into this engagement I practise great austerity. From the desire of obtaining him I resort to this severe observance.'

"Rāvana's passion is not in the least diminished by this explanation, and he urges that it is the old alone who should become distinguished by accumulating merit through austerity; prays that she who is so young and beautiful shall become his bride; and boasts that he is superior to Vishnu. She rejoins that no one but he would thus contemn that deity. On receiving his reply he touches the hair of her head with the tip of his finger. She is greatly incensed and forthwith cuts off her hair, and tells him that as he has so insulted her she cannot continue to live, but will enter into the fire before his eyes. She goes on: 'Since I have been insulted in the forest by

The marriage of Rāma to Sītā was brought about in this wise. In primitive times the maiden was often given in marriage to the victor in savage sports or trials of strength. In some aboriginal hill tribes in India to-day the bride is won by capture. The Rāja proclaimed that his fifteen year old daughter, Sītā, would become the prize of the Kshatriya, who could bend and string an enormous bow which was given him by Śiva as the reward of sacrifice. No other competitor was able even to lift the bow from the ground, but Rāma[1] not only strung it, but in bending it, snapped it in two, to the wonder and fright of the beholders. He thus became the husband of Sītā.

It is interesting to find in the description of their marriage that so many of the present Hindu marriage rites have the sanction of antiquity. In the Rāmāyana Rāma's marriage is described as celebrated in the old Aryan fashion. The bride and bridegroom stand before the sacred fire kindled on the altar. In the presence of the fire, symbol of Agni, the

---

thee who art wicked-hearted, I shall be born again for thy destruction.' Having thus spoken, she entered the blazing fire. Then a shower of celestial sparks fell from every part of the sky. 'She it is, lord, who has been born as the daughter of the King Janaka and has become thy bride; for thou art the eternal Vishnu. The Mountain-like enemy who was (virtually) destroyed before by her wrath has now been slain by her, having recourse to thy superhuman energy.'"

[1] The following passage in the Rāmāyana describes the character of Rāma:

"He was the delight of his father, his mother, friends, brothers, and the people at large; he was one who addressed everybody softly and gently; when addressed harshly himself he made soft answers. He ever delighted in the society of those who were advanced in learning, virtue, and age; he was wise, generous, and of sweet address. Valorous was he, but never boasting of his own valour; open-hearted, prudent, a respecter of the aged; one who was beloved by all his dependents, respected by the citizens, full of compassion, with his angry passions in subjection; not in the least covetous of the kingdom, though he knew that it was his lawful heritage; for he considered the acquisition of wisdom as more desirable than that of earthly power. A keeper of promises; one who could appreciate the merits of others; who had his own passions in control; who was firm of his own purpose; who preferred truth to life and happiness."

bridegroom takes the hand of the bride, and they are sprinkled with water, first consecrated by the priests. The bride then walks round the fire seven times. In marriage, as in funeral rites, the vast elemental forces of nature—fire and water—are the agents used to-day, as in the dim ages of the past.

The next event is the attempt to install Rāma as "Little Rāja," a recognition of his ultimate succession to the throne, and of his right to have some share in the administration of the State during his father's lifetime. The people, hearing of the king's intention, are delighted; the city is illuminated, and they spend the night in festivities. But the insidious influences of palace intrigue are also at work. A trusted female servant goes to Kaikeyī, the mother of Bhārata, and succeeds in exciting her jealousy to such an extent that she determines to have her son installed, and Rāma exiled. She gains her way by a mixture of Oriental deceit and the wiles and seductions of lovely womanhood. She secludes herself in a distant room of the palace and refuses to be comforted. The king visits her, and she makes him pledge his word to grant her request, no matter what it may be. The king foolishly promises to grant it. She then calls the gods to witness the oath of her husband, and threatens to kill herself before morn if he refuses to ratify the promise. When the king hears her demand he becomes nearly mad with grief, yet feels himself bound by oath to comply, and when on the morrow Rāma, gorgeously apparelled, was led into his father's presence, he receives, instead of the expected honour, the sentence of exile for fourteen years in the jungles of the South.

When Rāma returned in sorrow to break the news to Sītā, he found to his surprise that she cared little for the loss of the throne, or for the pain and privations of the lonely wandering life, so long as she was permitted to accompany her beloved. She is the ideal of wifehood, and her pleadings to accompany her husband are instinct with the highest devotion and the richest type of self-sacrifice. Sir Monier

Williams has translated the passage in which she pleads with Rāma into verse :

"A wife must share her husband's fate, My duty is to follow thee
Where'er thou goest. Apart from thee, I would not dwell in heaven itself.
Deserted by her lord, a wife is like a miserable corpse.
Close as thy shadow would I cleave to thee in this life and hereafter.
Thou art my king, my guide, my only refuge, my divinity.
It is my fixed resolve to follow thee. If thou must wander forth
Through thorny trackless forests, I will go before thee, treading down
The prickly brambles to make smooth thy path, walking before thee, I
Shall feel no weariness ; the forest thorns will seem like silken robes,
The bed of leaves, a couch of down. To me the shelter of thy presence
Is better far than stately palaces, and paradise itself.
Protected by thy arm, gods, demons, men shall have no power to harm me,
With thee I'll live contentedly on roots and fruits. Sweet or not sweet
If given by thy hand, they will to me be like the food of life.
Roaming with thee in desert wastes, a thousand years will be a day ;
Dwelling with thee, e'en hell itself would be to me a heaven of bliss."

At last Rāma consented to take her, but insisted that, as an additional protection, his brother Lakshman should accompany them. They left the city, walking with bare feet, clad in sorrowful garments, and made their way first to Prayāg (Allāhabād), and there they heard that Dasaratha had died of grief shortly after their departure ; and Bhārata rode in haste to persuade Rāma to return to his kingdom, but Rāma refused until the full term of his exile was completed. Bhārata therefore consented to reign in his stead, but always regarded him as the rightful king, and kept a pair of shoes of Rāma's, which were exposed to view on state occasions to indicate that he was only acting as Viceroy.

Then Rāma and Sītā continued their journeyings further

and further south, till they came to the Hill of Chitrakūta, in the jungles of Bundelkhand, and there they built a hut of leaves and tree-branches, and lived on forest-food—venison, fruits, and honey.

The Epic narrates that during their wanderings they visited the hermitages of many Brāhman sages, and found that these holy men were frequently attacked in their solitudes by the Rākshasas (see p. 289). Some historians have tried to identify these savages with the Buddhists of South India and Ceylon. Colour is given to this thought as Rāvana, their leader, was King of Ceylon, but it is probably the invention of the Brāhman priests, who tried everywhere to supplant and discredit Buddhism.

So we read that these Rākshasas tried to put a stop to the ceremonies of the Brāhmans, but Rāma became their champion, and in a great battle routed utterly 14,000 Rākshasa warriors. In revenge Rāvana determined to carry off the beloved Sītā, for

> " Reft of his darling wife, be sure
> Brief days the mourner will endure."[1]

The way Sītā was abducted by Rāvana is interesting. Mārīcha, one of Rāvana's demons, assumed the form of a beautiful golden deer with silver spots in order to attract Sītā's attention:

> " Doubt not the lady, when she sees
> The wondrous deer among the trees,
> Will bid her lord, and Lakshman take
> The creature for its beauty's sake."

The decoy was sufficient, and at Sītā's bidding Rāma started in pursuit, leaving Lakshman to guard his wife. He shot the deer with his arrow, and as the fiend was dying he mustered strength, and cried with a loud voice, imitating Rāma's tones: " Ho, Sītā ! Ho, Lakshman ! " They imagined that some evil had befallen Rāma, and Lakshman

[1] Griffith, *Rāmāyana*, iii. 143.

HANUMĀN, THE MONKEY GOD, at the Court of RĀMA and SĪTĀ.

THE CORONATION OF RĀMA AT AJODHYA.

(Note the significance of the Brāhman priest standing in front of the gods SIVA, BRAHMĀ, and GANESHA, &c., and crowning RĀMA.)

hurried towards the spot whence the cry proceeded, leaving Sītā an easy prey to Rāvana who was hiding close by; who mounted in the air and flew with her in his magical car to his fortress home in Lankā (Ceylon), where he tried in every way to persuade Sītā to become his wife.

The story strangely resembles that of the abduction of Helen by Paris and the consequent siege of Troy by the Greeks, with this exception—instead of Helen we have the stainless purity of Sītā who indignantly scorns and spurns all Rāvana's threats and entreaties.

Unfortunately the story becomes swollen with exaggerations and supernatural interventions, the truth (for it is quite possible this story had origin in a truth) is lost in the myth. Rāma, in his wild grief, sought the aid of Sugrīva, king of the Vānar or Monkey tribes (possibly the diminutive aboriginal hill tribes), and Hanumān, his commander-in-chief, promised support. Large armies of monkeys [1] bore great rocks from the Himālayas and built a bridge across the straits which separate India from Ceylon. The writer has seen these rocks stretching in regular order from the shore, and certainly their appearance to-day supports many a Hindu in his belief in this mythical undertaking. They are still known as "Rāma's Bridge."

Eventually, by the further aid of the monkeys and after a prolonged and terrible battle (described in article on Rāvana, see p. 291), the army of Rāma, under the able generalship of Hanumān, is completely victorious and Rāvana is slain.

[1] *Rāma and Hanumān's Army of Apes.*—Probably referring to the aborigines of the central plains—the Bhils, Kols, Santhals, &c., rude tribes that the Hindu of to-day still speaks of as "monkey people." In support of this we can instance the word *bunmanus* (Sanskrit *vana*= wood, *manusha*=man), "man of the woods." The *bunmanus* is an animal of the monkey kind. His face has a near resemblance to the human; he has no tail and walks erect. The skin of his body is black and slightly covered with hair. Further, this is the name of a well-known tribe of jungle folk in North India. (See mention of *bunmanus* in Campbell's *Kumaon and Nepal and Ethnology of India*, 1866, Part II, p. 46.)

Rāma at once despatched Hanumān to tell Sītā of the death of her oppressor, and she is sent to Rāma in a covered litter. He ordered the litter to be opened so that the army of monkeys may see the face of his wife for whom they had suffered so much. He said :

> " A woman's guard is not her bower,
> The lofty wall, the fences tower ;
> Her conduct is her best defence,
> And not a king's magnificence." [1]

This speech was the very opposite of the warm welcome Sītā expected, and she was heart-broken as Rāma went on to explain the reasons for which he fought :

> " Lady, 'twas not for love of thee
> I led my army o'er the sea.
> I battled to avenge the cause
> Of honour and insulted laws.
> My love is fled, for on thy fame
> Lies the dark blot of sin and shame ;
> And thou art hateful as the light
> That flashes on the injured sight.
> The world is all before thee ; flee ;
> Go where thou wilt, but not with me.
> For Rāvan bore thee through the sky,
> And fixed on thine his evil eye ;
> About thy waist his arms he threw,
> Close to his breast his captive drew ;
> And kept thee vassal of his power,
> An inmate of his ladies' bower." [2]

Poor Sītā, victim of this terrible and unjust suspicion, determines to prove her innocence by the great fire-ordeal, the resort of injured innocence in many ages and amongst many races. Lakshman prepares the sacred pyre which is either to vindicate or to destroy her. When all is ready

[1] Griffith, *Rāmāyana*, v. 271. [2] *Ibid.*, 273.

she walks round it and before entering the fire appeals to Agni:

"As this fond heart, by virtue swayed,
From Raghu's son[1] has never strayed,
So universal witness, Fire,
Protect my body on the pyre.
As Raghu's son has idly laid
This charge on Sītā, hear and aid."[2]

Sītā then entered the raging fire, but Agni also appeared, and taking Sītā by the hand, led her back to her husband, declaring her pure and spotless. Meanwhile the gods themselves had entreated Rāma, saying:

"Couldst thou, the Lord of all, couldst thou,
Creator of the worlds, allow
Thy queen, thy spouse to brave the fire
And give her body to the pyre?
Dost thou not yet, supremely wise,
Thy heavenly nature recognise?"[3]

Rāma, strange to narrate, had no idea of his immortal origin, whereupon Brahmā declares to him that he is Vishnu incarnated so that he might destroy the demon Rāvana who was oppressing the world. Sītā is thus amply vindicated and perfect reconciliation takes place.

Rāma and Sītā then return in triumph to Ajodhya, escorted by the faithful Hanumān and his legions of monkeys. They are crowned by the Brāhman priests; Bhārata willingly abdicates a position he never wished to fill, and Rāma reigns over the kingdom in great glory and prosperity for many years.

"Ten thousand years Ajudhia, blest
With Rāma's rule, had peace and rest;
No widow mourned her murdered mate,
No house was ever desolate.

---

[1] Rāma.
[2] *Ibid.*, 277.
[3] *Ibid.*, v. 278.

> The happy land no murrain knew,
> The flocks and herbs increased and grew,
> The earth her kindly fruits supplied,
> No harvest failed, no children died,
> Unknown were want, disease, and crime,
> So calm, so happy was the time."[1]

But alas! this idyll was rudely broken. The people of the place began again to poison Rāma's mind about his wife's purity. He, in spite of his heavenly origin, seems to have been quick to suspect her who had given him such signal proof of her constancy. He banishes her to a hermitage where her twin sons are born. When they came of age she personally brought them to court, and on her arrival Rāma demanded that she should prove her innocence before the assembled courtiers. But Sītā, the model of wifely patience and long-suffering, would not endure this. She calls on the earth which gave her birth to give her a home. The earth opens and receives her into its bosom. Rāma, worn with grief and remorse at his unworthy suspicion, grows tired of life, and Yama comes to tell him that his work is done. On hearing the Judge's call he goes to the banks of the sacred stream—the river Sārju (Ghagrā), a tributary of the Ganges—and, forsaking his body, ascends to heaven again as Vishnu.

In Ajodhya to-day, and in many places scattered over India, the epic is turned into a play, and the accompanying picture shows some of the actors of the tragedy. Around many a village fire the wondrous story is told—the woes of Sītā draw forth many a tear, the fortitude and heroism of the gentle Rāma excite deep regard, eyes glisten as the wiles and craft of the monkey-god are narrated, and the final deliverance of Sītā, and the reinstatement of Rāma into his kingdom, elicit many a grunt of approval and smile of relief.

The Rāmāyana is one of the world's great epics. It ranks with the *Odyssey* and the *Iliad* of the Greeks, and

[1] *Ibid.*, p. 314.

the *Æneid* of the Romans, and in its moral grandeur it surpasses them. Year by year it deepens its hold on the Indian peoples and lives more and more in their life and thought.[1]

[1] For the full story of Rāma and Sītā, see J. Talboys Wheeler, *Indian History*, vol. ii.; and Wilkins, *Hindu Mythology*, pp. 170–97, from whose accounts this presentation of the idyll is extracted.

CHAPTER VI

KRISHNA, THE HINDU APOLLO

> " Pond'ring spake the ancient Bhīshma, in his accents deep and clear :
> ' Greatest midst the great is Krishna ! Chief of men without a peer !
> Midst these monarchs pure in lustre, purest hearted and most high
> Like the radiant sun is Krishna, midst the planets of the sky ! ' "
>
> —A Hindu appreciation of Krishna :
> from Romesh Dutt's *Mahābhārata*, p. 35.

MEASURED by the gauge of religious development there must have been a considerable interval of time (estimated at 1000 years) between the Avatāra of Rāma and that of Krishna as incarnations of Vishnu. Both were earthly potentates, to both are ascribed miraculous powers and martial prowess ; but one was the type of virtue and modesty, the other of licentiousness and shameless immoralities. If penance and austerity be the leading feature of Śiva worship, and duty to one's home and family, country and god, that of Rāma worship, then love—spiritual and earthly—an ocean of love, is the element in which Krishna reigns. With it comes Bhakti, or faith, for the god is present to the true worshipper everywhere, but he is to be spiritually discerned—with this granted, Krishna can satisfy the love of thousands and each one regards his love as special and individual ; for it is love at once sensual and spiritual, love ecstatic and all-absorbing, that is the peculiar note of Krishna worship.

The name Krishna means " one who attracts or draws," and true to the name no god among the Hindus is now worshipped with the enthusiasm and devotion that Srī Krishna calls forth. He is the favourite deity of a large part of India,

THE DRAMA OF RĀMA AND SĪTĀ.
A dramatic representation of the Idyll, as played before the Mahārājā of Benares at Rāmnagar.

STATUES OF LAKSHMAN, RĀMA, SĪTĀ, AND HANUMĀN.
(Order left to right.)

KRISHNA AND RADHA.

KRISHNA DANCING WITH THE GOPIS (Milkmaids).
Note that he duplicates himself to dance the Rasa, in order to give each of them felicity, while he himself plays the flute standing in the centre.

and young India's ideal god.[1] Nor is this devotion confined to the ignorant. He is eulogised and worshipped by the great and learned. One of the prominent Hindus of the day describes him as "the greatest spiritual figure that has appeared in the religious drama of the world." Mrs. Annie Besant, an Englishwoman who has become a leader of neo-Hinduism, has selected him as her *ishta devata,* and in a letter to Dr. (now Sir H. S.) Lunn,[2] she "reaffirms" her profound reverence for Srī Krishṇa and "hopes that one day she may be fortunate enough to catch a glimpse of his divine beauty." In fact, Hinduism itself, driven from its age-long fastnesses of superstition and credulity by the progress of modern thought, has taken refuge under the figure of this dancing, pleasure-loving hero-god, and is endeavouring to reconstruct itself by spiritualising his sensual revelries. Even Mahādeva (Śiva) is represented as exalting Krishna in the following passage:

"Superior even to Brahmā is Hari the Eternal Purusha, Krishna, brilliant as gold, like the Sun risen in a cloudless sky, ten-armed, of mighty force, slayer of the foes of the gods, adored by all the gods. Brahmā is sprung from his belly, and I (Mahādeva) from his head, the luminaries from the hair of his head, the gods and Asuras (demons) from his hairs, and the Rishis, as well as the everlasting worlds, have been produced from his body. . . . He is the conferrer of honour, born to fulfil the purposes of the gods, and assuming a human body, will slay all the beings in battle. For all the hosts of the gods, destitute of Trivikrama (*i.e.* he who strode thrice) are unable to effect the purposes of the gods, devoid of a leader. . . . This

---

[1] Krishna (as Vishnu) is frequently identified with the Supreme Being. The following passages illustrate this:

"Thou art the source and the destruction of this universe, Krishna; it is thou who createst it in the beginning, and it is all in thy power, thou universal source; glory be to thee who wieldest the bow, the discus, and the sword."—*Mahābhārata Sāntiparva,* vv. 1514.

"The soul of all, the omniscient, the all, the all-knowing, the producer of all, the god whom the goddess Devakī bore to Vāsudeva (*i.e.* Krishna). In whom these worlds flutter, like birds in water," &c.—*Mahābhārata Sāntiparva,* vv. 1616.

[2] Quoted in the *Review of the Churches,* June 1894.

god is the lotus-eyed, the producer of Srī, dwelling together with Srī. . . . You, gods, should, as is fit, worship this deity, like the eternal Brahma, approaching him with reverential and excellent garlands of praise. For the divine and glorious Vāsudeva (Krishna) should be beheld by him who desires to see me and Brahmā the Parent. In regard to this I have no hesitation in saying that where he is seen I am seen, or the Parent Brahmā, the lord of the gods, know this ye whose wealth is austerity."[1]

Some Hindus have instituted a comparison between Krishna and Christ. Certain small resemblances founded possibly on the perusal in early times of the apocryphal Gospels, which may have found their way into India, have been seized upon, and Krishna has been proclaimed as the Hindu Christ. As such is the case let us institute a comparison between the Christian and the Hindu ideal. The facts of the life of Krishna as found in the Hindu Scriptures are sufficient in themselves, and they cannot be gainsaid.

It is very possible that if any real Hindu history could be discovered many of the recorded details of Krishna's life would be found to belong to a Hindu king of that name, for there is no doubt that Krishna was of mortal origin. Professor Goldstücker declares that " this is the most interesting incarnation of Vishnu on account of the opportunity it affords to trace in Hindu antiquity the gradual transformation of a mortal hero into the representative of one of the principal gods."

The steps by which this took place are clearly traceable in Hindu literature. First in the Brāhmanas there is a short reference to the warrior Krishna. The Mahābhārata is a very composite book containing many later interpolations. In the briefest, and, probably therefore, the earliest series of stories Krishna is represented simply as an heroic man, the Prince of Dwārka, remarkable for superhuman strength. In the more elaborate narrative of the Mahābhārata he appears as a demi-god acknowledging the greatness of Śiva. Later on he becomes an incarnation of Vishnu. Later still in the

[1] *Anusāsana Parva, Mahābhārata*, vv. 6806.

Bhagavad Gītā, written about A.D. 700, he is still further exalted and represented as the Supreme God, and his words in the Gītā are accepted as the utterances of the deity condescending to instruct men in bodily form. In the Gītā there is no reference to the conduct of Krishna as described in the Purānas. Krishna there describes his mission: "I am born from age to age, for the preservation of the good, the destruction of the wicked, and the re-establishment of Dharma" (religion). The Krishna of the Purānas and especially of the Prem Sāgar, the Hindi version of the tenth book of the Bhāgavata Purāna, the source from which the facts of his life as given in this chapter are mainly obtained, is a very different character from the pure, exalted Krishna of the Gītā. We will, however, accept the characterisation given in the Purānas as a detailed account of his life is not given in the Gītā.

There was a dreadful demon king Kansa whose tyranny became so unbearable that the whole earth groaned under it. The Earth, assuming the form of a cow, went to Indra and complaining of this said: "Evil spirits have begun to commit great crimes in the world; in dread of whom Religion and Justice have departed; and if you will permit me, I too will abandon the world and descend into the lower regions." Indra in company with the other gods sought redress for the Earth from Vishnu, and Vishnu, when entreated to become incarnate, plucked off two hairs from his head, one white, and one black, and said to the gods: "These my hairs shall descend upon the earth, and shall relieve her of the burden of her distress!" The white hair was impersonated as Balarāma, and the black hair as Krishna.

Shortly after this, Vāsudeva, a Rishi, and his wife Devakī were being driven by King Kansa in a chariot when "a voice in the sky, sounding loud and deep like thunder, addressing Kansa, said: 'Fool that you are, the eighth child of the damsel you are now driving shall take away your life!'" Kansa hearing this drew his sword to slay Devakī; but Vāsudeva interposed, saying: "Kill not Devakī, great warrior!

Spare her life and I will deliver up to you every child she may bring forth." Kansa, appeased by this promise, spared the lady, but to prevent any mistake he placed a guard, day and night over their apartments. Vāsudeva however found means to evade the vigilance of the soldiers and when Devakī gave birth to the eighth child he took the child and, eluding the palace guards, found opportunity to substitute Krishna with the child of a cow-herd called Nanda. Soon after this the cry of the new-born babe was heard by the guard, and Kansa, rushing into the room, dashed the child against a stone. As an additional safeguard he ordered, like Herod, that "search be made for whatever young children there may be, and let every boy in whom there are signs of unusual vigour be slain without remorse." Nanda, with his wife and the infant Krishna, eluded search by fleeing to Gokula.[1]

So far the details given resemble in main outline the birth

[1] Other stories of Krishna's childhood include the following:

When Krishna was seven days old, Kansa sent a nurse with poison on her nipple to destroy him, but his highness gave such a pull at it that the nurse dropped down dead. Kansa then sent a crane which caught up Krishna, who always looked very small for his age, and swallowed him as he would swallow a frog. But Krishna made such a commotion in the bird's stomach that he was immediately thrown up again. When seven years old his uncle invited him to a feast and got the largest and most ferocious elephant in India to tread him to death as he alighted at the door. But Krishna took the enormous beast by one tusk and, whirling him round in the air, dashed him to the ground and killed him.

When little Krishna was frisking about among the milkmaids of Govardhan, stealing their butter and cream, Brahmā, who had heard of his being an incarnation of Vishnu, visited the place and had some misgivings from his size and employment as to his real character. To test his divinity he carried away through the sky a herd of cattle which some of Krishna's favourite playmates were attending. Krishna, knowing how much the parents of the boys and owners of the cattle would be distressed, created in a moment another herd and other attendants so exactly like those that Brahmā had taken that the owners of the one and parents of the other remained ignorant of the change. Brahmā, now satisfied that Krishna was a true incarnation of Vishnu, restored to him the real herd and attendants. When Krishna saw the real ones returning he removed the others out of the way.

of Christ, but further details of his boyhood and youth show a marked divergence. Krishna was disobedient and mischievous as a boy. On one occasion he tormented the calves to such an extent that his foster mother tied him down to a heavy wooden mortar. At another time, when a mere infant lying under Nanda's waggon, he cried for the breast, and, being impatient because his mother did not come quickly, he kicked the waggon and, to the astonishment of the bystanders, overturned it. When Christ was teaching in the Temple and had already formed a high conception of "His Father's business," Krishna was playing all sorts of mischievous pranks, stealing butter, upsetting the pails of milk and curds. He is known quite commonly as the "butter-stealer," and represented as a child with a pat of butter in his hand.

In manhood more serious crimes than theft and disobedience are known to him. He is not above falsehood and deception. On one occasion there was a war between the Kurus, and the Pāndavas, and Krishna thought that if the report could be spread that the favourite son of the chief of the opposing side was dead he would be too distressed to fight. He said:

> "Casting aside virtue, ye sons of Pāndu, adopt now some contrivance for gaining the fight. . . . Let some man therefore tell him (the king) that Aswatthāman (the son) has been slain in battle."

Krishna also justifies five kinds of lying and calls them sinless:

> "On the occasion of making marriage arrangements, to deceive and beguile a woman, when life is in danger, or when one's entire property is about to be taken away, or for the sake of a Brāhman, falsehood may be uttered."

As an example of the above, Krishna's favourite mistress, the one with whom he is always represented in popular prints is Rādhā, but she was the wife of Ayanagosha. Her sister-in-law told her brother of his wife's misconduct, and Rādhā was in great fear lest her husband should murder her, but Krishna reassured her and promised that if at any time her husband should come he would instantly transform himself into an image of the goddess Kālī and instead of finding her with her lover, Ayanagosha would find her engaged in the worship of Kālī. Her husband happening to pass at the time he at once effected the transformation and so completely deceived him that Ayanagosha himself joined his wife in the worship of the goddess.

There is a well-authenticated story where murder and theft are attributed to Krishna. He was on his way to Muttra to destroy the demon King Kansa. As he approached the city Krishna felt ashamed at the meanness of his dress, and said to his brother, Balarāma: "All are going to the city elegantly dressed; we cannot go in this condition." Krishna then seeing a washerman by the river-bank sent his brother to him, but the washerman would on no account part with the clothes in his possession as they belonged to the king. A quarrel ensued in the midst of which Krishna killed the washerman and carried off his clothes. The brothers next went to a shop and stole two necklaces and so completed their toilet.

Of Krishna's moral outlook we have a curious quotation from one of the late Upanishads where he is represented as saying:

> "When I look upon chaste women of respectable families, I see in them the Mother Divine arrayed in the garb of a chaste lady; again, when I look upon the public women of the city, sitting in their open verandahs, arrayed in the garbs of immorality and shamelessness, I see in them also *the Mother Divine sporting in a different way*."

The story is narrated in the Prem Sāgar of how he found a woman on the roadside named Kubja, crooked and deformed, who gave him some fragrant ointment. His compassion was aroused, and lifting up her head with his thumbs and two fingers, and pressing down her feet with his feet, she stood before him upright as a palm tree. What a beautiful and Christlike miracle! Alas! the miracle is only the prelude to immorality, and the saviour of the body becomes its defiler.

It is usual in these cases for Hindus to excuse the doings of their gods and say that these can on no account be considered sinful. "To the mighty is no sin." In other words the gods are beyond and above moral obligation.[1]

We might pass on to other well-known incidents in Krishna's life, *e.g.* his stealing the clothes of the milkmaids of Vraj when they were bathing, and dancing with them in the famous circular dance; but sufficient has been given to show the general trend of the character of the so-called Hindu Christ.

[1] The following is the reasoning by which the author of the Bhāgavata Purāna attempts to quiet the scruples of some of the purer-minded among the devotees of Krishna:

"The King said: 'The divine lord of the world became partially incarnate for the establishment of virtue and the repression of vice. How did he, the expounder, author, and guardian of the bulwarks of righteousness practise its contrary, the corruption of other men's wives? With what object did the lord of the Yadus (Krishna) perpetrate what was blameable? Resolve, devout saint, this our doubt.'

"Suka said: 'The transgression of virtue, and the daring acts which are witnessed in superior beings, must not be charged as faults to these glorious persons, as no blame is imputed to fire, which consumes fuel of every description. . . . These beings, O King, who are beyond the reach of personal feelings, have no interest in good deeds done in this world, nor do they incur any detriment from the contrary. How much less can there be any relation of good or evil between the lord of all beings, brute, mortal and divine, and the creatures over whom he rules? (*i.e.* as Krishna is entirely beyond the sphere of virtue and vice how can any of his actions partake of the nature of either?) Since Murris (Yogis), who are satisfied by worshipping the pollen from the lotus of his feet, and by force of abstraction have shaken off all the fetters of works—since even they are uncontrolled, and act as they please, why should there be any restraint upon Him (Krishna) when he has voluntarily assumed a body? He who moves within the Gopis (milkmen's wives) and their husbands, and all embodied beings, is their superintendent, who only in sport assumed a body upon earth. Taking a human form out of benevolence to creatures, he practises sports such as that those who hear of them may become devoted to himself. The (male) inhabitants of Vraja harboured no ill-will to Krishna, since, deluded by his illusion, they each imagined that his own wife was by his side. When Brahmā's night had arrived, the Gopis, beloved and gladdened by Krishna, departed unwillingly to their own homes!'"

There is, however, another element that enters freely into all accounts of Krishna and makes it difficult to sift the true from the false. The supernatural and fabulous appears largely in stories relating to this god. Let us confine ourselves to a few illustrations, excluding his marvellous conflicts with various demons.

When only eight years old Krishna, in order to annoy Indra, the god of Rain, persuaded the cowherds of Vraj to worship the mountain Govarddhana, on which their cattle browsed, and abandon the worship of the Rain-god. This worship he diverted to himself as he appeared instantly on the summit of the mountain, saying: "I am the mountain, worship me." Indra, greatly angered at the disrespect shown to him, sent down floods of rain to sweep away the cowherds and their cattle, but Krishna raising the mountain aloft on one finger of his hand held it over them as an umbrella, and saved his friends from the fierce storm that raged for seven days and seven nights.[1]

The Vishnu Purāna narrates the following episode: "The river Jumna was the home of the serpent Kaliya who made its waters boil with the fires of his passion so that the trees on its banks were blighted and birds were killed by its fumes. Krishna, however, nothing fearing, plunged into the stream and challenged the great serpent to fight. He vanquished him and afterwards regaled himself with, and dispelled the sorrows of the serpent's wives by playing the flute while they danced to the music."

He also on another occasion overcame the demon King Naraka (or Bhun) and adopted the whole of his extensive marital obligations. He married no less than 16,100 of Naraka's widows, and had besides eight principal queens. Such was his marvellous power that he multiplied himself so that each lady imagined that she had him solely for her husband. He was blessed with a progeny of 180,000 sons and daughters! His career is indeed a romance!

[1] For this and preceding legends see Wilkins, *Hindu Mythology*, pp. 200–5.

And this career closes in an orgy by which he destroys his whole progeny. Krishna with numerous other princes went on a picnic to Prabhāsa, accompanied by many women of easy virtue. To further heighten the pleasure of the entertainment Krishna sent for the Apsaras (the dancing girls of Indra's heaven) to join in the revels. The princes were soon overcome with wine and pleasure. The Vishnu Purāna describes the closing scene :

"As the Yādavas (sons of Krishna) drank, the destructive flame of dissension was kindled amongst them by mutual collision and fed with the fuel of abuse. Infuriated by the divine influence, they fell upon one another with missile weapons. When these were exhausted they had recourse to the rushes growing high. The rushes in their hands became like thunderbolts and they struck one another with them with fatal blows. Krishna interposed to prevent them, but they thought he was taking part with them severally and continued to fight. Krishna then enraged took up a handful of rushes to destroy them, and the rushes became a club of iron, and with them he slew many of the Yādavas; whilst others, fighting fiercely, put an end to one another. In a short time there was not a single Yādava left alive except the mighty Krishna and Dāruka."

He is then accidentally wounded by a hunter. The hermit Durvāsa was once entertained by Krishna, but the latter omitted to wipe away the fragments of food which had fallen on the foot of the sage. For this slight Durvāsa foretold that Krishna was to die by a wound in the foot. After he left Krishna remained engaged in thought. Assuming one of the attitudes favourable to abstraction (*yogga*) he laid his left leg across his right thigh, by which means the sole of his foot was turned outward. By chance a hunter named Jara, whose arrow was tipped by a piece of iron, beholding from a distance the foot of Krishna, mistook it for part of a deer, and shooting his arrow pierced the sole. Jara, seeing his mistake, fell at Krishna's feet and begged forgiveness. To whom Krishna replied : 'Fear not in the least ; go, hunter, through my favour to heaven, the abode of the gods.' Immediately a celestial car appeared, in which the hunter ascended to heaven ; and Krishna then abandoned his mortal body.

The closing scenes in the life of Krishna suggest a feature in Vishnuism not often explained. He is present at the death of his brother, he sees his sons in fierce conflict and assists them to kill one another to the last man, and he himself perishes wounded in the heel, like Achilles, by the arrow of a hunter. Referring to this feature Barth says:[1] "Notwithstanding the amiable character with which the Muse has delighted to invest Krishna there is something sad and even cruel at the basis of the legend. It is in a smiling mood that he presides over all these acts of destruction, that he sees the end of his people approaching and prepares to meet it. . . . Though less fierce than Śiva, Vishnu is nevertheless, on one side of his character, an inexorable god; he too is that Time which devours everything."

These are the main facts of the life of a most amazing and incomprehensible character. Amazing and incomprehensible because the lofty sentiments of the Gītā harmonise ill with the records of Krishna in the older and therefore probably more authentic portions of the Mahābhārata and the Purānas. The Gītā, moreover, does not detail the life of its author and the Purānas give us what we know of Srī Krishna. The battle of neo-Hinduism to-day rages round the character of Krishna. He has many warm adherents amongst educated Hindus. Many regard him as the Supreme Being who, in his wondrous condescension, mingled in the affairs of human life, and naturally their one endeavour is to try to explain away and account for the stories of sensuality and libertinism which stain the fair name of their deity in the authoritative records of Hinduism.

The defence of Krishna is being carried on with great zeal and ability. The great point emphasized is that the loves of Krishna and the Gopis are given in terms of physical love because this is the only available means a poet or writer has of representing divine love. Just as in the Song of Solomon the lover has been supposed by some to typify Christ, and the loving woman the Church, so every incident

[1] *Religions of India*, p. 174.

of an amorous character in the life of Krishna should be spiritualised. The licentious loves of Rādhā and his many other mistresses is idealised into spiritual union with and full surrender to the Divine Being. Krishna says:

> "Fix thy mind upon Me, be my devotee,
> Sacrifice to me, prostrate thyself before Me
> And thou shalt come even to Me.
> I pledge thee my Troth, thou art dear to Me,
> Renouncing all Dharmas (religions), come to me alone for shelter,
> Sorrow not, I will liberate thee from all sins."

In this way one by one the incidents mentioned above are treated. His stealing the milkmaids' clothes and making them come out of the water to beg them from him is symbolical of the utter nakedness and humility of the soul before God, but surely the lesson could have been taught without such immodesty! True, he exhibited an appearance of excessive amatoriness, but it was all "Māyā" or "illusion," he was pure and chaste in reality. He danced the Rasa or circular dance with the milkmaids, and such was his power of reduplication that each imagined herself to be dancing with him alone: this is carefully explained, that he divided himself out of his kindness of heart to remove the deficiency of partners, so that none of the maidens should feel hurt by being omitted. The 16,100 wives that he married when he had slain their husband Bhun, the five-headed Asura (or demon), is disposed of in a wondrous manner by saying that Krishna was devoted to music and that there are 16,100 different musical modes or modulations to be obtained from a five-stringed native musical instrument typified by the five-headed Bhun.

The fact is that the educated classes of modern Hinduism have undertaken an exceedingly difficult task. They have to explain, in the light of the higher morality of the present day, the bacchanalian revels, inebriation, sensual love, the erotic gambols which have become an essential part of the legend of their national ideal, Krishna, and they can only explain and attempt to justify them esoterically. These amorous adventures represent, they say, the Supreme Soul in its relation to the human. The milkmaids and his numerous paramours are the various *vritis* or modifications of the human mind, and Krishna is the supreme self in whom all find perfect satisfaction and their ultimate rest.

With every desire to be scrupulously fair in our treatment of this difficult and complex character we are compelled to point out in conclusion:

The deplorable moral evils resulting from the widespread worship of so immoral a deity. The greater part of the licence and looseness of some types of present-day Hinduism centres round the names of Krishna, Śiva, and Kālī, but particularly that of Krishna. The most popular picture of Krishna—the one in which he is depicted sitting on the clothes of the milkmaids —is so indecent in character that it cannot be presented to English eyes, yet it is to be found in nearly every bazaar. The most popular Krishna festival is called the Rasa, and is held to commemorate the dance of the god with these maidens. Youths dressed to represent Krishna and Rādhā dance together, coarse jests are exchanged, revelry continues through the night, and only at daybreak does the crowd weary. Rādhā, Krishna's paramour, is deified by the Hindus. Her image is found in the temples by the side of Krishna and worshipped together with his. Indeed the act of looking at the two images together is said to be one of peculiar merit. Speaking of the profligacy of manners in Calcutta in days gone by a learned pundit said: "Every house contained a Krishna."

A sect called the Vallabhāchārya, or Mahārāj sect, betrays in an unmistakable form the immoral tendencies of Krishna worship. The spiritual leaders of this sect have had the audacity to assert that they were themselves incarnations of the youthful Krishna and that worship is to be paid to them by their votaries in the full and untrammelled gratification of their passions and desires. Needless to say this has led to the grossest immorality and debauchery. This may be fairly said to be the characteristic tendency of Krishna worship.

KRISHNA holding up Mt. GOVARDDHANA on his little finger to shelter his worshippers from the wrath of INDRA.

KRISHNA with the wives of the serpent KALIYA.
(See p. 138.)

THE BUDDHA OF BUDDHGAYA TEMPLE.

BUDDHIST PRIESTS OUTSIDE PAGODA, RANGOON.

Photo by Messrs. Hunds & Son, Jubblepore, C.P.

CHAPTER VII

BUDDHA, THE ENLIGHTENED ONE

" The Scripture of the Saviour of the World,
Lord Buddha—Prince Siddārtha styled on earth—
In Earth, and Heavens, and Hells, Incomparable,
All-honoured, Wisest, Best, most Pitiful;
The Teacher of Nirvāna and the Law."
—Introduction to Arnold's *Light of Asia*.

SOMEWHERE between the two conceptions of Rāma and Krishna there appeared on the stage a man, greater than either of them, possibly the greatest of mortals that ever trod the earth. Gautama Buddha was also of Warrior caste, the son of a petty king,[1] and he was born about 560 B.C. No man has left a deeper impress on the mind of humanity. His followers are numbered by millions, and around his name has sprung up a literature so voluminous that even to-day it has not all been traversed. It is found in Sanskrit, Pali, Tibetan, Burmese, Jāvanese, Siamese, Chinese, Mongolian, and many other languages.

His was a curious faith. It was a revolt from the Hinduism of the Brāhmans. It aimed at destroying caste, dethroning the priesthood, ignoring the Vedas and other sacred writings, abolishing at once sacrifice and the gods to whom the sacrifices were offered. On its constructive side it held out the highest ideal of morality and self-sacrifice, promising as the incentive—absorption into the deity. Buddha became the apostle of a passionless, hopeless form of atheistic morality—for beyond existence was extinction, and beyond death was Nirvāna—nothingness. " *Vanitas vanitatis, omnia vanitas.*"

[1] This is questioned by some scholars.

The following account of the life of Buddha is taken from a Buddhist work called the Lalita-vistara, translated by Max Müller.[1]

"Buddha, or more correctly '*The* Buddha,' for Buddha is an appelative meaning 'enlightened,' was born *c.* 560 B.C. at Kapilavastu, the capital of a kingdom of that name, situated at the foot of the mountains of Nepāl, north of the present Province of Oudh. His father, the king of that place, was of the family of Sākyas, and belonged to the clan of the Gautamas. His mother was Māyādevī, daughter of King Suprabuddha, and need we say that she was beautiful, as he was powerful and just? Buddha was therefore by birth of the 'Warrior' (Kshatriya) caste, and he took the name of Sākya from his family, and that of Gautama from his clan. The name of Buddha, or 'The Buddha,' dates from a later period of his life, and so probably does Siddhārtha ('he whose objects have been accomplished'), though we are told it was given him in childhood.

"His mother died seven days after his birth, and the father confided the child to the care of his deceased wife's sister, who however had been his wife even before the mother's death. The child grew up a most beautiful and most accomplished boy, who soon knew more than his masters could teach him. He refused to take part in the games of his playmates, and never felt so happy as when he could sit alone, lost in meditation in the deep shadows of the forest. It was there that his father found him when he had thought him lost; and, in order to prevent the young prince from becoming a dreamer, the king determined to marry him at once.

"When the subject was mentioned by the aged ministers to the future heir to the throne, he demanded seven days for reflection, and, convinced at last that not even marriage could disturb the calm of his mind, he allowed the ministers to look out for a princess. The princess selected was the beautiful Gopā, the daughter of Daudapani.

[1] *Chips from a German Workshop*, vol. i. p. 210 *et seq.*

"Though her father objected at first to her marrying a young prince who was represented to him as deficient in manliness and intellect, he gladly gave his consent when he saw the royal suitor distancing all his rivals in feats of arms and power of mind.

"Their marriage proved one of the happiest, but the prince remained, as he had been before, absorbed in meditations on the problems of life and death.

"'Nothing is stable on earth,' he used to say; 'nothing is real. Life is like the spark produced by the friction of wood. It is lighted and is extinguished—we know not whence it came, or whither it goes. It is like the sound of a lyre, and the wise man asks in vain from whence it came and whither it goes. There must be some supreme intelligence where we can find rest. If I attained it I could bring light to man; if I were free myself, I could deliver the world.'

"The king, who perceived the melancholy mood of the young prince, tried everything to divert him from his speculations, but all was in vain. Three of the most ordinary events that could happen to any man proved of the utmost importance in the career of Buddha.

"One day, when the prince with a large retinue was driving through the eastern gate of the city on the way to one of his parks, he met on the road an old man, broken and decrepit. One could see the veins and muscles over the whole of his body; his teeth chattered, he was covered with wrinkles, bald, and hardly able to utter hollow and unmelodious sounds. He was bent on his stick, and all his limbs and joints trembled. 'Who is this man?' said the prince to his coachman. 'He is small and weak, his flesh and his blood are dried up, his muscles stick to his skin, his teeth chatter, his body is wasted away; leaning on his stick, he is hardly able to walk, stumbling at every step. Is there something peculiar in his family, or is this the common lot of all created beings?'

"'Sir,' replied the coachman, 'that man is sinking under old age, his senses have become obscure, suffering has destroyed his strength, and he is despised by his relations.

He is without support and useless, and people have abandoned him like a dead tree in the forest. But this is not peculiar to his family. In every creature youth is defeated by old age; your father, your mother, all your relations, all your friends, will come to the same state: this is the appointed end of all creatures.'

"'Alas!' replied the prince, 'are creatures so ignorant, so weak and foolish, as to be proud of the youth by which they are intoxicated, not seeing the old age which awaits them? As for me, I go away. Coachman, turn my chariot quickly! What am I, the future prey of old age—what have I to do with pleasure?' And the young prince returned to the city without going to the park.

"Another time the prince was driving through the southern gate to his pleasure-garden, when he perceived on the road a man suffering from illness, parched with fever, his body wasted, covered with mud, without a friend, without a home, hardly able to breathe, and frightened at the sight of himself and the approach of death. Having questioned his coachman, and received from him the answer which he expected, the young prince said: 'Alas! health is but the sport of a dream, and the fear of suffering must take this frightful form. Where is the wise man, who, after having seen what he is, could any longer think of joy and pleasure?' The prince turned his chariot and returned to the city.

"A third time he was driving to his pleasure-garden through the western gate, when he saw a dead body on the road, lying on the bier and covered with a cloth. The friends stood about crying, sobbing, tearing their hair, covering their heads with dust, striking their breasts, and uttering wild cries. The prince, again calling his coachman to witness this painful scene, exclaimed: 'Oh, woe to youth, which must be destroyed by old age! Woe to health, which must be destroyed by so many diseases! Woe to this life, where a man must remain for so short a time!' Then, betraying for the first time his intentions, the young prince said: 'Let us turn back, I must think how to accomplish deliverance.'

"A last meeting put an end to his meditation. He was driving through the northern gate on the way to his pleasure-garden, when he saw a mendicant, who appeared outwardly calm, subdued, looking downwards, wearing with an air of dignity his religious vestment, and carrying an alms-bowl.

"'Who is this man?' asked the prince.

"'Sir,' replied the coachman, 'this man is one of those who are called *bhikshus* or mendicants. He has renounced all pleasures, all desires, and leads a life of austerity. He tries to conquer himself. He has become a devotee. Without passion, without envy, he walks about asking for alms.'

"'This is good and well said,' replied the prince. 'The life of a devotee has always been praised by the wise. It will be my refuge, and the refuge of all other creatures. It will lead us to a real life, to happiness and immortality.' With these words the young prince turned his chariot and returned to the city.

"After having declared to his father and his wife his intention of retiring from the world, Buddha left his palace one night when all the guards that were to have watched him were asleep. After travelling the whole night, he gave his horse and his ornaments to his groom, and sent him back to Kapilavastu. 'A monument,' remarks the author of the Lalita-Vistara, 'is still to be seen on the spot where the coachman turned back.' Hiouen Thsang, a Chinese pilgrim who visited India 629–648 A.D., saw the same monument at the edge of a large forest, on his road to Kusinagara, a city now in ruins, and situated over fifty miles E.N.E. from Gorakhpur.

"Buddha first went to Vaisali, and became the pupil of a famous Brāhman, who had gathered round him 300 disciples. Having learnt all that the Brāhman could teach him, Buddha went away disappointed. He had not found the road to salvation. He then tried another Brāhman at Rājagirha, the capital of Magadha, or Behār, who had 700 disciples, and there, too, he looked in vain for means of deliverance. He left him, followed by five of his fellow-students, and for six years retired into solitude near a village named Uruvilva, near Buddh Gayā, subjecting himself to the most severe penances, previous to his appearing in the world as a teacher. At the end of this period, however, he arrived at the conviction that asceticism, far from giving peace of mind and preparing the way to salvation, was a snare and a stumbling-block in the way of truth. He gave up his exercises, and was at once deserted as an apostate by his five disciples. Left to himself, he now began to elaborate his own system. He had learned that neither the doctrines, nor the austerities of the Brāhmans were of any avail for accomplishing the deliverance of man, and of freeing him from the fear of old age, disease, and death. After long meditations and ecstatic visions, he at last imagined that he had arrived at the true knowledge which discloses the cause, and thereby destroys the fear, of all the changes inherent in life, and sang this song of triumph:

'Through countless births have I wandered, seeking but not discovering the maker of this my mortal dwelling-house, and still again and again have birth and pain returned. Now at length art Thou discovered, thou builder of this house. No longer shalt Thou rear a house for me. Rafters and beams are shattered, and with destruction of DESIRE (tanhā) deliverance from repeated life is gained at last.'

"Buddha hesitated for a time whether he should keep his knowledge to himself or communicate it to the world. At that moment we may truly say that the fate of millions of millions of human beings trembled in the balance. Compassion for the sufferings of man prevailed, and the young prince became the founder of a religion which, after two thousand years, is still professed by many millions of people.

"Buddha then turned his steps to Benares,[1] where he met his five former disciples and explained to them his new beliefs in his first sermon:

'There are two extremes, O recluses, which he who has gone forth ought not to follow: the habitual practice on the one hand of those

[1] Here the narrative of the Lalita-Vistara closes.

things whose attraction depends upon the pleasures of sense, and especially sensuality (a practice low and pagan, fit only for the worldly-minded, unworthy and of no abiding profit); and the habitual practice, on the other hand, of self-mortification (a practice painful, unworthy and of no abiding profit). There is a *Middle Way*—a path which opens the eyes and bestows understanding, which leads to peace of mind, to the higher wisdom, to full enlightenment, to Nirvāna.'

"The four noble truths which Buddha claimed to have discovered are:

(1) Existence is suffering.
(2) The desire of existence is the origin of suffering.
(3) The destruction of this desire of existence is the destruction of suffering.
(4) The noble eightfold path to the destruction of suffering is: Right Faith, Right Resolve, Right Speech, Right Action, Right Living, Right Effort, Right Thought, Right Meditation.

"On hearing his teaching his five former disciples were the first to join him, and within five months of his arrival at Benāres he had no less than sixty followers. Calling them together, he sent them out to proclaim the new doctrine:

'Go ye now, O Bhikshus, and wander for the gain of the many, out of compassion for the world, for the welfare of gods and men.'

"After this Buddha went about teaching and preaching for forty-five years, spending his time largely at his friend the King of Magadha's capital, Rājagirha, and at Srāvasti, the capital of the King of Kosala, who became a convert. At the end of this time he was attacked by a serious and painful illness. Turning to a disciple he said:

'O Ānanda, I am now grown old and full of years, my journey is drawing to its close. I am turning eighty years of age, and so, just as a worn-out cart, this body, with only much additional care, can be made to move along. Therefore, O Ānanda, be lamps unto yourselves. Hold fast to the truth as a lamp. Look not for refuge to anyone besides yourselves.'

"His last words to his disciples were:

'Behold now brethren, I exhort you saying, Decay is inherent in all component things. Work out, with diligence, your own perfections.'

"Shortly afterwards he became unconscious and passed away:

'Unto Nirvāna. He is one with Life,
Yet lives not. He is blest ceasing to be.
Om, mani padme, Om! The Dewdrop slips
Into the shining sea!'[1]"

So passed one who, for good or ill, has left a deep and lasting influence on the lives of millions of the human race. There is much that fascinates and much to admire in the character of Buddha as described in Buddhist writings. He is unquestionably the grandest character in Indian history. Deeply in sympathy with human needs, he sought, according to the measure of light granted to him, with unwearied diligence to benefit his fellow-creatures and supply an answer to the problems of life. All this should not blind us to the fatal defects of his system. This book does not attempt to discuss the doctrines of the systems of religion in India, but we may be permitted to close this account with the words of a famous Buddhist scholar, Professor Oldenburg of Berlin, who characterises Buddhism as "a proud attempt to create a faith without a God, to conceive a deliverance in which man delivers himself." If Hinduism is God without morality, Buddhism is morality without God—and therein lies its inherent weakness and the cause of its decline in the world to-day.

[1] Arnold's *Light of Asia.*

A TEMPLE RATH OR CAR.

This car is used to carry the idol in procession through the town. An umbrella, the insignia of royalty in the East, is seen above the canopy. The ropes for drawing the car are already grasped by the devotees. Note the "V" shaped mark in the centre of the canopy. (See p. 96 for explanation of this sign.)

BALBADRA, SUBHADRA, and JAGANNĀTH (order left to right).

Reproduced by kind permission of Rev. R. L. Lacey from his book "The Holy Land of the Hindus."

CHAPTER VIII

JAGANNĀTH, LORD OF THE WORLD

" A thousand pilgrims strain
Arm, shoulder, breast, and thigh, and might and main
To drag that sacred wain,
And scarce can draw along the enormous load,
Prone fall the frantic votaries on its road,
And, calling on their god,
Their self-devoted bodies there they lay
To pave his chariot way ;
On Jagannāth they call—"

—SOUTHEY, *Curse of Kehanna.*

JAGANNĀTH'S image is repulsively ugly—a more gruesome representation can scarcely be imagined—a head altogether out of proportion to the rest of its body, huge goggle eyes, no legs, no hands, only the stumps of arms. And yet this deity is so highly considered that he is not reckoned an Avatāra (descent) of Vishnu, but a manifestation of Vishnu himself, and not, as in the case of Rāma and Krishna, an incarnation of only a portion of his essence.

The great shrine and special centre for the worship of this deity is at Puri in Orissa, one of the seven most sacred places in all India. This temple has an interesting history. It had originally no connection with Vishnu. It was built on the site of an ancient Buddhist shrine, where the tooth of Buddha was kept before its removal to Ceylon. It is possible that when the famous tooth was removed, the image of some local divinity took its place, and this image—called Jagannāth —was presently admitted into the Hindu Pantheon as another manifestation of Vishnu. Whatever may be the origin of the image there are too many indications of the influence of Buddha at Puri to doubt the original connection of the place with Buddhism.

A Hindu (Lāla Baij Nāth) contributes an interesting note on the temple at Puri :

> "The temple of Jagannāth is not mentioned in the older Hindu Sāstras, nor even in the Purānas, though attempts have been made to trace the institution to the Vedas. The place seems from all accounts to be an adaptation of Buddhism or Śaktism, or both, to Vaishnavism. There is nothing to correspond to the images of Jagannāth, Balbhadra, and Subhadrā in any of the Sāstras, nor is that absence of caste restriction and freedom in the matter of eating and drinking, which forms such a unique feature of that temple, recognised elsewhere. The temple at Puri dates only from the twelfth century, and the first mention of Jagannāth is in the fourth century. When I visited the place I tried to find out some more historical facts connected with the institution, but could not do so. And yet it is a wonderful institution, both for its wealth, its grandeur, and its hold on the minds of the people. I do not think it is an adaptation of any non-Aryan institution or deity. On the contrary, from the fact that Durgā has to be first worshipped in the temple before you can see the great God, it appears that the worship is borrowed from Śakta sources. The absence of caste distinction also points to the same conclusion.
>
> ". . . It is visited by lacs of people every year. The income of the temple is estimated at 4 or 5 lacs a year (a lac is £6666) from landed property, but the offerings of pilgrims make it thrice as much more. It has a staff of 60,000 priests and servants. The Rāja of Puri is its hereditary sweeper."

"The strange, unfinished state of the image is explained by the following legend. When Krishna was accidentally shot by Jara, the hunter, his bones were collected by some devotee and placed in a box. It happened that Indrahumma, a king who was earnestly striving to propitiate Vishnu, was directed by that deity to form an image and place Krishna's bones inside it with the assurance that if he did so he would afterwards be richly rewarded. The king asked Visvakarma, the artificer to the gods, to help him in the preparation of this image. This he was ready to agree to do, but he made the stipulation that if anyone looked at him, or disturbed him before the twenty-one days required to finish the work were over, he would immediately desist. The king consented to this condition, but his curiosity was too strong, and after fifteen days of waiting he opened the door of the room where the image was. The heavenly artisan disappeared, and the result is the present ugly ill-shaped deity now resident at Puri. On one side of the idol Jagannāth there is an image of Krishna's favourite brother Balarāma, and his sister Subhadrā is seen between the two."[1]

"One peculiarity of the worship of this deity is that the image is not only worshipped in the temple, but is taken out of doors, and for three days in the year is exposed to public view. On the first of these days the idol is taken from its shrine, and on a lofty platform, in sight of vast multitudes, is bathed by the priests. This exposure is supposed to be productive of a 'cold,' and for a fortnight it is taken to the sick chamber where it is carefully tended. After this a change of air is believed to be beneficial, so the image is placed on an immense car and taken to pay a visit to the temple of another god. This car is drawn by the worshippers through the excited crowds of people. In olden days devotees may have voluntarily laid down in the pathway of the car, or have fallen under the car by pressure from the enormous crowds around it. Unless such a practice did take place it is difficult to account for the tradition of bloodshed that has gathered round the Rath Jattra (Car Festival). After waiting a few days the Return Festival is held, and 'the Lord of the World'—for so his name reads—is once again dragged back to his home.'"[2] To *see* the image cleanses from all sin, but considerable religious merit is obtained by assisting in dragging the car. Many large Bengal towns and villages keep these cars, and hold a yearly festival in honour of the god when the cars are used.

The following account of the great temple at Puri is given by the well-known travellers, Dr. and Mrs. W. Hunter Workman :

"Early accounts of the god are vague, and later ones

[1] Wilkins, p. 252. [2] *Ibid.*, p. 253.

conflicting, but reliable authorities seem to agree that the origin of the three images seen at Puri is Buddhist. The Buddhist wheel and monogram as seen at Sānchi suggest the form of the wooden images of Jagannāth, Balarāma, and Subhadrā. It seems probable that when Hinduism supplanted Buddhism a Hindu temple was built on the site of the old Buddhist one, and the emblems found in the ancient shrine were taken as models for the present Vaishnava gods. Certainly these wooden blocks more closely resemble Buddhist deities than the familiar deities of Hinduism. Jagannāth leads a busy life, for, outside the special festivals, he has daily to be bathed, dressed, undressed, and put to bed, besides presiding at four meals served him by temple attendants. Each meal is concluded with music and dancing in the hall of the temple, and this means the maintenance by the temple of a large number of dancing girls, stated to be one hundred and twenty.

"Pilgrims are taught it is of vital importance to partake of, and carry away with them, portions of the specially consecrated food served to the god. From the sale of this food a large revenue is derived. The pilgrim who eats this food is absolved from the direst sin. Jagannāth recognises no caste, and any orthodox Hindu, whatever be his caste, may discard all restrictions and eat the consecrated food with Hindus of other castes. Here, again, we trace the influence of Buddhism.

"Whatever it may have been in the beginning, the worship of Jagannāth has now become a business which furnishes employment to thousands of attendants. At festival time the railway is taxed to its fullest capacity. A railway official stated that more than 300,000 rupees worth of tickets had been issued in a single day. When 100,000 pilgrims are at times assembled, many priests are required to officiate, many attendants to direct the movements of the multitude, and many cooks to prepare their food.

"In addition to those employed in, and around the temple, it is said that agents are sent to all parts of India to induce pious Hindus to make the pilgrimage. These agents inform themselves carefully as to the pecuniary circumstances of their intended victims, and approach only those who are wealthy or well-to-do. The information thus gathered, and the names of those who agree to go, are forwarded to the temple priests, who thus know what demands they can make on the purses of the devotees when they arrive.

"When the temple is reached it is a question of rupees whether the pilgrim beholds Jagannāth from near or from far, or indeed at all. He is told that the sight of the god cleanseth from all sin, and the nearer the view of the god the greater the efficacy of the pilgrimage. His privileges are regulated by the amount of means known to be at his disposal. But to obtain even an ordinary view he must pay a good round sum. If he has not the sum demanded with him in money, he is required to sign a bond for it binding on him and his descendants, which is collected to the last anna. Many a Hindu family has been impoverished for several generations by the drain thus created by the religious fervour of an ancestor.

"Deception is also practised. A pilgrim, on entering the East or Lion gate, is required to walk round the temple from the left, six or seven times. In going round, pilgrims are attended by cicerones, who direct their attention to its outer ornaments and towers. The glare of the sunlight on its white-washed exterior so dazzles their eyes that when they reach the interior and look into the sanctuary they can see nothing. They are told this inability to see is caused by their sin-laden conscience, and the usual demand follows.

"For a sum of five hundred to five thousand rupees a special permit is given allowing the pilgrim to go into the inner sanctum where the god is, all others being excluded.

"The story of the Calcutta Rāja is typical. Having seen nothing at his first visit he was reminded that he must be purged of sin by prayer and do something substantial for the temple. He thereupon prayed for a day and a night, and promised, should he see the god, to make at his own expense a metalled road from Cuttack to Puri, and build rest houses and dispensaries for pilgrims at various points. On being taken again, this time without circumambulation of the temple, into the sanctum, he beheld the god in all his beauty. He kept his promise at the cost of several lakhs of rupees, and to him we owe the excellent road from Cuttack to Puri."

KĀMADEVA, THE HINDU CUPID.

CHAPTER IX

KĀMADEVA, THE HINDU CUPID

> " He bends the luscious cane, and twists the string
> With bees, how sweet! but ah! how keen the sting!
> He with five flow'rets tips his ruthless darts,
> Which through five senses pierce enraptured hearts."
>
> —*Extract from Brij Sonnet.*

According to the Vedas, Desire is said to have been the first outflow of the act of creation, the primal germ of the mind, and the origin of all subsequent action. Little wonder then that Kāmadeva, the god of love, who excites desire, should be highly esteemed among the Hindus. He is generally regarded as the son of Vishnu and Lakshmī in their incarnations as Krishna and Rukminī, but some accounts represent him as springing from the heart of Brahmā. The former descent is the most probable, for Lakshmī is the " Śakti " of the agent for preservation, and so is regarded as the general principle of attraction, which unites in love all animated beings, and gives coherence to the atoms of the physical world.

Kāma is represented as a beautiful youth armed with bow and arrows. The bow is of sugar cane strung with a line of honey bees, and each arrow is tipped with a beautiful flower. He rides on a parrot, attended by Apsaras, or heavenly nymphs of great beauty, over whom he rules. One bears before him his banner, on which is the device of a fish mounted on a red ground. He is accompanied by Rati, his wife, the goddess of affection, and with him go to escort him in his wanderings through the three worlds—the cuckoo, the humming bee, and the gentle breezes. His greatest friend is Vasanta or Spring personified, denoting love's season. His victims are thus addressed: "May Kāma, having well directed the arrow which is winged with pain, barbed with longing, and has desire for its shaft, pierce thee to the heart!"[1]

This dread god, owing to the far-reaching operation of the passion he inspires, and its mysterious origin, has accumulated a number of names. He is called "the destroyer of peace," "the bewilderer," "the lamp of spring," "the crackling fire," "the teacher of the world," "the stalk of passion," "he whose arrows are flowers," "who intoxicates with love," "who conquers all."

Many stories are told of him. He was destroyed by a burst of flame from Śiva's third eye, because he wounded the god while wrapped in meditation and devotion, and caused him to forsake his ascetic life and fall in love with Pārvatī. Poor Śiva, though he burnt up Kāma, had received his arrow in the heart. The Vāmana Purāna[2] gives a lengthy account of his sufferings, from which we extract the following: "The wounded god could find no rest. He threw himself into the Kalindi river, but the waters were dried up and changed into blackness, and ever since, its dark stream, though holy, has flowed through the forest like the black string that binds a maiden's hair." He wandered from hermitage to hermitage, but was ill at ease. The hermits' wives from the forest of Daruvanam followed him from place to place, and their husbands cursed Śiva, and deprived him of his strength. At last he had to yield to the invincible passion, and returned, conquered by love, to marry Pārvatī.

Great was the grief of Rati on the death of the god of Love. She entreated Pārvatī to intercede with Śiva to restore him to life. Pārvatī told her how her wish would be gratified. He would be born again as the son of Krishna! Rati became a servant in the house, and when the child was born she tended him with the greatest care, being fascinated by his beauty. Her affection deepened into passion as the child advanced to youth and manhood. Kāma observed

[1] Atharva-Veda, iii. 25.
[2] Kennedy's *Hindu Mythology*.

this and said: "Why do you indulge in feelings so unbecoming the character of a mother?"—thinking that she who for so long had cared for him must be his mother. To which she replied: "Thou art no son of mine, thou art the son of Krishna." Krishna, when appealed to, agreed to this, and gave Kāma the handmaid Rati to be his wife. So Rati rejoiced in receiving her husband Kāma again.[1]

Even the great Buddha is said to have been tempted by Kāmadeva. The incident is pictured in glowing verse by Sir Edwin Arnold:[2]

"Next there drew
Gallantly nigh a brave Tempter, he,
Kāma, the King of passions, who hath sway
Over the gods themselves, Lord of all loves,
Ruler of Pleasure's realm. Laughing he came
Unto the tree, bearing his bow of gold
Wreathed with red blooms, and arrows of desire
Pointed with five-tongued delicate flame, which stings
The heart it smites sharper than poisoned barb:
And round him came into that lonely place
Bands of bright shapes with heavenly eyes and lips
Singing in lovely words the praise of Love
To music of invisible sweet chords,
So witching, that it seemed the night stood still
To hear them, and the listening stars and moon
Paused in their orbits."

No images are made to represent Kāmadeva in Bengal, but at the time of marriage when a wife leaves her father's house to go to her husband's for the first time petitions are addressed to this god for happiness in the married state and offspring. A festival is held in Kāma's honour on the 13th and 14th of March, on which occasion the following verses are chanted:

1. Hail! God of the flowery bow: hail, warrior, with a fish on thy banner; hail, powerful Divinity, who causeth the firmness of the sage to forsake him, and subduest the guardian deities of the eight regions!

---

[1] Wilkins, *Hindu Mythology*, p. 159.
[2] *Light of Asia*, p. 166.

2. O Kāmadeva! thou son of Mādhava! O Mara! Thou foe of Sambara! Glory be to thee, who lovest the goddess Rati; who springest from the heart!

3. Glory be to Madana; to Kāma; to him who is formed as the God of gods; to him by whom Brahmā, Vishnu, Śiva, and Indra are filled with emotions of rapture!

4. May all my mental cares be removed! all my corporeal sufferings terminate! May the object of my soul be attained, and my felicity continue for ever.[1]

[1] Moor, *Hindu Pantheon*, p. 451.

CHAPTER X

CHAITANYA, THE MENDICANT GOD

"I choose
To tread its paths with patient stainless feet,
Making its dust my bed, its loneliest wastes
My dwelling, and its meanest things my mates.
This will I do because the woeful cry
Of life and all flesh living cometh up
Into my ears, and all my soul is full
Of pity for the sickness of this world.

—ARNOLD'S *Light of Asia*, p. 106.

THIS incarnation of Vishnu is of great interest because, like that of Krishna, we can trace the means by which a human being came to be regarded as divine. Chaitanya's principal centre of worship is Nadiya in Bengal, and it is a singular fact that at his shrine there is a very small image of Krishna, of whom he was a disciple and apostle, whilst the image of Chaitanya is large and conspicuous. The Hindus who acknowledge his divinity form a large community—about one-fifth of the entire population of Bengal. These declare that amongst the many incarnations of Vishnu four are most important—the white incarnation named Ananta, the red Kapila, the black Krishna, and the yellow Chaitanya.

One of the two masters (Prabhus) of the sect of which Chaitanya was the most illustrious member was a Brāhman, named Adaitya, who lived at Santipore in Bengal. Another leader, named Nityānanda, was born at a village named Ekachakra, in the district of Birbhum, a short time before Chaitanya. The god himself was born in A.D. 1484 at Nadiya, and died at Puri in 1527. His father was a Brāhman named Jagannāth Misra, and his mother's name was Suchi. Their first son, Visvarūpa, became a religious mendicant.

When their second son, Chaitanya, was born, his mother was advanced in years. Consequently the child was very weak, and continued for three days without taking the breast. In accordance with the cruel custom that then prevailed, his parents hung him out in a basket suspended to a branch of a tree to die. Adaitya, happening to pass at the time, and imagining that the child thus exposed might be the incarnation of the deity that he was expecting and had foretold, wrote with his toe on the soft earth under the tree the incantation employed in the initiation of a disciple into the mysteries of Krishna-worship: "Hari Krishna; Hari Krishna; Krishna, Krishna, Hari, Hari; Hari Rāma; Hari Rāma; Rāma, Rāma, Hari, Hari." The mother, greatly impressed by this act, lifted the child from the tree, who immediately took kindly to his food and showed signs of vigour and strength.

Chaitanya as a youth made great progress in learning. He married twice, first at the age of eleven a girl named Lakshmī, and on her early decease he married when sixteen years of age Vishnupriyā, with whom he lived till he was twenty-four years of age, when "he felt moved to the heart by the distresses of mankind" and was constrained to renounce his *poita* (Brāhmanical thread) and join the ascetic life. This was a great act of self-renunciation as at one stroke he lost his high position as a Brāhman. Leaving his home, his parents, and wife, he spent the next six years as a Bairāgi (wandering Sādhu) travelling all over India teaching his doctrines, acquiring followers, and extending the worship of his lord Krishna.

Like most such holy men he eventually reached Benares and there he converted to his faith the chief pundit of the place, Prakāshānanda, and many others. He called his disciples Vaishnavas (*i.e.* followers of Vishnu) and gave them as their initiatory rite the incantation already quoted. Many of his teachings are opposed to orthodox Hinduism, yet in spite of this he made many disciples. His success may be traced to his extraordinary fervour and his love for men.

He preached causeless or utterly unselfish love to Vishnu (Krishna). "Worship," he said, "from interested motives (viz. the attainment of happiness, or the expiation of sin) was not worship at all, but shopkeeping—barter." Self-sacrifice was also urged with passionate insistence. "A man must attain the nature of a tree, which lives solely for the benefit of others, before he can become a true worshipper." The chief tenets of his faith were :

1. A disregard of caste distinctions—"The mercy of God regards neither tribe nor family."

2. Emphasis was laid on the mendicant life.

3. His followers must as a means of God-realisation honour Vishnu in his incarnation of Krishna, using in their prayers a rosary made from the wood of the Tulsaī-tree (Holy Basil) sacred to Vishnu. "He also recommended Rādhā worship and taught that the best form of devotion was that which Rādhā, as the beloved mistress of Krishna felt for him." [1]

4. They must exercise *Bhakti* (*i.e.* fervent devotion founded upon implicit faith) in Krishna as the only means of salvation. This devotion contains five degrees of intensity: (1) quiet contemplation of the deity (*śānti*) ; (2) service, the devotion of a servant to his master (*dāsva*) ; (3) friendship to him (*sākhya*) ; (4) love to him resembling the love of children to their parents (*vātsalya*) ; (5) passionate attachment, as of a girl to her lover, or as the Gopis felt for Krishna (*mādhurya*).

Chaitanya was in advance of his times as a social reformer. He allowed widows remarriage, and he forbade the drinking of intoxicants, and the eating of fish and flesh, and the offering of animal sacrifices, and included a prohibition to his disciples to hold no fellowship with those who offered such sacrifices. "The bacchanalian orgies of the Tantrics," writes a Bengali,[2] "and their worship of a 'shamefully exposed female' provoked the abhorrence of Chaitanya and roused his energy to remove the deep blots upon the national character. He commenced his labours by holding meetings of his immediate

[1] Bhattacharjee, *Hindu Castes and Sects*, p. 469.

[2] *Travels of a Hindu*, by Bholanāth Chunder, pp. 29–30.

friends. At these meetings he expounded the life and acts of Krishna. Passages in the Bhagavat which everyone understood in a literal sense, he construed figuratively, and, by striking upon the emotional cord of our nature, he thought of putting down sensualism by sentiment. In a little while his enthusiasm affected hundreds and gathered around him a body of disciples."

His great doctrine was *Bhakti*,[1] and it is a curious coincidence that Martin Luther preached salvation by faith in Europe about the time that Chaitanya in Bengal was giving prominence to a very similar doctrine. He spent the last eighteen years of his life at Puri, the great shrine of Jagannāth, where he proclaimed his doctrines to the many pilgrims who visited the place. "But this was not his only occupation. He insisted on the importance of singing (*sankīrtana*) and dancing, as well as of contemplation, to fit the mind for ecstatic communion with the deity, and his followers often swooned away in their fits of religious emotion."[2] His excitable, neurotic, emotional temperament led him into many vagaries, and at times to actual insanity. Oman says that he had many of the characteristics of what may be called to-day "the higher degenerates." He imagined he saw visions of Krishna and his attendant Gopis, and terminated his life by walking into the sea in one of these fits of ecstasy to join Krishna sporting with the maidens in the waves.

Chaitanya before his disappearance gained many adherents and honours. The independent King of Orissa became his disciple and not the least of his honours was the boon the gods granted to him, so the popular legend runs, of four additional arms (additional limbs are always a sign of a god's increase of power and reputation among the Hindus). As Chaitanya left no issue, Adaitya and Nityānanda, his Brāhman coadjutors, became, on his death, the great leaders of the new faith. They remained some years in Benares following the religious life, but afterwards returned to a secular life. Their

[1] See previous page and p. 7.
[2] Monier Williams, *Hinduism*, p. 147.

FOLLOWERS OF CHAITANYA DANCING THE RASA.

(See p. 164 and compare p. 141.)

ŚIVA, PARVATĪ, AND GANESHA.

ŚIVA is represented as seated on Mt. Kailasa. He grasps in one hand the Trident, sign of the august Hindu Triad. MĀ GANGA appears from his hair. See p. 177 for explanation of all details.

ŚIVA, THE DESTROYER.

Note the necklace of human skulls and the snake, representing Eternal Time, coiled round his neck, and the river Ganges flowing from his hair. See p. 177 for full description.

descendants to-day are greatly respected and acknowledged as the spiritual heads of the community. They are called Gossains, and are very wealthy. Some of them derive a large revenue from the marriage of low castes, and from the estates of all disciples who die intestate. This revenue is also derived from the estates of immoral women who profess the religion of Chaiṭanya in order to be entitled to funeral rites, as by their conduct and life they have excommunicated themselves from orthodox Hinduism. The image of Chaitanya is that of an almost naked mendicant painted yellow.[1]

[1] Extracted mainly from Wilkins' *Hindu Mythology*, pp. 253–6; and Ward's *Hindoos*, pp. 134–7.)

CHAPTER XI

ŚIVA, THE DESTROYER, AND PANCHĀNANA

"Is that the King of Dread,
With ashy, musing face;
From whose moon-silvered locks famed Gangā springs?"
—Sir WM. JONES.

"I am the god of the sensuous fire
That moulds all nature in forms divine;
The symbols of death and of man's desire,
The springs of change in the world are mine;
The organs of birth and the circlet of bones,
And the light loves carved on the temple stones.

"I am the lord of delights and pain,
Of the pest that killeth, of fruitful joys;
I rule the currents of heart and vein;
A touch gives passion, a look destroys;
In the heat and cold of my lightest breath
Is the might incarnate of Lust and Death."
—Sir ALFRED LYALL.

"Thine are these orbs of light and shade;
Thou madest Life in man and brute;
Thou madest Death; and lo! Thy foot
Is on the skull which Thou hast made."
—TENNYSON, *In Memoriam.*

THE third of the great gods of the Hindu Triad is the personification of destruction. The work of creation and preservation being undertaken it was necessary to provide an agent for that of disintegration or destruction, as things created are by an inexorable law liable to decay and dissolution. Strange to relate the emblem by which this god is generally worshipped represents in a rude and unattractive form the forces of re-creation and re-production. For Hindu philosophy, untinged by Buddhism, excludes the idea of non-being or annihilation. Śiva therefore represents Time, endless and inexorable. Death itself is only a turning of the glass of Time, a rearrangement of indestructible atoms, and a gateway from one court of Life to another. To destroy, therefore, is practically to recreate, and Death stands at the gates of Life. Hence the name given to the agent of destruction is Śiva, "the Bright and Shining One," "the Propitious."

The worship of Śiva is alluded to by Megasthenes and must therefore date back to a period earlier than Buddhism (600 B.C.), but it is unknown in the Vedas. To gain for him greater reverence the Brāhmans have connected him with the Vedic god, Rudra, which name means "roarer" or "howler." Rudra is a storm deity whose chief function is that of directing and controlling the rage of the hurricane. As god of the gale or tempest he is the father of the Maruts, the destructive storm-winds. In this character he is closely connected with the Rain-god Indra, and still more so with Agni which as an agent of destruction, fire, rages and crackles like the roaring tempest. He is also nearly related to Time (Kāla), the all-consumer, and afterwards becomes identified with him. He is the awful being whose thousand shafts bring death or disease to men and cattle.[1] In the Yajur-Veda a

[1] "We approach first (with our worship) the god who has horses, is dark, black, destroying . . . reverence be to him. Do not hurl at us thy harrow, thy celestial bolt; be not incensed at us, Pasūpati; reverence to thee. Brandish thy celestial arrow over some other than us. Slay us not; intercede for us; avoid us; be not angry with us; let us not contend with thee.—Do not covet our cattle, our men, our goats and sheep. Fierce god, betake thyself elsewhere, slay the off-spring of the wicked (v. 26). Do not assail us, Rudra, with consumption or with poison or with celestial fire; cause this lightning to descend elsewhere than upon us (v. 29). Slay neither our great nor our small, neither him who carries (?) nor those who shall carry (?), neither our father, nor our mother; injure not, Rudra, ourselves. I have offered this reverence to Rudra's wide-mouthed howling dogs who swallow their prey unchewed. Reverence, O deity, to thy shouting, long-haired, devouring hosts. May blessing and security be ours."—*Atharva-Veda*, xi. 2, 18.

hymn is addressed to Rudra, and in it he is described, with that confusion of ideas that characterises Hindu thought, in many contradictory and incongruous aspects. As a killer and a deliverer, as both tall and dwarfish, he dwells in mountains and owns troops of servants, spirits, who traverse the earth obeying his orders. He is lord of ghosts and goblins, patron of thieves and robbers, and is himself one of them. He also is a benevolent and auspicious being who heals while he destroys. He is the master of life as of death.

Most of these characteristics are continued, deepened, and intensified in Śiva, who in late Hinduism becomes an exceedingly important deity. He is bewildering in the range and variety of his many-hued nature.

"In Hindu writings no less than 1008 different names are given to him, and most of them indicate separate functions. Yet some attempt may be made to disentangle the confusion by pointing out that there are six chief characteristics that Śiva most prominently assumed:

1. *He personifies the forces of destruction and disintegration.* He destroys even the gods themselves and wears their skulls as his necklace." He delights in destruction for its own sake, haunting burning grounds and places of death. All the terrors of a fierce consuming wrath are his, and constitute his normal condition of mind. On the slightest provocation they break forth and overwhelm his enemies, hence the attribute "terrible" (*bhairava*) given to him. A characteristic story is told in the Mahābhārata: "One day as Śiva was seated on the Himālayas engaged in austerities, Umā, attended by her companions and dressed as an ascetic, came up behind and playfully put her hands over his eyes. Instantly the world became darkened, lifeless, destitute of oblations. The gloom, however, was dispelled by a great flame which burst from Śiva's forehead, in which a third eye, luminous as the sun, was formed. By the fire of this eye the mountain was scorched and everything upon it consumed." This flame will one day, it is declared, devour the world.

2. "*He personates the eternal reproductive power of Nature*

perpetually recreating itself after disintegration. In this character he is commonly known and worshipped all over India under the symbol of the Linga stone."

The Linga, or Greek Phallus, and Roman Priapus, with its usual accompaniment, the Yoni, is the universal emblem of Śiva-worship. That this has always been the case we do not know, but we know as a fact that at the time of the raids of Mahmud of Ghaznī (eleventh century) there existed twelve celebrated linga shrines, one of which at Somnāth he destroyed. Some have asserted that this worship is of non-Aryan origin—borrowed from the aboriginal tribes found in India, but to this it is replied that no trace of it is found in any existing non-Aryan people and that there is no proof of such a derivation. Hindus assert that there is nothing indecent meant or understood in this symbol, and its usual clumsy representation is considered free from suggestion of indecency, and it may be regarded as a type of Nature-worship. "The spiritualisation, exaltation, and even deification of natural desire, of the sexual instinct in fact, has been in the East from the earliest times an object of certain sect founders, impressed no doubt and fascinated by the mystery of generation. And so it has come about that this mystery, which the West has regarded with the greatest suspicion and dread, has been invested by the subtle mysticism of the Orient with the sanctifying garment of religion." [1]

There exists a Saivite sect, the Lingāyats (or Lingaits)—founded in twelfth century by Basava, a native of the Deccan—who in theory reject caste [2] and Brāhmanical authority and all idolatry except the worship of the linga, a model of which, usually in a silver box, they bind to their arms or tie to their necks.[3]

[1] Oman, *Mystics, Ascetics, and Saints of India*, p. 110.

[2] "In the 1901 Census the Lingayats asked to be recorded as Lingayat Brāhmans, Lingayat Vaisyas, Lingayat Śūdras, thus claiming the very caste distinctions which their founder had repudiated."—Holderness, *People and Problems of India*, p. 103.

[3] The Census Reports of the Mysore State give reliable information about this sect which has spread through South India and is more

Several legends explain how the Linga came to be the representative of Śiva. The Padma Purāna says that it was the result of a curse pronounced by Bhrigu. When Bhrigu was sent by the Rishis to discover which of the three gods was the greatest, he came to Śiva's abode. Wishing at once to enter, he was prevented by a doorkeeper, who informed him that as his master was with Devī his wife, it was impossible for him to enter at present. After waiting for some time, Bhrigu's patience being exhausted, he said: "Since thou, O Sankara, hast treated me with contempt in preferring the embraces of Pārvatī, your forms of worship shall be the Linga and Yoni."

3. "*He is the typical great ascetic and self-mortifier* (Yogi). In this character he sits naked, motionless, with ash-besmeared body, matted hair, and beggar's bowl under a banyan-tree. By so doing he teaches mankind by his example to mortify the body and suppress passion so that the loftiest spiritual knowledge and union with himself may be attained." He himself attained the highest perfection in meditation and self-mortification. In the Vāmana Purāna we read that when Śiva was enwrapped in meditation, Pārvatī, oppressed by the great heat, remonstrated with him: "O Īsha, the heat increases in violence. Hast thou no house to which we might repair and there abide, protected from the wind, the heat, the cold?"

Sankara (Śiva) replied: "I am, O lovely one, without a shelter, a constant wanderer in forests." Having thus spoken they remained during the entire hot season under the trees, and when it was passed, the rainy season with its dark clouds

---

especially prominent in the Mysore. It appears from Abbé Dubois' testimony that the use of *arrack*, or native liquor, is prohibited among them under penalty of exclusion from their caste or sect, but they supply its place by using opium and other drugs. They keep Monday in every week as a day of rest for their cattle and pay special homage to the Sacred Bull, as Basava is said by his followers to be an incarnation of Nandi, Śiva's bull. A noteworthy custom of this sect is "its abstinence from whatever has had the principle of life," and its practice of interring its dead in place of burning them.

succeeded, and still Śiva remained immovable and indifferent to the heavy showers.

Another legend relates how he burnt up in a blaze of wrath the god of Love (Kāma), when that deity attempted to disturb his devotions.

4. *As a philosopher and learned sage.* In this character he is represented as a Brāhman wearing the Brāhmanical thread, and as being skilled in the knowledge of the Vedas. He is represented as seated on Mount Kailāsa discussing with Pārvatī the most abstruse problems of philosophy. It is remarkable to note in this connection that he has a peculiar hold upon the higher classes of the Hindu community. In fact an ancient version of Manu is often quoted: " Śiva is the god of the Brāhmans, Krishna (Vishnu) of the Kshatriyas, Brahmā of the Vaisyas, and Ganesha of the Śūdras."

5. *Śiva is also exactly the opposite of the two preceding characters.* He is a wild, jovial, wine-drinking hunter addicted to dancing and jollity—fond of good living and often inebriated. The worshippers of Śiva in this character generally belong to those who worship the Śakti or female energy of the gods, and are given to self-indulgence and sensual pleasures. This is in many respects the most degraded form of Hinduism."[1]

6. *Śiva is also the Lord of Demons.* " When he offended Daksha by not rising to salute him on his entrance into the audience-chamber of the gods, Daksha grew angry and complained :

> ' He roams about in dreadful cemeteries, attended by ghosts and spirits, like a madman with dishevelled hair. . . . He is the lord of Bhūtas (spirits), beings whose nature is essentially darkness.'

It is over the countless hosts of spirits and demons that Śiva exercises sovereignty. These are primarily subject to his authority ; but the actual command over them is delegated to his sons Ganesha, Skanda (Kārtikeya), and Ayenār."[2]

[1] Monier Williams, *Religious Thought and Life in India,* pp. 80–5.
[2] *Arsenal,* p. 259.

Millions of the peoples of South India are devoted to Śiva-worship, and in the North, his shrines and temples are numberless. His great centre is Benares, the most sacred city of Hinduism. Sacred because it is said to be placed on the prong of his trident. It is the chief of the seven most holy cities of India, in any one of which, if a man chances to die, no matter how sinful his past life may have been, he will instantly attain salvation. The other six cities [1] are Muttra and Dwarka in Gujerāt (both sacred to Krishna), Buddh-Gayā (to Buddha), Ajodhya to Rāma, Puri to Jagannāth, and Ujjain. The following story shows the sanctity of Benares and explains the reason why it is regarded as the seat of Śiva: "On one occasion Brahmā and Śiva quarrelled about their respective positions in the Hindu hierarchy. As Brahmā continued to declare that he was supreme, Śiva to show his power cut off Brahmā's fifth head, and thus was guilty of a most heinous crime. This was instantly seen, for the head of Brahmā adhered to Śiva's hand and could not be shaken off. He tried every austerity and device to get rid of it and made many pilgrimages, but all was in vain until he came to Benares and there the head instantly fell off his hand."

The writer has often seen Śiva-worship as it is practised in the temples at Benares and in similar shrines scattered over North India. It has little in it to attract the reverent mind. First of all the popular representation of Śiva, the linga stone, is a rude primitive emblem.

Then the course of worship itself offers nothing to excite devotional interest or to arouse the imagination. A brief description will make this clear. A Hindu temple is divided into two parts—the vestibule and the shrine itself, and these are often surrounded with courts. The temple courts are large, but the central shrine is generally small. The worshipper begins by circumambulating the temple court as many times as he pleases, always remembering to keep his

[1] Some lists omit Puri and Buddh-gayā and insert Hardwar, where the Ganges first enters the plains, and Conjevaram near Madras.

WORSHIPPING THE LINGA OF ŚIVA.

These upright, rounded, and conical stones are worshipped by pouring water upon them. The dark stains on the stone are caused by water. In front of the principal stone is seen a diminutive Nandi.

Photo by Messrs. Saeed Bros., Benares.

BULL SAÇRED TO ŚIVA.

right hand towards the shrine. He then enters the vestibule or porch of the innermost shrine where the image is kept, and into which only the priest (*pūjāri*) is allowed to go. Generally there is suspended from the roof of the vestibule a bell which the worshipper strikes in order to arouse the attention of the god. The priest often blows a conch shell kept for the same purpose. The worshipper then advances to the threshold of the shrine and presents his offering to the idol within (it may be a few faded flowers, some Bilva (Bel) leaves, an offering of grain or food stuffs, or water to cool and refresh the hot and excited god). This done he mutters a short prayer begging the god's acceptance of his worship, accompanied with the act of prostration, or simply that of lifting the hand to the forehead. The worship now is over and the man departs. It is to be noted that throughout the whole there is nothing like a religious service, no moral instruction is given. All is done rapidly and often mechanically. The quick succession of worshippers, the pouring out of water, the scattering of leaves or flowers, the muttering of a hurried prayer—all this fails to favourably impress the Occidental observer.

Domestic worship is also offered to him. First of all the place where the worshipper sits is purified by reciting a *mantra* to the Earth (*Prithivī*). The worshipper then makes an extemporised clay image of Śiva in the form of a linga. He performs certain rites while making it, and after washing it, with salutation he performs the ceremony of animation, by which he believes that its nature is changed from that of the mere materials of which it is formed, and that it not only acquires life but supernatural power. Whenever a Hindu purchases an idol from the market the same " rite of animation " is undertaken, and the idol is consecrated. The linga being made and consecrated is solemnly placed on an untorn Bilva leaf, and the same *pūjā* or worship is offered to it as already described in the public worship.

A much more elaborate and complex type of Śiva-worship is described by Dr. Rājendralāla Mitra. This is an account of the ceremonies (twenty-two in number) offered to the linga in a great Saivite temple in Orissa:

"(1) At the first appearance of dawn bells are rung to rouse the deity from his slumbers; (2) a lamp with many wicks is waved in front of the stone; (3) the god's teeth are cleaned by pouring water and rubbing a stick about a foot long on the stone; (4) the deity is washed and bathed by emptying several pitchers of water on the stone; (5) the god is dressed by putting clothes on the stone; (6) the first breakfast is offered, consisting of grain, sweetmeats, curds, and cocoanuts; (7) the god has his principal breakfast, when cakes and more substantial viands are served; (8) a kind of little lunch is offered; (9) the god has a regular lunch; (10) the midday dinner is served, consisting of curry, rice, &c., while a priest waves a many-flamed lamp and burns incense before the stone; (11) strains of noisy discordant music arouse him from his afternoon sleep at 4 P.M.; (12) sweetmeats are offered; (13) the afternoon bath is administered; (14) the god is dressed as in the morning; (15) tiffin is served; (16) another bath is administered; (17) the full-dress ceremony takes place; (18) another offering of food follows; (19) after an hour's interval the regular supper is served; (20) five masks and a *damaru* (drum) used in dancing are brought in and oblations made to them; (21) waving of lights before bedtime; (22) a bedstead is brought into the sanctuary, and the god composed to sleep."[1]

This is a daily series of ceremonies. Can anything more puerile or more wearisome be imagined?

Śiva's great festival is held about the middle or the end of February. A fast is observed during the day and a vigil kept at night. A priest reads in the temple a list of his names, and as each is mentioned the worshipper throws a leaf of the Bilva (Bel) tree on the linga in order to secure heaven. The origin of the sacredness of this festival is related in the Skanda Purāna: "In Jambu Dwīpa, on the Himālayan Mountains, there lived a hunter. One day while hunting he was overtaken by nightfall. As he was anxious not to become a prey to the wild beasts he climbed a tree. Tormented by cold and hunger he passed a miserable night in strict wakefulness. The night happened to be Śiva-rātri

[1] Dr. Murdoch, *Śiva Bhakti*, pp. 19–20.

night, and at the foot of the tree, which fortunately was a Bilva, the leaves of which are sacred to Śiva, was a linga. His discomforts obliged him to change his position frequently, and the shaking of the tree caused some leaves to fall on the linga. This involuntary worship pleased Śiva exceedingly. When a few days after the hunter died Śiva put Yama to flight after a violent quarrel and carried off the hunter to his heaven. When Yama complained to Nandi (Śiva's vehicle) of his treatment Nandi replied: 'This man has been a great sinner who has not scrupled to shed blood; but before he died he fasted, watched, and offered Bilva leaves to the linga. This action has cleansed him from his sins.'"[1]

Śiva, in his efforts to get rid of the dissevered head of Brahmā, adopted the ascetic life and wandered about for many years from holy place to holy place and shrine to shrine. In virtue of this he is to-day the patron god of the vast number of religious mendicants, Sādhus, Sannyāsis, Yogis, India's holy men, who practise great austerities and resort to all kinds of self-torture to gain his favour. Wandering through the country are many Sannyāsis or pilgrims, devotees, who subsist on charity, expose themselves equally to heat and cold and to many discomforts in hope of future reward. Some of these are naked, others inflict on themselves such tortures as the following.—Retaining their limbs in one position for years until it is impossible to move them. Gazing on the sun until blindness ensues. Growing their finger nails through the flesh of the palm of the hand till they appear on the outside. Swinging on bamboos, having hooks forced between the muscles of the shoulder—these are some of the cruel practices in which Śiva is supposed to delight.[2]

Another characteristic of his worship is representative of his character of master of revelries, "lord of mad frantic folly, who, clad in the blood-stained skin of an elephant, dances the wild tāndava dance."[3] Dancing girls are "con-

[1] *Arsenal*, p. 411.

[2] See also p. 240.

[3] Barth, *Religions of India*, p. 164.

secrated" to his service. Dubois says: "Throughout South India Saivite temples are often the abode of troupes of dancing girls who are kept to delight the god's hours of leisure, and gratify the profligacy of those who come to worship him. Next to the priests they are the most important persons about the temples, as they are connected with the management of most temple affairs and the performance of ceremonies. These girls are called '*devadāsis*,' or 'servants,' or 'slaves of the god.' They are bred to an immoral life from infancy, and often their mothers and fathers, in fulfilment of a vow to devote their child to the service of the god, think they honour the god by devoting her to a life of infamy." It is gratifying to record that efforts are being made by the Hindus themselves against the continuance of this custom. The Mysore Government has pronounced against the employment of temple girls,[1] and in the case of official entertainments, all over India public protest is often made against the Nautch, and there is a sensible diminution of the practice amongst the educated classes.

"Each god is represented as having special fondness for some bird or animal, on which he is supposed to travel, and which therefore is called his *vāhan* or vehicle. The bull is Śiva's; and the image of his favourite bull, Nandi, is seen in most of his temples and in front of many of his shrines. Owing probably to this circumstance a curious custom prevails, similar in many respects to the setting loose of the scapegoat by the Israelites. At the death of a worshipper of Śiva, if his friends are pious and can afford it, they set a bullock loose and allow it to wander at will. By the Hindus generally it is considered a meritorious act to feed these sacred bulls, and a sin to injure them. In country places many of them are seen, and they become a great nuisance to the cultivators into whose fields they wander; for as they have no owner compensation cannot be obtained. If a man were specially devout, or his friends eminently pious, as many

[1] This was in 1909—the first official action taken by any Indian Government to deal with this disgraceful practice.

PANCHĀNANA (the five-headed form of Śiva)
To his left sits Umā, his Śakti, and to his right are seen the Trimūrti or triple form (see p. 82) and Ganesha, recognisable by his elephant trunk. Below the steps are found Nandi, Śiva's bull, and the tiger sacred to Durga. The Ganges springs from his hair.

SAKTIS, OR FEMALE ENERGIES OF THE GODS.

In this photo are seen the goddesses Kālī, Lakshmī, Sītā, Sarasvatī, and other consorts of the various gods. Originally there were ten representations, but one has been omitted, as it was too indecent to publish.

as seven bulls are set loose at his decease. The idea seems to be this: as Śiva was delighted with Nandi, he will graciously receive into his presence those on whose behalf these bullocks were given." [1]

The following is a full description of Śiva:

"In the first place he has sometimes five faces (see Panchānana), sometimes only one, but always three eyes; these are said to denote his insight into the past, present, and future. The third eye is in the middle of the forehead, and a moon's crescent above it marks the measuring of time by months according to the phases of the moon, while a serpent round his neck denotes the endless cycle of recurring years, while a necklace of skulls symbolises the successive dissolution and regeneration of the races of mankind. His body is generally covered with ashes said to be the remains of gods he destroyed. His hair is thickly matted together and gathered above his forehead into a coil, so as to project like a horn. On the top of it he bears the personified river Ganges, the rush of which he intercepted in its descent from Vishnu's feet. His throat is blue from the stain of the deadly poison which would have destroyed the world had not Śiva in compassion undertaken to drink it up on its production at the churning of the ocean. He rides a white bull, Nandi, images of which are always found outside his temples. He sits on the skin of a tiger alleged to have been killed by him when the Rishis tried to destroy him by it. As Śiva is constantly engaged in battle he is armed with a weapon suitable to his needs. He carries a three-pronged trident, thought by some to denote that he combines in his person the three attributes of Creator, Destroyer, and Regenerator. In the opposite hand he holds a kind of rattle or drum, shaped like an hour-glass, called *damaru*, which he uses as a musical instrument to keep time while dancing. A begging-bowl at his side typifies another side to his character—the ascetic." [2]

Panchānana—The God of Five Faces

This is a form of Śiva which represents the god as having five faces, and each face with three eyes; the customary necklet of snakes and the naked ascetic's body being added. This deity is largely worshipped, particularly by ignorant

[1] Wilkins, *Hindu Mythology*, p. 277.
[2] Murdoch, *Śiva Bhakti*.

villagers. Usually a stone is placed under certain trees and painted red at the top and anointed with oil. Sometimes several stones are so placed and offerings of flowers, fruits, water, sweetmeats are made to them.

There is a more than considerable element of demonolatry in the worship paid to this god. Hindu women are terrified with it, and in time of sickness, although not ordinarily worshippers of Śiva, render the most abject worship. Children in fits of epilepsy are supposed to be seized by this god until they foam at the mouth, &c. The mother asks the evil spirit his name, who answers through the child: "I am Panchānana—your child has cast dust on my image, kicked it, and is the ringleader of the village children in this wickedness. I will certainly take away his life." The priestess is then called, who comforts the weeping family and addresses the god thus: "O Panchānana, I pray thee restore this child. If thou restore this child the parents will sacrifice a goat to thee and present to thee many other offerings." If this fails to make the god propitious they take the child to the image, before which they sit down and offer the most excessive flattery to the god, causing the child to beat its head on the ground. After using every contrivance they retire, and at the close of the fit, believing that Panchānana has cured the child, they present to him offerings according to their ability.[1]

Some shrines of this god in Bengal have acquired considerable celebrity, and women of the lower orders resort to them to obtain the gift of children and other blessings.

[1] Ward, *Hindoos*, p. 144.

CHAPTER XII

ŚIVA'S CONSORT, OR ŚAKTI

" O Durgā ! thou hast deign'd to shield
Man's feeble virtue with celestial might,
Gliding from yon jasper field ;
And, on a lion borne, hast brav'd the fight :
For when the Demon Vice thy realms defy'd,
And armed with death each arched horn,
Thy golden lance, O goddess ! mountain-born,
Touch'd but the pest—he roar'd and died ! "
—Sir WM. JONES, *Hymn to Durgā.*

THE worship of the Śaktis, or female energies or counterparts of the gods, forms a religion by itself. It has its special doctrines, its special forms of initiation, and its own peculiar devotees. The roots of this worship are hid far away in ideas, as old as India itself, of a sexual dualism. The bright spreading Heavens have as their counterpart the broad fertile Earth, and each succeeding god has his own energy, the god loftily quiescent, the goddess active and virile, the embodiment of rude energy.

It is in Śaivism that these ideas have found a soil most favourable for their growth. Whilst Vishnu has his Śakti in Lakshmī, his worship and influence have retained their supremacy, but over half of the adherents to Śiva have largely transferred their allegiance to the cult of his female counterpart. This great goddess (often called Devī or Mahādevī) has a thousand names and a thousand forms. She is not merely Śiva's counterpart, but she intensifies the attributes of the dread lord of destruction. " As a destructress she is Kālī ; as a reproducer she is symbolised by the Yoni ; as a type of beauty in Umā ; as the mother of the Universe in Jagan-Mātrī ; as a malignant being, delighting in blood,

Durgā; as a mountaineer, Pārvatī.[1] This by no means exhausts the list of names commonly applied to her, each name having some special significance. She is Satī, Ambikā, Gaurī, Tārā, Bhavānī, and many others.

Fortunately there is a clear division line in these various manifestations. We can distinguish between the "white" or mild, benevolent nature, and the "black" or fierce, cruel nature. Our purpose will be amply served if we concern ourselves solely with Umā and Pārvatī, representatives of the "milder" nature, and Durgā and Kālī, deities of the fiercer type. It is by these four names that she is best known. Umā (meaning Light), Daksha's daughter, is distinguished for her severe austerity, her charity, knowledge, and beauty. As Pārvatī she is beautiful, gentle, faithful, and full of womanly qualities. But alas! when she appears as Durgā and Kālī she exhibits a very different spirit. Nothing is sadder in Hinduism than the transformation of the gentle Umā and Pārvatī into the cruel, bloodthirsty Durgā and Kālī. The goddess, as represented in Durgā, has still the calm features and golden colours of Pārvatī, combined with the fiercer, untamable characteristics of Kālī; but Kālī is wholly given over to cruelty and blood. She drinks the blood of her victims. She lives in an orgy of horror.

I. Umā

Daksha, son of Brahmā, and one of the Divine Rishis, was at first very unwilling to give his daughter Umā in marriage to the wandering mendicant, Śiva, but his scruples were overcome by the persuasion of Brahmā, and Umā became Śiva's wife. Daksha, however, never overcame his first repugnance of the unclean habits and ash-smeared form of his son-in-law. This led to the great tragedy of Umā's life and made her the earliest example of Satī or self-immolation. She is frequently called Satī, which means "the true or virtuous woman." The name is given to widows

[1] Monier Williams, *Hinduism*, p. 95.

who ascend the funeral pyre and undergo a terrible death [1] voluntarily so that in death they shall not be separated from their husbands. Daksha refused to invite Śiva to the great sacrifice he was making to the gods, and because of this reproach cast on her husband Umā voluntarily entered the fire.

II. Pārvatī

Śiva was inconsolable on hearing of Pārvatī's death, and fainted from grief, and like a man lost to sense he wandered forth as an ascetic seeking her everywhere. One day in his agony he fainted under a banyan-tree. The gods hastened to his aid. Vishnu placed the head of the senseless Śiva on his bosom and wept aloud; he spoke to him words of cheer: "O Śiva! recover thy senses and listen to what I say. Thou wilt certainly recover Satī (Umā), since thou art as inseparable from her as cold from water, heat from fire, smell from earth, or radiance from the Sun." Umā then appeared before him as Pārvatī seated in a gem-adorned car, accompanied by various attendants and arrayed in costly garments, and said: "Be firm, O Mahādeva! lord of my soul! In whatever state I exist I shall never be separated from my lord; and now I have been born as Pārvatī the daughter of Himavat (Himālayas) in order to become again thy wife; therefore no longer grieve on account of our separation." Then she departed.[2]

Whilst still a girl in her mountain home Pārvatī heard a voice from heaven saying: "Perform a severe course of austerity, in order to regain Śiva for thy husband, as he cannot be otherwise obtained." But Pārvatī, proud of her

[1] When this rite was suppressed by the British the Brāhman priesthood resisted to the uttermost and appealed to the Vedas as sanctioning the ordinance. The leading Sanskrit scholar of the day, Professor H. H. Wilson, proved that the priests had actually falsified the text of their sacred Veda in support of this horrible rite. It has not the sanction of antiquity and was unknown in Vedic days.

For further reference to Satī, see p. 247 ff.

[2] Kennedy, *Hindu Mythology*, p. 331.

youth and in the full lustre of her beauty, was confident that he would come to her without self-denial on her part. Her hopes, however, were disappointed. Śiva was by that time confirmed in the practices of his ascetic life. Finally she performed the required austerities and with the aid of Kāmadeva (the Indian Cupid), who wounded him with his arrows, she was united to her husband.[1]

Pārvatī and Śiva are usually represented as living in felicity in their mountain home, Kailāsa. She was the mother of Ganesha and Kārtikeya, and was Śiva's constant companion and faithful wife. Grieved often at his immoralities, she never deserted him except on one occasion when he reproached her for the blackness of her skin. This so incensed her that she retired into the depths of the forest and performed a severe course of austerities until Brahmā granted her as a boon that her countenance should be golden. From this circumstance she is known as Gauri (the Golden One).[2]

Pārvatī is a beneficent goddess, represented as a fair and beautiful woman with no superfluity of limbs. Few miraculous deeds are ascribed to her, but her influence on the fierce and evil-minded Śiva is always for the good. Very different is she in character from Durgā, Kālī, &c., the "black" manifestation of the goddess. Hence the supposition that in very early times they were distinct deities.[3]

III. Durgā

Śiva's consort now assumes a very different character. As Umā and Pārvatī she acts as an ordinary woman replete with womanly virtues. As Durgā she is a powerful warrior who overcame the formidable giant of that name. She is still represented as a golden-faced woman of beautiful countenance, but she has ten arms. In one hand she is holding a

[1] Wilkins, *Hindu Mythology*, pp. 292–3.
[2] Muir, *O.S.T.*, iv. pp. 403–6.
[3] Wilkins, *Hindu Mythology*, p. 296.

spear, with which she impales the giant, and her other hands are filled with various weapons. Her lion leans against her left leg, and the giant himself lies under her right.

The Skanda Purāna[1] gives an account of the slaying of giant Durgā, whose name means "difficult of access." Kārtikeya was once asked by a sage why his mother Pārvatī was called Durgā. His reply was the following: "A giant named Durgā having performed great penances and austerities in honour of Brahmā, obtained his blessing, and grew so mighty that he conquered the three worlds, dethroned the gods, whom he sent from heaven to live in the forests; at his nod they came and worshipped him. He abolished all religious ceremonies. The Brāhmans, through fear of him, forsook the reading of the Vedas, rivers changed their courses, fire lost its energy, and the terrified stars retired from sight.

"The gods at length applied to Śiva. Indra said, 'He has dethroned me;' Sūrya said, 'He has taken my kingdom;' and one by one all the gods related their misfortunes. Śiva, pitying them, asked Pārvatī to go and destroy the giant. She accepted the commission willingly, calmed the fears of the gods, and first sent Kālarātrī (Dark Night), a female of great beauty, to command Durgā to restore things to their ancient order. He, full of fury, sent soldiers to seize her, but by the breath of her mouth she reduced them to ashes. Durgā then sent 30,000 other giants, such monsters in form and size that they covered the face of the earth. At the sight of these giants Kālarātrī fled to Pārvatī, followed by the giants. Durgā then with 100,000,000 chariots, 120,000,000 elephants, 10,000,000 swift horses, and innumerable horsemen went to fight Pārvatī on the Vindhya Mountains. As soon as the giant drew near, Pārvatī assumed 1000 arms, called to her assistance a great array of beings of different kinds (a list covering half a page is given in the Purāna), filled her hands with weapons, and sat on the Vindhya Mountain waiting his arrival. The troops of giants poured their arrows upon her like drops of rain in the storm. They even tore up the

[1] Ward, *Hindoos*, p. 64.

trees and mountains, and hurled them at the goddess, who, however, threw a weapon, which carried away many of the arms of Durgā. He, in return, hurled a flaming dart at the goddess, which she turned aside. Another was resisted by the discharge of a hundred arrows. He next let fly an arrow at Pārvatī's breast, but this she saved herself from. At last Pārvatī seized Durgā, and set her left foot on his breast. . . . She pierced him with her trident . . . seized him with her thousand arms, and carried him into the air, whence she threw him down with terrific force. This, however, did not kill him; so she pierced his breast with an arrow, when blood issued in streams from his mouth, and he expired. The gods were delighted, and regained their former splendour, and gave her, in gratitude for the deliverance, the name of Durgā."

The great festival called the Durgā Pūjā is celebrated yearly throughout Northern India in honour of this goddess. It is the most popular of all the Hindu festivals, and is considered the great holiday of the year. For three days all business is laid aside, and people living at a distance go home to celebrate it. Sacrifices of buffaloes and goats are made to her, and immense sums are spent by wealthy persons on this occasion. Brāhmans are entertained and sumptuously fed. Dancing girls, richly dressed, and covered with jewels, sing and dance before the idol. The songs are grossly indecent, and the dances more so. An English spectator says: "The whole scene produced on my mind sensations of the greatest horror. The dress of the singers—their indecent gestures—the abominable nature of the songs—the horrid din of the drums—the lateness of the hour—the darkness of the place—with the reflection that I was standing in a heathen temple, and that this immense multitude of rational and immortal beings were, in the act of worship, perpetrating a crime of high treason against the God of heaven, while they themselves believed they were performing an act of merit—excited ideas and feelings in my mind which can never be obliterated."

This festival lasts for fifteen days. The first four nights are allotted to the decoration of the goddess; the fifth is for the preparation of her dress; on the sixth she is awakened; on the seventh she is invited to a bower formed of the leaves of nine trees and plants, of which the Bel (Bilva) tree, sacred to Śiva, is the chief. The seventh, eighth, and ninth are the great days, on the last of which the beasts sacrificed in her honour must be slain. The directions given in the Kālikā Purāna are, "The sacrificed beasts must be killed with one blow of a broad sword or sharp axe." The next day the goddess is reverently dismissed and her image returned to its shrine. On the fifteenth day, that of the full moon, her devotees pass the night in merriment and revelry. It is unlucky to sleep, for on this night the fiend led his army against Durgā, and on this night the goddess Lakshmī descended on earth, promising wealth to all who keep awake.

IV. Kālī

"Hail, Kālī, three-eyed goddess, of horrid form, around whose neck a string of human skulls is pendant! Salutation to thee with this blood!"—*Mantra used in Kālī-worship.*

The "black" manifestations of Śiva's consort culminate in the portrayal of Kālī, the horrible goddess of blood. Human invention or imagination, however depraved and brutalised, cannot equal elsewhere the terror of this conception of deity. The Tantras tell us:

"One should adore with liquors and oblations Kālī, who has a terrible gaping mouth, with eyes red as those of a drunkard and uncombed hair; who has four hands, and a splendid garland formed of the heads of the giants she has slain, and whose blood she has drunk; who holds a sword in her lotus-like hands; who is fearless, and awards blessings; who is black as the large clouds; who has a throat smeared with blood; who wears earrings consisting of two dead bodies; who carries two dead bodies in her hands; who has terrible teeth and a smiling face; whose form is awful; who dwells in burning grounds, and stands on the breast of her husband, Śiva."

After her victory over the giant she began to dance. She danced till the earth shook and began to crumble away. At the request of the gods Śiva asked her to stop, but owing to her excitement she did not notice him. He then lay down among the dead at her feet. She continued her wild orgy till she caught sight of her husband under her feet; upon seeing him she thrust out her tongue in dismay, and ceased.

There is no question that in days gone by, human sacrifices were offered to Kālī. In the great temple of Kālighāt —the central shrine of Hinduism in Calcutta (which city takes its very name from Kālī)—there are two stones to the right and left of the main porch, red with the blood of sheep and goats, but it is well known that, before the prohibition of the British Government, the blood of human beings was the sacrifice offered. In tracts of Central and Northern India the innocent traveller was often in former times waylaid by numerous bands of Thugs, who strangled and buried their victims, and became the scourge and terror of the land. The patron goddess of the Thugs, now finally suppressed,[1] was Kālī. In the Kālikā Purāna [2] nothing can be clearer than the instruction regarding human sacrifice:

> "The flesh of the antelope and the rhinoceros give my beloved (Kālī) delight for five hundred years. By a human sacrifice attended by the forms laid down, she is pleased for a thousand years; and by the sacrifice of three men, a hundred thousand years. . . . An oblation of blood, which has been rendered pure by holy texts, is equal to ambrosia; the head and flesh also afford much delight. . . . Let the sacrifice repeat the word Kālī twice, and say, 'Hail, Devī, goddess of thunder; hail, iron-sceptred goddess!' Let him then take the axe in his hand, and again invoke the same by the Kālarātri text, as follows: 'Let the sacrifice say, "Hrang, Hrang! Kālī, Kālī! O horrid-toothed goddess! Eat, cut, destroy all the malignant; cut

---

[1] Suppressed by the efforts of General Sleeman and staff, acting under the orders of Lord William Bentinck, Governor-General, in 1829 and following years. A special department for the suppression of Thuggee was instituted, so widespread was the evil.

[2] Moor, *Hindu Pantheon*, p. 144.

with this axe ; bind, bind ; seize, seize ; drink blood. Spheng, spheng ! secure, secure. Salutation to Kālī !"'

"Let princes, ministers of State, councillors, and vendors of spirituous liquors make human sacrifices for the purpose of attaining prosperity and wealth. On these occasions this is the mantra to be used, 'Hail, three-eyed goddess, of most terrifying appearance, around whose neck a string of human skulls is pendant, who art the destroyer of evil spirits, who art armed with an axe and a spear! Salutation to thee with this blood!'"

An enemy may also be murdered by proxy if the worshipper substitutes a goat or a buffalo and calls the sacrifice by the name of his enemy throughout the whole ceremony. In this case the sacrificer says :

"O goddess of horrid forms ! Eat, devour such an one, my enemy. Consort of fire ! salutation to fire ! This is the enemy who has done me mischief, now personated by this animal—destroy him, O Kālī !"

Of the Karhada Brāhmans of Bombay Sir J. Malcolm wrote : "This tribe had formerly a horrid custom of annually sacrificing to the Śaktī (Kālī) a young Brāhman. The Śaktī is supposed to delight in human blood, and is represented with fiery eyes, and covered with red flowers. The prayers of her votaries are directed to her during the first nine days of the Dasara festival, and on the evening of the tenth a grand repast is prepared, to which the whole family is invited. An intoxicating drug is mixed with the food of the intended victim, who is often a stranger whom the master of the house has for several months treated with the greatest kindness and attention, and sometimes, to lull suspicions, given him his daughter in marriage. As soon as the poisonous and intoxicating drug operates, the master of the house, unattended, takes the devoted person to the temple, leads him three times round the idol, and on his prostrating himself before it takes the opportunity of cutting his throat. He collects with the greatest care the blood in a small bowl, which he first applies to the lips of the ferocious goddess, and then sprinkles it over her body ; and a hole having been dug at the foot of the idol for the corpse, he deposits it with great care to prevent discovery. After this the Karhada Brāhman returns to his family, and spends the night in mirth and revelry, convinced that by the bloodthirsty act he has propitiated the goddess for twelve years.[1]

There seems reason to suspect that even at the present day sacrifices are occasionally performed secretly in the shrines of Kālī or Durgā Dēvī. There are numerous modern instances in Nepāl. At Benares one recently occurred. At Chanda and Lanji, near Nāgpur, there are shrines of Kālī at which human sacrifices to the goddess have been offered almost within the memory of the present generation.[2]

[1] Malcolm, *North Indian Notes and Queries*, i. 112–148.

[2] In the dark past, human sacrifices were offered for many reasons, and in a variety of ways. Sleeman gives the following examples:

"The city of Sāgar, in the Central Provinces, occupies two sides of a very beautiful lake, formed by a wall which unites two sandstone hills on the north side. This wall was, according to tradition, built by a wealthy merchant of the Banjara caste. After he had finished it the bed of the lake still remained dry, and he was told in a dream, or by a priest, that it would continue so till he should consent to sacrifice his own daughter, then a girl, and the young lad to whom she was affianced, to the tutelary god of the place. He accordingly built a little shrine in the centre of the valley, which was to become the bed of the lake, put the two children in, and built up the doorway. He had no sooner done so than the whole of the valley became filled with water, and the old merchant, the priest, the masons, and spectators made their escape with difficulty. From that time the water of the lake has been inexhaustible, but no living soul of the Banjara caste has ever since been known to drink its waters."—Sleeman, vol. i. p. 122.

"The Mahādeo sandstone hills overlook the Nerbudda to the south, and rise to between 4000 and 5000 feet above the level of the sea. In one of the highest parts a fair was formerly held for the enjoyment of those who assemble to witness the self-devotion of a few young men who offer themselves as a sacrifice to fulfil the vows of their mothers. When a woman is without children she makes votive offerings to all the gods who she thinks can assist her, and promises still greater in case they should grant what she wants. Smaller promises being found of no avail, she at last promises her first-born, if a male, to the god of destruction, Mahādeo (Śiva). If she gets a son she conceals her vow from him till he attains the age of manhood, and then solemnly enjoins him to fulfil it. He believes it to be his paramount duty to obey his mother's

PĀRVATĪ (UMĀ) ŚIVA'S CONSORT,
the mild manifestation.

DURGA, ŚIVA'S CONSORT (fierce manifestation)
The goddess is represented as fighting with the demon king. DURGA, whose name the gods gave her when she killed him.

KALĪ, ŚIVA'S CONSORT (fierce manifestation).
The points to be noted are the necklace of human skulls, and the human hands suspended from her belt, while she dances on her husband's body.

call, and considers himself as devoted to the god. He then puts on the mendicant robes, visits all the celebrated temples dedicated to this god in different parts of India, and at the annual fair on the Mahādeo Hills throws himself from a perpendicular height of 400–500 feet, and is dashed to pieces upon the rocks below. This rite is called Bhrigupāta (*i.e.* throwing oneself from a precipice)."—Sleeman, vol. i. p. 125.

CHAPTER XIII

SONS OF ŚIVA AND PĀRVATĪ

I. GANESHA, THE PROPITIOUS

"And on the middle porch god Ganesha,
With disc and hook—to bring wisdom and wealth,—
Propitious sate, wreathing his sidelong trunk."
—ARNOLD'S *Light of Asia*, p. 59.

THE name is derived from Gana-Īsa, or "Lord of the Ganas," *i.e.* troops of inferior deities and evil spirits, and more especially those subordinate deities who are in attendance on Śiva, who has delegated the command of them to Ganesha. He is known by this name in the North, but in South India he is worshipped as Pulliyār. There is little doubt that this deity is the most widely worshipped of all the Hindu gods. His grotesque, unwieldy figure is found over the lintel of the door of countless Hindu dwellings. English people may well wonder at so hideous a deity becoming so popular. The explanation probably is that Ganesha is the embodiment of success in life. His form strongly resembles the familiar figure of the corpulent, well-fed *buniya* (banker or money-lender) seated at the receipt of custom, supremely at his ease, with his legs folded under him. He is the beau-ideal of a satiated appetite and of superb self-complacency. Success in life to the Hindu is synonymous with good-living, plenteousness, prosperity, and ease. Ganesha's image, smeared with red ochre, monstrous, and corpulent, conveys this idea to the rustic mind. To the poor hard-worked villager he represents the height of successful achievement and the reward of a life-long struggle.

It is difficult to find occasions which Ganesha is not called in to bless with his favour. He is the god of good luck, and of all fortunate enterprise, prudent and sagacious and full of policy. Hence his quaint image is found over the entrance doorways of thousands of Hindu homes, and he presides over the undertakings of most Hindu shopkeepers. He is invoked by the Hindu at the outset of any business. If he build a house, an image of Ganesha is previously propitiated and set up near the spot. Before money-lenders open their account books of a morning, or travellers start on a new journey, they supplicate his welfare, and invoke his aid. The average Hindu on entering a temple will first pour out water, scatter flowers, or offer a small oblation to Ganesha to obtain his assistance, before he proceeds to worship his own special deity.

Most especially is Ganesha invoked by authors in the writing of books. The reason for this is that the writing of a book is considered to be a very serious and solemn undertaking, peculiarly liable to obstruction from spiteful and jealous evil spirits; so the words, "Salutation to Ganesha," are found at the beginning of every volume. The following is the preface to the Prem Sāgar, a famous book:

> "Reverence to the Holy Ganesa!
>
> "Obstacle-cleaving, most famous, elephant-faced, resplendent, grant the boon that much advanced (by this book) may be pure speech and intellectual delight."

Is it surprising to find that the chief failing of this portly divinity is gluttony? Schoolboys, when they seek his aid at examination times, flatter him with presents of sweetmeats, and by telling him how much he can eat. At one time, it is said, Śiva was in trouble because one of the gods was offering great sacrifices, and undergoing great austerities to accomplish his destruction. He sought the aid of Ganesha, but his wily enemy delayed Ganesha's arrival on the scene by throwing sweetmeats in his way, and Ganesha waited to pick these up and eat them, and so arrived too late to be of any assistance.

Notwithstanding all this, Ganesha has a distinguished ancestry. He is regarded as the elder son of Śiva and Pārvatī, but she is said to have produced him from the *scurf*, or, some say, excreta of her body. At his birth all the gods came to tender their congratulations, and were permitted to see the infant. Amongst the number was Sani (the planet Saturn), who, to everyone's surprise, kept his eyes fixed on the ground. Pārvatī was naturally annoyed at this, and demanded the reason. He told her of a quarrel he had had that morning with his wife. She was annoyed because he had disregarded her caresses. He excused himself, and said that he was so wrapped up in meditation on Vishnu that he had eyes for no one else. She thereupon solemnly cursed everyone on whom he should gaze that day. Pārvatī laughed at the curse, and exhorted him to look at her son. He looked, and instantly the child's head was severed from his body. Taking the headless trunk in her arms, she cast herself, weeping, on the ground, but Vishnu, mounting Garuda, flew off to the banks of a river, where he found an elephant asleep. He cut off its head, and flying back with it restored Ganesha to life by crowning his dismembered trunk with this new appendage. Pārvatī was very little appeased by the change of head, but Brahmā, to soothe her, told her that Ganesha would be the first worshipped of all the gods.[1]

There is one peculiarity about his elephant's head. It has only one complete tusk. The reason for this is also given. " Paraśurāma, who was a favourite disciple of Śiva, went to Kailāsa to visit his master. On arriving at the inner apartment his entrance was opposed by Ganesha, as his father was asleep. The two came to blows, because Paraśurāma insisted on urging his way in. Ganesha at first had the advantage, for he seized his antagonist with his trunk and gave him a twirl that left him sick and senseless. On his recovery Paraśurāma threw his axe at Ganesha, who, recognising it as his father's weapon—Śiva having given it to

[1] Like many other Hindu myths, this story is told with many variations.

GANESHA.

WORSHIPPING IMAGE OF GANESHA.

Photo by Messrs. Saeed Bros., Benares.

his pupil—received it with all humility upon one of his tusks, which it immediately severed, and hence he has but one tusk." [1]

The following extract from the Ganapati [2] Upanishad will serve as a specimen of the way Ganesha is honoured and worshipped by his followers. Imagine any educated, refined people, after gazing on his manifold beauties, addressing him thus:

> "Praise to thee, O Ganesha! Thou art manifestly the Truth; thou art undoubtedly the Creator, Preserver, and Destroyer, the Supreme Being, the Eternal Spirit. . . . We acknowledge thy divinity, O Ekadanta (single-tusked one), and meditate on thy countenance; enlighten, therefore, our understanding. He who continually meditates upon thy divine form, conceiving it to be with one tusk, four hands, bearing a rat on thy banner, of a red hue, with a large belly, anointed with red perfumes, arrayed in red garments, worshipped with offerings of red flowers, abounding in compassion, the cause of this universe, imperishable, unproduced and unaffected by creation, becomes the most excellent of Yogis, *i.e.* religious devotees. Whoever meditates upon this figure will never be impeded by difficulties, will be liberated from the five great sins, and all the lesser ones, and will acquire riches, the objects of his desires, virtue, and final beatitude."

As to the origin of Ganesha, Crooke says: "There can be little doubt that he is an importation from indigenous mythology. His elephant head and the rat as his vehicle suggest that his worship arose from the primitive animal cultus." The elephant's head is the symbol of wisdom and prudence, and the rat on which he rides is the type of perseverance. Both qualities are needed to ensure success.

The sect of those who exclusively worship him are called the Ganapatyas, as Ganapati is the name given to this deity in Western India. There is said to be at Chikur, near Poona, an hereditary living Ganesha. The story is briefly this, that the god, gratified at the devotion and piety of a

[1] Kennedy, *Hindu Mythology*, p. 353.
[2] Ganapati is another name for Ganesha.

man called Muraba, rewarded him by incarnating himself in his person, and covenanted that the divinity should descend in his children to the seventh generation, and empowering its incumbent to work miracles and foretell future events. Six out of seven of the inheritors of this covenant have already died, and the Brāhmans say that the Avatāras (Incarnations) will end with the life of the last Ganesha, unless there is a renewal made by a further expression of the divine will.

II. Kārtikeya, the God of War

> "Lead us as the martial Skanda led the conquering gods of old,
> Smite the foe as angry Indra smote the Danavs, fierce and bold."
> —Romesh Dutt, *Epic of Ancient India.*

We will now pass on to the younger son of Śiva and Pārvatī, Skanda or Kārtikeya—the Hindu "Mars," as Ganesha is the Hindu "Janus." He is the commander-in-chief of the armies of the gods, which he often leads in battle against the demon hosts. The Rāmāyana says: "While Śiva, the lord of the gods, was performing austerities, the other deities went to Brahmā and asked for a general in his place. 'He,' said they, 'whom thou didst formerly give as a leader of our armies is now performing great austerities, along with Umā.' The request was granted by the birth of Kārtikeya."

The Śiva Purāna tells us that there was a demon king of Tripura, by name Tārika, who was exceedingly ambitious and oppressive. He forced Brahmā by his austerities to grant any boon he should demand. A list of these austerities is interesting, as devotees in Benāres and Ajodhya may be seen to-day practising many of them. Tārika went through eleven mortifications, extending over a hundred years:

1. He stood on one foot, holding the other, and both hands up towards heaven, with his eyes fixed on the sun.
2. He stood on one great toe.
3. He took only water as sustenance.
4. He lived on air.
5. He remained in water.

6. He was buried in earth, but continued in incessant devotion.
7. He was burned in fire.
8. He stood on his head.
9. He hung on a tree by his hands.
10. He bore the weight of his body on one hand.
11. He hung on a tree head downwards.

Such merit was irresistible, and Brahmā granted his request. The boon asked was that he should be unrivalled in strength, and that no hand should slay him but that of a son of Śiva. Tārika now became so arrogant that Indra was forced to yield him his white eight-headed horse, Kuvera his thousand sea-horses; the Rishis were compelled to resign the cow Kāmadhenu, that yielded everything that could be wished. The sun in dread gave no heat, and the moon in terror remained always at full; the winds blew as he dictated; and, in short, he usurped the entire management of the universe.[1]

At length Śiva was persuaded to deliver the world from the thraldom of Tārika, and Kārtikeya (Subramanya) was born on the banks of the Ganges. It is said that the six daughters (*i.e.* Pleiades), coming to bathe, saw the boy, and each one was so enraptured with him that she sustained him from her own breast; hence his six heads.

Another myth makes him the offspring of the union between Agni and Swāhā (narrated on page 300), who took in turn the form of the wives of the Divine Rishis, with whom the god of fire had become enamoured. Yet another describes that the sparks from Śiva's eyes became six infants, whom Pārvatī embraced with such rapture that their bodies became one, though their six heads remained.

In due course a conflict ensued between Kārtikeya and Tārika, in which the demon was slain. Many further accounts are given of his prowess. It is related how in pursuit of his calling he was once delayed on his journey by beautiful damsels, who entertained him by dance and song. Hence, alas! it is the custom for some of the dancing girls now

[1] Moor, *Hindu Pantheon*, p. 51.

attached to many southern Hindu temples to be betrothed and married to Kārtikeya.

He is not nearly so much worshipped as Ganesha, his elder brother. In South India, where his cultus more generally prevails, he has ceased to be worshipped as a martial hero, but is worshipped under the name of Subramanya, which means " very devotional or very favourable to Brāhmans." His temples are frequented by those who hope through his intervention to be delivered from evil spirits, or else by women who hope by propitiating him to obtain handsome sons.

III. Ayenār, a Guardian Deity

This god is the son of Śiva and Vishnu. The Skanda Purāna (Stanza 48) says: " This Ayenār, the author of our prosperity, was born when the holy Śiva, whose colour is that of the red sky, had intercourse with Vishnu under the form of Mohinī." Mohinī is represented as being a woman of surpassing beauty. The combination of the two deities is represented by the image of Hari-Hara, where one half represents a female form, and the other Śiva, surmounted by half a head-dress twisted into a matted coil, with the lunar crescent conspicuous on it.

" Like Ganesha and Skanda, the popular deity Ayenār (worshipped exclusively in South India) is a lord and leader of the demon host, and his province is to guard the fields, crops, and herds of the peasantry, who are ever on the watch to inflict disease, blight, and other calamities. Accordingly, outside many villages in Southern India, and generally among a group of trees to the west of the village, may be seen the shrines of Ayenār, surrounded by rude clay or terra-cotta figures of horses and other animals—often life-size—on which he is supposed to ride when keeping guard. This is his distinction—unlike Ganesha, he is never asked for any positive good, he protects from harm, and his worship is solely propitiatory. His image is that of a human form, painted a reddish colour and roughly carved. He rides on horseback, and with him are his two wives (Puranī and Pudkalā), who generally sit on each side of him, and take an active part in driving away the demons at night. It is on this account that no villager in Southern India likes to be out in the fields at night. If he should cross the path of Ayenār and his wives when they are careering about the fields, he is liable to be taken for an evil spirit and killed.

"After recovery from sickness, or to commemorate any piece of good fortune, the villagers place fresh clay horses round the shrine of Ayenār as thank-offerings. He is also to be propitiated by offerings of the blood of swine, goats, sheep, cocks, &c., cooked food, and libations of strong liquor. If cholera or pestilence of any kind breaks out the villagers redouble their offerings."[1]

In so many characteristics is Ayenār a typical village godling that he really should have been described under that heading. He merits, however, a higher place in view of his adulterous but distinguished ancestry. He forms, therefore, a suitable link to the following section of the book.

[1] Monier Williams, *Religious Thought and Life in India*, p. 218.

PART IV

INFERIOR DEITIES AND GODLINGS

CHAPTER I

INTRODUCTORY SKETCH TO SECTION ON INFERIOR DEITIES AND GODLINGS

" Gods, partial, changeful, passionate, unjust ;
Whose attributes are rage, revenge, and lust."
—ALEXANDER POPE.

IT is beyond question that in modern times the worship of the great gods of the Hindu Pantheon has suffered much degradation. Of all the number existing in the past, Hindus of to-day largely confine themselves to half a dozen deities—Śiva and his female counterparts, Vishnu and his incarnations, Ganesha, and the Sun-god. Throughout the length and breadth of India Brahmā, the Creator, has hardly more than a couple of shrines, Indra has become a vague weather godling, and Agni survives only in the fire sacrifice of the Brāhmans. Many others, once famous and powerful, are now forgotten, save by the learned priests and pundits.

Generally speaking, the greater gods of Hinduism are the property and the objects of worship of the richer and higher classes, and are to the ordinary villager little more than mere names. He does, it is true, occasionally bow at their shrines. He will pour water, or lay flowers on, or before, their images, but his allegiance and devotion are given to the inferior deities and godlings, of which there are thousands and thousands scattered over the land. Crooke[1] says that "this class of deities—often of mere local celebrity—has a distinct advantage over the greater gods in the eyes of the village community. They will help to recover a lost drinking-vessel,

[1] W. Crooke, *Popular Religion and Folk-Lore in N. India*, ii. p. 36.

will restore the sick baby to health, or will smite your neighbour's cow with disease, if suitably appealed to, which the great Śiva or Vishnu will hardly do."

Crude and primitive indeed is this type of deity. A red flag fluttering on a Pīpal tree, below which is a rough heap of stones, or a red-daubed splash on the trunk, is the customary shrine. Here dwells a godling of disease—cholera or small-pox—a local Mother with a reputation for cruelty, a village guardian in whose keeping are the herds or crops, or a deified saint or hero.

Hinduism is wonderfully assimilative. It is quite prepared to receive and acknowledge the village godling, provided that its worshippers observe caste-rules and obey the Brāhman priesthood. It has opened its doors to a vast amount of demonolatry, fetish-worship, and merely local belief. These constitute now the popular religion of the masses in contrast with the official faith of the upper classes in the greater deities of the Hindu Pantheon.[1] In some cases these godlings have become so popular that a place has had to be found for them in the ranks of the subordinate deities of the regular Pantheon.

Nature-worship, too, is widely prevalent—the deity of the mountain, wood, stream, or river, the Sun, the Earth Mother, and the sacred Tree.[2] Animals also come in for their

[1] "The high and mighty deities of Brāhmanism would never draw upward the peasant and the woodlander if he were not invited to bring with him his fetish, his local hero or sage, his were-wolf and his vampires, all to be dressed up and interpreted into orthodox emanations. In one part of Rājputāna the Minas (an aboriginal tribe) used to worship the pig. When they took a turn towards Islām they changed their pig into a saint called Father Adam, and worshipped him as such; when the Brāhmans got a turn at them, the pig became identified as the famous Boar Avatāra of Vishnu, whose name is Varāha."—Lyall, *Asiatic Studies*, Part I, p. 50.

[2] *Godlings*.—Macpherson says of the local deities of the Khonds of Orissa: "They are the tutelary gods of every spot on earth, having power over the functions of nature, which operate there, and over everything relating to human life in it. Their number is unlimited. They fill all nature, in which no power or object, from the sea to the

VILLAGE SHRINE AND ITS CUSTODIAN.
(Note the Linga stone and bull of Śiva, together with the local gods.)

Photo by Messrs. Hands & Son, Jubblepore, C.P.

A DEMON GUARDIAN OF BENARES.

Photo by Messrs. Saced Bros., Benares.

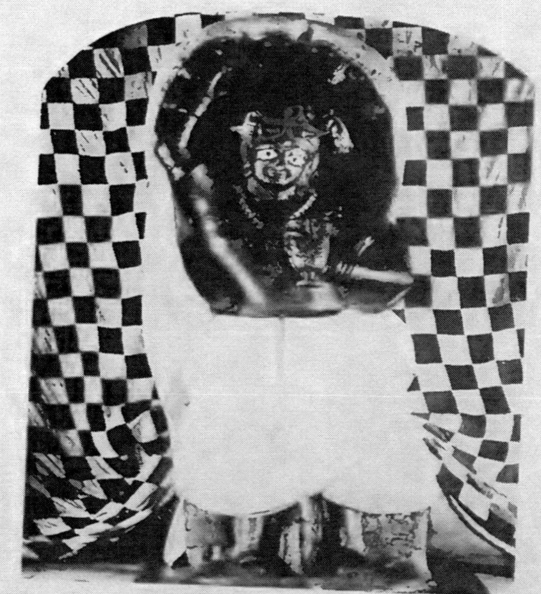

A VILLAGE DEMON.

THE SHRINE OF A VILLAGE GODLING.
The rude figure represents Bhairon (p. 272), and in front appeal is made to the mighty Brāhmanical deities. Note the Trident and Linga stone of Śiva.

share of worship, especial reverence being paid to the Cow and the Monkey. Ayenār, in the South, and Hanumān, the Monkey-god, in North and South India, are famed as guardian deities. In fact there is scarcely a village in India without its tutelary divinity. Usually its only shrine is the mud platform or heap of stones, already described, but sometimes the godling rises to the dignity of a building. In North India it is generally a small square shrine with a bulbous head and an iron spike as a finial. The walls are decorated with rude unshapely frescoes, or remain plain. Broken bits of statuary from ruined and dismantled temples are often found in it, but it is very rarely that a real image is seen there. Interior lamps are sometimes lighted, and fire sacrifices and petty offerings presented. Very frequently near the shrine, on a rough mud platform, little clay images of elephants and horses are found in rows. These are said to form the equipage or vehicle of the god, and are sometimes placed there in fulfilment of vows, or as a substitute for the real article, a very economical arrangement.

The votaries of the village godlings are looked upon with good-natured contempt and pity by their more intelligent neighbours, who worship the regular deities, but no active hostility is shown to them. In times of trouble, when the clouds withhold the rain, when the pestilence walketh in darkness, or when murrain devastates the herds—then the patron deities of the village are appealed to, and the worship at the shrine under the banyan or pipal tree becomes a factor of first importance.

---

clods of the field, is without its deity. They are the guardians of hills, groves, streams, fountains, paths, and hamlets, and are cognisant of every human action, want, and interest in the locality where they preside."—Macpherson, *India*, p. 90.

In considering the domination of the above, compare Milton's lines :

> " Millions of spiritual creatures walk the earth,
> Unseen, both when we wake and when we sleep."

CHAPTER II

THE TALE OF THE FIVE BROTHERS

(DEMI-GODS OF THE MAHĀBHĀRATA)

"The Epic, the Mahābhārata, is one continued allegory between man's virtues and his vices, the former personified by the five sons of Pāndu, of whom Bhīma, Yudhishthira, and Arjuna are personifications of Strength, Fortitude, and Prudence, and Nakula and Sahadeva are of Temperance and Chastity. Man's manifold vices are personated by the hundred sons of Kuru, who was Pāndu's brother, thus showing the near relationship existing between Vice and Virtue."—MOOR'S *Hindu Pantheon*, p. 92.

THE Tale of the Five Brothers is found in the Mahābhārata, so called because these five princes were descendants of King Bharata. They belonged to the Lunar race of kings, whereas Rāma was the representative of the Solar race. These are the two main races of ancient Hindu kings, and there are princes still reigning in Rājputāna who claim descent from the Sun. King Bharata reigned in ancient Delhi (Hastinā-pura), and his authority stretched over a great part of India; so from earliest times Delhi was a royal city.

His descendant was King Vyāsa, who wrote the Epic, and who lived a life of prayer and meditation. As his elder brother died childless, according to the ancient custom he married the two widows, in order that the line of kings might not fail. His sons were Dhritarāshtra and Pāndu, and as the elder was born blind the younger son succeeded to the throne. The elder son, however, married, and his wife miraculously became the mother to one hundred sons, of whom the eldest and leader was Duryodhana. Pāndu's wife, on the other hand, was childless until she obtained a boon from a powerful sage, who taught her an incantation, by means of which she could have a child by any god she cared to invoke.

Out of curiosity she called upon the Sun, and had a child, the first of the Pāndu princes, who was born clothed in shining armour. The other sons were Bhīma, the Hindu Hercules,[1] born, like Hanumān, a son of Vāyu, the Wind-god. It is said that soon after his birth his mother accidentally let him fall, and the child falling on a rock shivered it to atoms. Arjuna was Indra's son, and the most beautiful and perfect in character of the five. At his birth showers of flowers fell, celestial minstrels filled the air with harmony, and a heavenly voice sounded his praises and future glory. The other two were the sons of the Asvins, the twin charioteers of the Sun. So each of the five princes, having gods as their fathers, are regarded and worshipped by the Hindus as among the minor deities of the Pantheon.

The interest of the story of these princes lies in their conflict with their cousins, the hundred sons of Dhritarāshtra, commonly called the Kuru princes. The contrast between them is great. The Kuru princes were notorious for their mean, spiteful, and vicious characters, whereas the Pāndavas were upright and honourable, of undoubted bravery, and with a capacity for tender chivalry. In this story, as in the case of Rāma and Rāvana, we mark the conflict, keen and never-ending, between the great elemental forces of good and evil. The Hindus regard Duryodhana "the unfair fighter," and his ninety-and-nine brothers as visible types of Vice, or the evil principle in human nature. This is for ever waging war with Virtue, or the good principle, symbolised by the five sons of Pāndu.

Continuing the allegory, the good and evil princes spent their youth together, studying at the same school under the same Brāhman teacher. When manhood came to them they employed their growing strength in tournaments and deeds of skill. Arjuna covered himself with glory, as on one occasion

[1] See p. 271.

he shot twenty-one arrows in succession into the hollow of a cow's horn suspended in the air by a string. There was a natural rivalry in these tournaments between the cousins, and this keen competition, alas! deepened into hatred when the Kuru princes saw that the five Pāndavas everywhere excelled. They spitefully sought their revenge by setting fire at dead of night to their cousins' house, but the Pāndavas, warned of their intention, escaped to the jungles, where they lived as mendicant Brāhmans, wandering from place to place.

Then came their supreme test, the trial of skill and strength by which they won great renown. In ancient times maidens of high degree were often given to suitors who excelled in manly vigour, and were victors in the lists. Drupada, king of Panchāla, proclaimed that his daughter would be given to the prince who could shoot five arrows through a revolving ring into the target beyond. An immense bow was brought into the arena, which was filled from end to end with cadets of princely families and their retainers from all Hindustān. When expectation was at its height, drums and trumpets sounded, and Draupadī, as radiant and graceful "as if she had descended from the city of the gods," took her seat on the raised dais. The princes, one by one, tried their strength, but failed even to bend the bow. The hundred sons of Dhritarāshtra—the Kuru princes—strained every nerve to bend the ponderous weapon, but without effect. Its recoil dashed them to the ground, and made them the laughing-stock of the crowd. At last Arjuna, Indra's son, like the Grecian hero Ulysses, took up the bow:

> "A moment motionless he stood and scanned
> The bow, collecting all his energy;
> Next, walking round in homage, breathed a prayer
> To the Supreme Bestower of good gifts;
> Then fixing all his mind on Draupadī,
> He grasped the ponderous weapon in his hand,
> And with one vigorous effort braced the string.
> Quickly the shafts were aimed; they flew—
> The mark fell pierced; a shout of victory

Rang through the vast arena ; from the sky
Garlands of flowers crowned the hero's head,
Ten thousand fluttering scarfs waved in the air,
And drum and trumpet sounded forth his triumph."[1]

Then, alas ! the defeated suitors' rage overstepped all bounds. A real conflict took place, and the five brothers hastened to protect the newly-won bride and her father. They wrought prodigies of valour. Bhīma, uprooting a tree, used it as a club. The onslaught of Arjuna speedily routed the attacking party, who surrendered Draupadī as Arjuna's bride. The Pāndu princes then threw off their disguise as Brāhman priests, and entered into an alliance with King Drupada, by means of which Dhritarāshtra was induced to restore to them their share in his kingdom.

When they returned in triumph, bringing the beauteous maiden Draupadī to their mother's house, they found their mother inside her private apartments. They called out to her that they had brought her a great prize. Unwittingly she replied, " Share it between you." When she beheld Draupadī she exclaimed, " Oh, what have I said ? " But the word of a parent is a command that cannot be set aside with impunity ; so Draupadī became the joint wife of the five brothers. Polyandry is very rare in India, and practically is only found amongst the remote hill-tribes ; but this marriage is justified by Hindus on the grounds that being divine in origin, the five brothers possessed the divine essence equally, and so were really only one person. Naturally Drupada objected to his daughter's strange alliance, but was overruled on hearing of the brothers' semi-divine nature, and Draupadī lived for two days successively in each brother's house.

What the Kuru princes could not gain by force, they now tried to achieve by guile, and in order to overthrow their successful rivals they proposed a game of chance. Few Hindus can resist gambling. At one great festival every year

[1] Monier Williams, *Indian Epic Poetry*, p. 22.

gambling is openly practised in the streets, in houses, and everywhere; even the poorest can be seen gambling. The eldest of the five brothers, admirable as he was in every other respect, had this one great fault—a passion for the dice. By degrees, tempted by the Kurus, he lost all. He staked his wealth, his kingdom, his palaces, his brothers, himself, and, last of all, the beauteous Draupadī. She was brought into the assembly, and humiliated by being handed over to the Kuru princes as their slave, but she pleaded with their father to be allowed to accompany Yudhishthira and his brethren, who by the decree of their victorious cousins were compelled to go forth and wander in exile for thirteen long years. Her request was granted and the Five Brothers went out and hired themselves as servants to King Virāta: Yudhishthira as a professional gamester, Bhīma as a cook, Arjuna as a teacher of music and dancing, Nakula as a horse-trainer, and Sahadeva as a herdsman. They acquitted themselves so well in these various employments that, when the sentence of exile had expired, King Virāta gladly became their ally in the attempt to recover their lost kingdom.

Preparations for war were rapidly pushed forward, and the armies met on that vast plain north-west of modern Delhi which has since so often been the arena on which the fate of India has been decided. As the hosts advanced a tumult filled the heavens. Thunders roared, lightnings flashed, but the Pāndavas and Kurus, regardless of these portents, "pressed on to mutual slaughter, while the peal of shouting hosts, commingling, shook the world." The scene can be vividly imagined, although to a Western there is always a ponderous and unwieldy character about Oriental battle scenes, often brought to the verge of the ridiculous by the grotesque exaggerations of the Eastern writers. "Monstrous elephants career over the field, trampling on men and horses, and dealing destruction with their huge tusks; enormous clubs and iron maces clash together with the noise of thunder; rattling chariots dash against each other; thousands of arrows hurtle in the air, darkening the sky; trumpets, kettle-

THE DISPUTE BETWEEN THE PĀNDU AND KURU PRINCES.

KRISHNA adjudicating.

drums, and horns add to the uproar; confusion, carnage, and death are seen everywhere." After several days of incredible exertions the army of the Five Brothers was successful. They recovered their lost possessions, and the eldest brother was elevated to the throne.

All surely now should have ended in general content, with the brothers in peaceable possession of their own, but the dramatist has not so learned human nature in its deeper and sublimer phases. A European poet would have closed the volume here, the Eastern poet with the passion for renunciation, self-denial, and devotion to a higher end, that characterises so much of Eastern religion, continues the story to teach us the sublimer lessons of his faith.

The old blind King Dhritarāshtra could not forget nor forgive the dreadful slaughter of his sons—the hundred Kuru princes. He mourned especially for the eldest Duryodhana. At length he, his wife, and ministers of state retired to a hermitage in the woods, where after two years residence they perished in a forest fire. Deep remorse and sorrow then seized upon the Five Brothers. They renounced their kingdom and departed on a pilgrimage to the Himālayas, where they hoped to find Indra's heaven in Mount Meru, and by penances and self-denials to atone for the sorrow and suffering which they had caused to others.

The description of the pilgrimage is translated word for word by Monier Williams and set to verse:

"When the four brothers knew the high resolve of king Yudhishthira,
Forthwith with Draupadī they issued forth, and after them a dog
Followed; the King himself went out seventh from the royal city,
And all the citizens and women of the palace walked behind;
But none could find it in their heart to say unto the king, 'Return.'
And so at length the train of citizens went back, bidding adieu.
Then the high-minded sons of Pāndu and the noble Draupadī
Roamed onwards, fasting, with their faces turned towards the east, their hearts
Yearning for union with the Infinite; bent on abandonment
Of worldly things. They wandered on to many countries, many a sea

And river. Yudhishthira walked in front, and next to him came Bhīma,
And Arjuna came after him and then, in order, the twin brothers.
And last of all came Draupadī with her dark skin, and lotus-eyes—
The faithful Draupadī, loveliest of women, best of wives—
Behind them walked the only living thing that shared their pilgrimage,
The dog—and by degrees they reached the briny sea. There Arjuna
Cast in the waves his bow and quivers.[1] Then with souls well-disciplined
They reached the northern region and beheld with heaven-aspiring hearts
The mighty mountain Himavat (Himālayas). Beyond its lofty peak they passed
Towards the sea of sand, and saw at last the rocky Meru, king
Of mountains. As with eager steps they hastened on, their souls intent
On union with the Eternal, Draupadī lost hold of her high hope,
And faltering fell upon the earth!"[2]

One by one the others also drop, till only Bhīma, Yudhishthira, and the dog are left. Still the king walks steadily in front, calm and unmoved, looking neither to the right hand nor to the left, and gathering up his soul in inflexible resolution. Bhīma, shocked beyond measure at the death of his companions, appeals to his brother and inquires the reason why beings so guileless should meet so cruel a fate. Yudhishthira, without looking back, explained that sins and moral defects had proved fatal to the pilgrims. Draupadī fell, "too great was her love for Arjuna," next Sahadeva, "who esteemed none equal to himself," then Nakula, for "ever in his heart was this thought, there is none equal in beauty to me." Arjuna's fault was a boastful confidence in his power to destroy all his enemies. Bhīma then feels himself falling, and, asking the reason, is told he suffers death for his selfishness, pride, and too great love of enjoyment. The sole survivor now is Yudhishthira, who still walks steadily onward,

[1] He had a celebrated bow and quivers given him by the god Agni.

[2] *Indian Epic Poetry*, p. 29.

followed only by the faithful hound—he reaches the gate of heaven:

"When with a sudden sound that rang through earth and heaven came the god
Towards him in a chariot, and he cried, 'Ascend, O resolute prince.'
Then did the king look back upon his fallen brothers, and addressed
These words unto the Thousand Eyed (Indra) in anguish—'Let my brothers here
Come with me. Without them, O god of gods, I would not wish to enter
E'en heaven; and yonder tender princess Draupadī, the faithful wife,
Worthy of happiness, let her too come. In mercy hear my prayer.'"[1]

Upon this Indra informs him that the spirits of Draupadī and the four brothers are already in heaven, but that he alone is permitted to enter there in bodily form. Again he refuses to enter unless, in the words of Pope, "admitted to that equal sky, his faithful dog shall bear him company." Indra remonstrates, "You have abandoned your brothers and Draupadī, why not forsake the dog?" To this he haughtily replies, "I had no power to bring them back to life; how can there be abandonment of those who no longer live?" Now the dog was really his own father Dharma in disguise, who, reassuming his proper form, praises Yudhishthira for his constancy, and they enter heaven together.

One sharp and unexpected trial remains. To his utter astonishment he finds his enemies, the hateful Kuru princes, there, but looks in vain for Draupadī and his four brothers. He absolutely declines to remain in heaven without them. An angel is then sent to conduct him across the Indian Styx to the hell where they are supposed to be. He is taken to the uttermost depths of this hell. It is a dense wood, whose leaves are sharp swords, and its ground paved with razors. The way is strewn with foul and mutilated corpses. Hideous shapes flit across the air and hover over him. There is the horror of palpable darkness. There the wicked are burning

[1] *Indian Epic Poetry*, p. 30.

in flames of blazing fire. Suddenly he hears the voices of his brothers imploring him to assuage their torments, and not desert them. His resolution is then taken—he will not abandon his brothers in their misery. He bids the angel leave him there and return to heaven.

Then comes the crowning triumph. This whole scene, it is explained to him, is a mere illusion, given to test his constancy to the utmost. His brothers are not there but in the real heaven to which as yet he has not been admitted. He is now directed to bathe in the sacred Ganges, and then he enters the real heaven, where he, his brothers, and Draupadī dwell with Indra in full content of heart and life for ever and ever.[1]

[1] The whole story is found in Monier Williams' *Indian Epic Poetry*, pp. 19, 31; and Dowson's *Classical Dictionary of Hindu Mythology*, under word Mahābhārata, pp. 183–90, from which this account has been extracted.

CHAPTER III

THE WORSHIP OF THE SACRED RIVERS

Mā Gangā (the Ganges), the Nerbudda, and Other Rivers

> "Daughter of Vishnu, thou didst issue forth
> From Vishnu's foot, by him thou art beloved.
> Therefore remove from us the stain of sin—
> From birth to death protecting us thy servants."
>
> —*Hymn sung whilst bathing in Ganges, translated by* Monier Williams.

The deification of the Ganges is not surprising. To the Hindu she is what the Nile is to the Egyptian and the Volga to the Russian. To know the history of the land through which the Ganges flows is to know the history of India. She has been a potent influence in the spread of the only civilisation that India knows, and what a mighty civilisation it is! On her banks arose those two great systems of Theology, Philosophy and Social law, which we speak of as Hinduism and Buddhism; and which, with all their defects, constitute the peculiar claim of India to the attention of the thinking world. The arts of civilisation flourished here when Britain was in a state of barbarism. Over 3000 years have passed since the advent of the early Aryans on the Gangetic basin, and during all these centuries the mighty river has unfailingly brought life and plenty to the toilers on her alluvial plains. She has spoken to them of an Eternal Beneficence, of a never-failing Providence. Mighty kingdoms, races of heroes and men have passed away like the bubbles on her bosom, glittering for a moment in the sunlight and then bursting, vanishing into oblivion—but the great flood has ever remained, a permanent source of blessing, and a lasting token of the Creator's goodness.[1]

Gangā, the personified Ganges, was the elder daughter of Himavat (the Himālayas), lord of the mountains, her younger sister being Umā, Śiva's wife. Sāgara, King of Ajodhya, had two queens, one of whom gave birth to a single son and the other in a mysterious way to 60,000. These were directed to search for a horse which had been stolen by a Rākshasa (demon) at a horse sacrifice. Having searched the earth for the missing steed without success, they proceeded to dig up the ground bordering on the infernal regions, but meeting with the sage Kapila they accused him of the theft. This so enraged the Rishi that without more ado he reduced them all to ashes. Sāgara's grandson some time afterwards found the ashes and began to perform the funeral ceremonies. To do this, water was required and he was told that only Gangā could successfully complete the sacred rites. Neither Sāgara nor his grandson were sainted enough to devise any means of effecting the descent of the holy river from heaven. Great austerities and manifold devotions were required, and it was reserved for Bhagīratha, Sāgara's great-grandson, to bring down to earth the sacred river from where she issued from the foot of Vishnu in heaven. In her descent she fell with greatest fury on the head of Śiva, hoping to sweep him to destruction, but that great god to quell her pride and punish her presumption entangled her in the thick folds of his hair and compelled her to wander for many years in the orb of his Jata (top knot).[2] Then by a still further course of austerity Bhagīratha obtained her release:

> " When Gangā from his brow, by heavenly fingers prest
> Sprang radiant and descending, graced the caverns of the West."

---

[1] According to the Greek geographer Strabo, the Indians worshipped Jupiter Pluvius, the river Ganges, and the gods of the country. This Jupiter Pluvius was, no doubt, Indra (Strabo, xv. 1, 69). Note the early importance of the Ganges.

[2] Educated Hindus nowadays say that the foot of Vishnu from whence the Ganges issued is the Himālayas; that when she was received

MĀ GANGĀ (the Ganges Goddess) standing on the back of her vehicle the crocodile, and crossing the Ganges.

DESCENT OF MĀ GANGĀ ON ŚIVA'S HEAD.
Pārvatī and the bull Nandi and a Brāhman worshipper are seen in front

Pilgrim returning from the Ganges carrying baskets containing large water-pots, full of holy water, for sale in distant villages.

Photo by Rev. C. P. Cape, Benares.

Brass vessels used for carrying and sprinkling sacred Ganges water.

Photo by F. Deaville Walker.

Bhagīratha compelled her to follow him over the earth, thence to the ocean, and from there to the infernal regions, where she watered the ashes of Sāgara's sons and became the means of conveying their souls to heaven.

Several other legends are told about the Ganges. In the Mahābhārata we read of the wise Sāntanu, who, while hunting on her banks, found a very charming nymph with whom he fell in love. Before she consented to live with him, she put him under oath that he would never question her actions. After marriage she bore him eight sons, seven of whom, one by one, she threw into the river. Her husband dared not remonstrate with her, but when she was about to throw in the eighth son, he broke his oath and challenged her to tell him who she was, and why she committed such a crime. She then told him she was Gangā personified, and that these seven sons were the divine Vāsavas, who being thrown into the stream were liberated from the curse of human existence. Until the beginning of the last century the custom of offering a first-born child to the Ganges was very prevalent. Especially was it the case with women who had long been barren and who made a vow to devote their first child to the sacred river if made fruitful. This legend points to the origin of this dreadful practice.

Another tale narrates how that Balarāma, in a state of intoxication, called on Mā Gangā to come to him that he might bathe in her refreshing waters; and as she refused to obey him, he in his rage seized his ploughshare and by making a furrow dragged her to him and compelled her to follow him wherever he chose to wander through the forest. The river, hearing its dreadful fate, assumed a human form and begged the god's forgiveness, but it was some time before he

by Śiva into his locks and compelled to wander there for years, what is typified is the twists and turns the river makes in the sub-Himālayan regions before gaining the plains; finally, when King Bhagīratha prayed for her descent and brought her to the plains, what is represented is the fairly straight course made by the river from Hardwar to the sea.

relented. Her early crooked course to the sea is regarded as sufficient evidence of the truth of this story.

When Rāma reached the river bank on his famous pilgrimage he, having bathed, found a hermit there and began to question him :

> "O saint, I yearn
> The three-pathed Gangā's tale to learn.
> Thus urged, the saint recounted both
> The birth of Gangā and her growth,
> The mighty hill with metals stored,
> Himālaya, is the mountain's lord,
> The father of a lovely pair
> Of daughters, fairest of the fair. . . .
> Gangā was the elder born ; then came
> The fair one known by Umā's name,
> Then all the Gods of heaven, in need
> Of Gangā's help their vows to speed,
> To great Himālaya came and prayed
> The mountain king to yield the maid.
> He, not regardless of the weal
> Of the three worlds, with holy zeal
> His daughter to the Immortals gave—
> Gangā, whose waters cleanse and save,
> Who roams at pleasure, fair and free,
> Purging all sinners to the sea.
> The three-pathed Gangā thus obtained
> The gods their heavenly homes regained." [1]

India is the land of mighty rivers, and high on the list of river deities are Gangā and her sister stream the Yamunā (Jumna). Their banks are dotted with temples and shrines, and thousands upon thousands worship daily the sacred streams. The principal centres of worship on the Ganges are Gangotri, the source of the Ganges in the mountain ; Hardwar, where she forsakes her mountain home ; Allāhabād, where she joins water with the Jumna and that mythical stream, the Sarasvatī ; Benares, the holy city, and Sāgar Island, where she mingles with the ocean.

[1] Griffith's *Rāmāyana*, p. 72.

The characteristic feature of Ganges worship, and one that impresses every beholder, is the vast Bathing Mēlas [1] held at certain special festivals. It has been computed that as many as two million people gather on special occasions at the great Kumbh Mēla at Allāhabād. At Benares uncounted crowds are often seen.[2]

These pilgrims plunge their bodies in the sacred river believing that, as water cleanses their bodies from physical pollution, so the water of the Ganges will purify their souls from all past sin and its defilement. The following is a prayer often addressed to the River:

> "O Mother Gangā! I now bow at thy feet, have mercy on thy servant. Who can describe thy virtues? Were the greatest of sinners, the perpetrator of endless crimes, to pronounce the word Gangā, he, being delivered from all his sins, shall be translated to the blissful abode of the celestials."

No words can define the fascination and mystery of the giant stream as, at full moon or during eclipses, the people gather from all the country round. The ardour and intensity of their worship, their simple faith in the mighty flood that, as it flows, bears on its breast their sins and sorrows, and carries them into oblivion—these fill the mind with wonder and awe.

Naturally Ganges water is highly prized. It is carried in baskets and bottles long distances into the interior. It is

[1] The Hindu's life is marked by recurring ceremonial purification from the time when his first appearance in the world brings uncleanness on the household, requiring ablution and clean garments to remove it, and henceforth through his years, from youth to old age, bathing is a part of the long minute ceremonial of daily worship. At last the day comes when his kinsfolk, on the way home from his funeral, when his ashes have been thrown into the sacred river, cleanse themselves from their contamination by his remains. "Take away, O Waters, whatsoever is wicked in me, what I have done by violence or curse, and untruth" is a Vedic prayer repeated often to-day (*Rig-Veda*, i. 22–3).

[2] The day of Gangā's supposed descent on earth, the 10th of the light half of Jeshth (June), and the day of the full moon of Kārttik (October) are observed as festivals in her honour by all Hindus.

used in many religious ceremonies, as a remedy for disease, as a form of stringent oath,[1] and as a viaticum it is poured into the mouth and on the eyes of the dying.

The dead are brought many miles, sometimes hundreds of miles, for cremation on the banks of Mother Ganges, and allied to this custom is the Gangā Jātra. When a Hindu gets seriously ill, or appears to be near the end of life, relatives carry him to the banks of the sacred stream. There he sometimes lies for days with his body half immersed, and his mouth half filled with water, waiting for the final deliverance. The Agni Purāna declares that "those who die when half their body is immersed in the Ganges water shall be happy thousands of thousands of ages and resemble Brahmā." Undoubtedly by this cruel custom many lives are shortened and in some cases manslaughter is committed. These customs with the spread of enlightenment and knowledge of medical science are fast dying out, but they have not entirely ceased.

In addition to the Ganges there are many other rivers which are regarded as sacred by the Hindus. The Nerbudda is the only river that in any way disputes the pre-eminence of the Ganges. While only the northern bank of the Ganges, the bank on which Benares is situated, is efficacious for ceremonial bathing and the cremation of the dead, both banks of the Nerbudda can be so used. According to some authorities the Nerbudda is even more sacred than the Ganges, because while it is necessary to bathe in the Ganges for the forgiveness of sins, the mere sight of the Nerbudda, like that of the idol Jagannāth, is sufficient.

It is curious to note that the whole length of the banks of all the chief rivers of India, from their source to the sea,

[1] So strong is the popular belief in the sanctity of the river that both in private life as well as in the law-courts people often give up cherished claims if their opponents deny them when holding Ganges water in their hands or swearing by the Ganges. In the Mahābhārata it is said that the "Gītā comprises all the Sāstras, *i.e.* sacred writings, Hari (Vishnu), all the gods, and the Ganges all the sacred places."

PILGRIMS BATHING IN THE GANGES.

The large plaited umbrellas shelter Brāhman priests, who direct the worship of the bathers, and bless them on their return from the water.

Photo by Messrs. Sacred Bros., Benares.

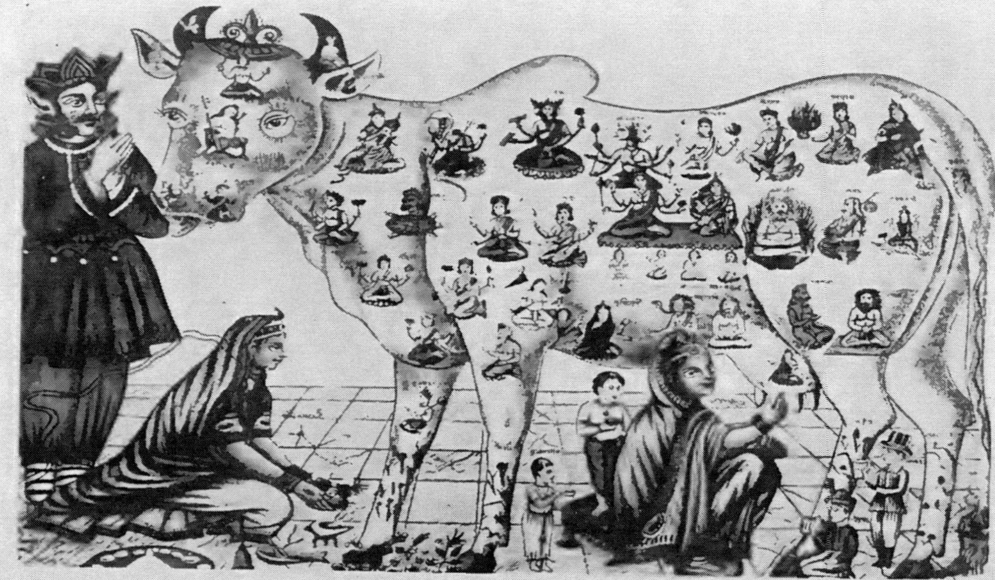

WORSHIP OF THE SACRED COW.

The Hindu Cow of Plenty enshrines all the deities. Most of the important gods and goddesses of the Pantheon are depicted on the surface of her body.

Note the worship offered by the woman in front, the reverence paid by the man, while her utility is seen by the woman milking her.

is regarded as holy ground. To follow their course on foot is considered a highly meritorious act. A pilgrim, for example, sets out from the source of the Ganges at Gangotri, and walks by the left bank of the river to its mouth, at Gangā-Sāgara; then turning round, he proceeds by the right side back to Gangotri, whence he departed. This takes six years to accomplish. In the same way a pilgrim starts from the source of the Nerbudda, a peak on the Vindhya chain of mountains, and walks to the mouth near Broach and back. This takes three years. The rivers Godāvarī and Krishna require only two years for the same process. Of course the merit accumulated is in proportion to the time occupied in pilgrimage and the sacredness of the ground traversed.[1]

Some of the rivers of India are considered male and some female deities; the two male rivers are the Brāhmaputra and the Sona (Sone) and the female rivers, in addition to those already mentioned, are the Kāvērī, Atreyī, Gomatī, Sārju (Ghagrā), Taptī, Gandakī, Varahī, Sabarmatī (Sabhramatī), and others. These are all sacred streams.[2]

Not only rivers but certain lakes and tanks are considered inherently holy. There are five such lakes, of which the holiest is Mānasa (commonly called Māna-Sarovar) in the Himālayan Mountains. The Well of Salvation in Benares is also supremely holy.

[1] Monier Williams, *Hinduism*, p. 173.

[2] This is a parallel to Hindu river worship in classical mythology. Gen. Sleeman (vol. i. p. 11) points out that among the Romans and ancient Persians rivers were propitiated by sacrifices. When Vitellius crossed the Euphrates with the Roman legions to put Tiridates on the throne of Armenia, he propitiated the river by the sacrifice of a hog, a ram, and a bull. Tiridates himself sacrificed a horse. Tacitus does not praise the river god, but the stream itself (see *Annals*, Book VI, ch. 37). Plato makes Socrates condemn Homer for making Achilles behave disrespectfully towards the river Xanthus in offering to fight him (*Iliad*, xx. 73); and towards the river Spercheus, another acknowledged god, in presenting to the dead body of Patroclus the locks of his hair which he had promised to the river, (*Iliad*, xxiii. 140–53.)

CHAPTER IV

ANIMAL AND BIRD WORSHIP

" Hari [1] himself, present in tortoise form,
Became a pivot for the churning staff.
There did they churn the sea of milk ; and first
Out of the waters rose the sacred cow,
God-worshipped Surabhi—eternal fountain
Of milk and offerings of butter."

—MONIER WILLIAMS, " The Churning of the Ocean," *Indian Wisdom*, p. 499.

THE origin of the Hindu worship of animals may be traced to various sources. In the first place no savage fixes the boundary line between man and the lower forms of animal life very definitely. The animal, in his belief, has very much the same soul, much the same feelings, as man has. The doctrine of the transmigration of souls holds out the possibility of any man being reborn as an animal, or an insect, possibly even a flea! To him again the belief is familiar that the spirits of his ancestors appear in the form of animals and birds ; perchance as a tiger, which attacks the surviving relatives, or as a chicken, which leaves the marks of its footsteps in the ashes when it revisits its former home.

Many animals and reptiles therefore are worshipped through fear, others again are respected and worshipped because of their use to man—or as scarers of demons, like the cow ; as possessors of wisdom, like the elephant ; as able to destroy him by the slightest puncture, like the snake ; as semi-human in origin or character, as the ape. In Vedic times great honour was paid to the horse, and the Asvamedha, or horse sacrifice, was the best mode of winning the favour of

[1] Name for Vishnu.

the gods. The sacrifice of one hundred horses entitled the sacrificer to displace Indra from his heaven, and in later times we meet the belief in the coming deliverer, Kalki, whose white horse reminds us of the white horse of the Book of Revelation.

Many animals are regarded as sacred by the Hindus because they are the *vāhans* or vehicles by which the gods travel. For instance Indra rides on an elephant, Śiva on his bull Nandi, Yama on a buffalo, Ganesha on a rat, and Durgā on a tiger, but there are two animals held in special veneration though not associated in this way with any god—the Cow and the Monkey.

I. COW-WORSHIP

Of all animals the cow is most venerated by the Hindus. She typifies the all-yielding earth from whom all plenty flows. It is said that Brahmā created Brāhmans and cows at the same time, the Brāhmans to conduct the rites of worship, and the cows to supply the products necessary for so many ceremonies. There is no doubt that the Hindu worships the cow because he is profoundly grateful for the services she renders him. She supplies his nourishment in a land where flesh foods are prohibited to the caste Hindus. Cakes of cow-dung mixed with mud are the universal fuel. All agricultural labour depends on the ox, for no horses are used at plough in India.

Monier Williams says: [1] "The cow is of all animals the most sacred. Every part of her body is inhabited by some deity or other. Every hair on her body is inviolable. All her excreta are hallowed. Not a particle ought to be thrown away as impure. On the contrary the water it ejects ought to be preserved as the best of all holy waters—a sin-destroying liquid which sanctifies all it touches. Nothing purifies like cow-dung. The filthiest place plastered with it is at once cleansed and freed from pollution, while the ashes produced by the burning of this hallowed substance are of such a holy

[1] *Religious Thought and Life in India*, p. 318.

nature that they not only make clean all material things, however previously unclean, but have only to be sprinkled over a sinner to convert him into a saint."

An example of the foregoing is cited. In the Agra Fort there is an image of a man named Mukunda. He was a celebrated saint who felt compelled to commit suicide by throwing himself in the river Jumna, which flows by the Fort, because he had accidentally swallowed the hair of a cow by drinking milk without straining it. This voluntary death, though, was not thought sufficient punishment, for he was condemned to become a Muhammadan in the next birth, but in view of his sanctity the harshness of the sentence was partially mitigated and he was born again as the Emperor Akbār!

The Sāstras appoint that images of the gods shall be anointed with the five products of the cow: milk, curds, clarified butter, cow-dung, and cow's urine, whereby they are free from all impurity. The gods themselves are exhorted to destroy their sins by eating clarified butter. Brahmā declared the cow to be a proper object of worship, and many Brāhmans to-day will not go out of doors of a morning until the doorway has first been rubbed over with cow-dung.

The cow is worshipped by all Hindus annually, but some of them worship her daily. No image is used, for the cow itself supplies that. "The worship is performed in the cowhouse before a jar of water. The ceremonies are the same as those before the images of the gods; the prayers are necessarily peculiar to the object worshipped." Another form of worship is used for those who worship daily. After bathing they throw flowers at her feet and feed her with fresh grass, saying: "O Bhagavatī, eat!" and then walk round her three or seven times making obeisance.[1]

"An interesting form of cow-worship is preserved in many of the Central Indian States. It is called the Maun Charāun, or 'silent tending of cattle.' The celebrants rise at day-break, wash and bathe, anoint their bodies with oil, and hang garlands of flowers round their necks. All this time they

[1] Ward, p. 154.

remain silent and communicate their wants by signs. When all is ready they go to the pasture in perfect silence. Each of them holds a peacock's feather over his shoulder to scare demons. They remain in silence with the cattle for an hour or two and then return home. This rite is celebrated in commemoration of Krishna feeding the cows in the pastures of Braj."[1]

Cow-worship is comparatively modern. It was unknown in Vedic times, but when the Institutes of Manu was compiled, a thousand years later, it had become recognised popular belief. Manu classes the slaughter of the cow or bull among the deadly sins, and even says " The preserver of a cow, or of a Brāhman, atones for the crime of killing a priest." One of the greatest problems of the Government of India lies in the slaughter of cows or bulls for food purposes by Christians and Muhammadans. To an orthodox Hindu this is anathema. Even the accidental killing of a cow is a serious matter and involves the feeding of Brāhmans and the performance of pilgrimages. Many serious riots have been caused by this divergence of practice between the Hindu and Muslim peoples. The most recent and one of the most serious was in Calcutta in 1910.

It is curious to find many instances of the use of the cow's tail in Hindu ceremonial.

A pious Hindu touches the cow's tail in the moment of dissolution, and by its aid he is carried across the dread river of death. More than one criminal has ascended the scaffold with the utmost composure when allowed to grasp a cow's tail. It is also used in the marriage ritual, and in ancient times the tail of the wild cow was once a symbol of regal power and waved over the ruler to protect him from evil spirits. Quite recently one of the chief Brāhman priests at the sacred pool of Hardwār kept a cow's tail to wave over his clients while they were bathing in the pool underneath. A legend relates how Śiva once manifested himself in his fiery form, and Vishnu and Brahmā went in various directions to see

[1] Crooke, *Popular Religion and Folk-Lore of N. India*, ii. p. 232.

how far the light extended. On their return Vishnu declared he had been unable to find out the limit where the light ceased to prevail, but Brahmā said he had gone beyond its limits. Vishnu then called upon the great legendary cow, Kāmadhenu, "the cow of plenty," to bear testimony, and she corroborated Brahmā with her tongue, but shook her tail by way of denying the statement. So Vishnu ruled that her mouth should be impure, but her tail should remain holy for ever.[1]

In the Srāddha (see page 278), or the obsequies for deceased ancestors, a milch cow is sometimes given to the Brāhmans who stand in place of the deceased ancestors, as by propitiating the Brāhman it is believed that the celestial bliss of the deceased is assured. The Brāhman having accepted the gift holds the cow by its tail and recites on behalf of the dead man the following prayers:

> "May the goddess, who is the Lakshmī of all beings, and resides among the gods, assume the shape of a milch cow and procure me comfort.
>
> "May the goddess who is Rudrānī (Pārvatī) in a corporeal form, and who is the beloved of Śiva, assume the shape of a milch cow and procure me comfort.
>
> "Since thou art Swadhā (*i.e.* the celestial food of the departed ancestors) and Swāhā, the consuming power (*i.e.* fire) of solemn sacrifices, therefore, being the cow that expiates every sin, procure me comfort.
>
> "I pray to that auspicious goddess for immortality and happiness."

The boon-granting cow so honoured in the preceding invocation is called Surabhi. She, like Lakshmī, was produced at the Churning of the Ocean, and her descendants are greatly honoured by the Hindus to-day. It is common for Brāhmans and others to feed the cow before they take their own breakfast, ejaculating, as they present her food: "Daughter of Surabhi, framed of five elements, auspicious, pure, holy, accept this food given by me; salutation unto thee!" This, too, is repeated when he leads the cow to grass![2]

[1] Crooke, *Popular Religion and Folk-Lore of N. India*, ii. p. 233.

[2] Moor, *Hindu Pantheon*, pp. 138–9.

II. The Monkey and Hanumān, the Monkey God

> " Hanumān, best of monkey kind,
> Was son of him who breathes the wind ;
> Like thunderbolt in frame was he
> And swift as Garud's [1] self could flee."
> —Griffith's *Rāmāyana.*

This god has become one of the most popular gods throughout the Deccan, Central and North India, because by his aid Rāma recovered Sītā after she had been abducted by Rāvana and carried off to Ceylon. He was commander-in-chief of the monkey host who were Rāma's great allies in the mighty struggle. He leaped from India to Ceylon in one bound to reconnoitre for the invaders. He tore up trees, carried away huge boulders from the Himālayas to build the famous bridge by means of which Rāma's army crossed the straits and reached the island. In one of his fights with Rāvana and the Rākshasas they captured him, greased his tail and set it on fire, but with his burning tail he destroyed their capital city. At another time, after a grievous battle, he flew to the Himālayas and brought from thence medicinal herbs with which he restored the wounded.

It is related that Hanumān in early youth longed for the rosy radiance of the rising sun, in lieu of his customary nourishment. He accordingly flew like the wind to seize the glorious luminary. Sūrya, affrighted at the bold attempt, fled with his complaint, pursued by Hanumān, to Indra. The god of Thunder, placing Sūrya in safety, launched a flash of lightning and smote the Monkey god almost lifeless to the earth.

For these and many other exploits he is often called Mahābīr, or the " great hero," and Rāma on his return to Ajodhya rewarded him with the gift of perpetual life and youth.

[1] Garuda, Vishnu's mythical bird.

Learning is not often associated with the monkey tribe, but Hanumān is described in the Uttara Kānda of the Rāmāyana as a being possessed of great learning. "The chief of the monkeys, measureless, seeking to acquire grammar, looking up to the sun, bent on enquiry, went from the mountain where the sun rises to that where he sets, apprehending the mighty collection. The chief of the monkeys is perfect: no one equals him in the Sāstras, in learning, and in ascertaining the sense of the Scriptures. In all sciences, in the rules of austerity, he rivals the preceptor of the gods."[1]

It must not be forgotten that the Monkey god is one of the greatest village godlings. His rude image, smeared with oil and vermilion, meets one's gaze in many a fair-sized Hindu village. He is often the guardian deity, and is considered the embodiment of virile strength, the conqueror of evil spirits, while women implore his aid as the giver of offspring.

A probable explanation of the prevalence of monkey-worship is that it is a matter of common belief that monkeys were once human beings who have suffered degradation. Hanumān was thought to be the chief of some such aboriginal tribe like those who to-day dwell almost like wild animals in the hill-tracts of Central India. If so, then hero and animal worship have become strangely mixed in the legend of the Monkey god.

Hanumān does not often rise to the dignity of a separate temple devoted to his honour, but in Rāma's birthplace, Ajodhya, the greatest temple is the Hanumāngarhi. It is a fortress-temple rising solidly from the surrounding plain, and is provided with a regular priesthood of Khāki ascetics. In the last census over a million persons in the United Provinces alone returned themselves as worshippers of Hanumān.

One of the main reasons why this god is so widely worshipped over a large part of India is that he is regarded as the type and model of faithful, unselfish, and devoted service. India is the land of servitude and nowhere is service so ungrudgingly given for such meagre wages. The lowly village

[1] Muir, *O.S.T.*, iv. 490.

THE DURGĀ TEMPLE, BENARES.
Sometimes called the Monkey Temple.

Photo by Messrs. Saeed Bros., Benares.

HANUMĀN, THE MONKEY GOD.
Returning to India to report to Rāma after the burning of Lankā with his tail.

GARUDA, VISHNU'S BIRD-VEHICLE.
The god is seen with Lakshmī (duplicated) and Garuda's power over the snake is also portrayed.

toilers from early childhood to old age reverence the arduous labours of Hanumān, and are never tired of narrating his wondrous accomplishments. He forms the favourite subject for their crude dramatic representations. At the Dasara—one of the most popular festivals of the year—Hanumān, clothed in gorgeous attire, marches along the stage at the head of his army of monkeys and bears, plays his part valiantly in the assault of Lankā, and the play ends with the destruction of Rāvana whose great body, formed of wickerwork and coloured paper, is blown up with fireworks amid the enthusiastic plaudits of the audience. Hindus worship Hanumān on their birthdays to obtain from him the gift of long life.

Living monkeys too are honoured and worshipped as Hanumān's representatives, and the feeding of monkeys is part of the regular ritual at some temples, notably the Durgā Temple at Benares, often called for this reason "the Monkey Temple." There is a king of monkeys there who is treated with much respect. It is remarkable with what impunity monkeys are allowed to steal grain and fruits and sweets from shops on the main roads. Very little resentment is shown, and as for killing them—the idea to a Hindu would be sacrilege, no matter how great the mischief and harm caused. In fact General Sleeman tells a story of a Muhammadan Nawāb of Oudh who died of fever, the result, it was said, of his father killing a monkey: "Mumtaz-ud-daula might have been king of Oudh," said his informant, "had his father not shot that monkey." [1]

Ward tells a remarkable story of the Rāja of Nadiya who spent a lac of rupees (£10,000 in those days) in marrying two monkeys. There was a magnificent parade. In the procession were seen elephants, camels, horses, all richly caparisoned; palanquins carried the guests whose path was lit by torches and fairy lamps. The male monkey was fastened in his palanquin with a silver chain. He wore a golden crown on his head and servants stood on either side to fan him with

[1] Sleeman, *Journey through Oudh*, ii. 133.

punkahs. There followed numbers of dancing girls in carriages. Every kind of musical instrument was pressed into use to celebrate the occasion, and at the time of marriage no less than twelve learned Brāhmans were employed to read the Sāstras.

III. Worship of Birds—Garuda—Vishnu's Vehicle

Birds also serve as the equipage or vehicle of the gods and goddesses, and are worshipped as such. The goose is the *vāhan* of Brahmā, the peacock of Kārtikeya and Sarasvatī; the planet Sani of ill-omen, rides appropriately on a vulture, and Vishnu mounts Garuda.

Garuda is a mythical being half man, half bird. He is represented as having the head, wings, talons, and beak of an eagle, and the body and limbs of a man. His face is white, his wings red, and his body golden. Though not strictly divine he appears so frequently in Vishnu's exploits that he is worshipped together with his lord.[1]

He is the king of birds, and is descended from Kasyapa (the Pole Star) the progenitor of gods and men, and Vinatā one of the daughters of Daksha. He is the great enemy of serpents, having inherited his hatred from his mother, who quarrelled with her co-wife Kadru, the mother of a thousand powerful many-headed snakes. Garuda obtained permission from the gods to devour these whenever he could find them. The mother of Garuda is said to have laid an egg; hence her son assumed the form of a bird—as soon as he was born his body expanded till it touched the sky; all other animals were terrified at him; his eyes were like lightning; the mountains fled with the wind of his wings; and the rays which issued from his body set the four quarters of the world on fire. The affrighted gods sought the help of Agni, con-

[1] Wilkins, *Hindu Mythology*, p. 449.

ceiving that Garuda must be an incarnation of the god of Fire.[1]

Another legend makes Garuda the son of Kasyapa and Diti. This all-prolific dame laid an egg, which, it was predicted, would yield her a deliverer from some great evil. After the lapse of five hundred years Garuda sprang from the egg, flew to Indra's abode, extinguished the fire that surrounded it, conquered the guards, and bore off the Amrita, the nectar giving immortality, which enabled him to liberate his captive mother. A few drops of the immortal liquid falling on some Kusa grass gave it eternal consecration ; the serpents greedily licking the grass so lacerated their tongues that they have ever since remained forked. But the boon of immortality was ensured them by their partaking of the Amrita.[2]

Yet another legend is related in the Mahābhārata of how Garuda liberated his mother from servitude and became Vishnu's carrier or vehicle. Ward tells the story thus: "His mother was reduced to a state of servitude to her co-wife and the innumerable brood of serpents. These were anxious to become immortal and promised to release her on condition that Garuda should bring them Chandra (Soma) the moon, whose bright spots were filled with Amrita. Before starting on his quest he asked his mother for some food. She instructed him to go to the seashore and gather up whatever he could see ; but entreated him to beware of eating a Brāhman, adding: 'Should you at any time feel a burning heat in your stomach, be sure you have eaten a Brāhman.'

"After receiving this warning he set forth, and passing through a country inhabited by fishermen, he, at one inspiration, drew into his mouth houses and trees, cattle, men, and other animals. But alas ! a Brāhman was among the inhabitants he swallowed, and he caused him such an intolerable burning in his stomach that Garuda, unable to bear

[1] Ward, *Hindoos*, p. 158.

[2] Moor, *Hindu Pantheon*, p. 341.

it, called on him to come out. The Brāhman refused unless his wife, a fisherman's daughter, might also be released. To this Garuda consented.

"Pursuing his journey Garuda met his father, Kasyapa, who shines in the firmament as the Pole Star. He directed him to appease his hunger at a certain lake where an elephant and a tortoise were fighting. The tortoise was eighty miles long and the elephant one hundred and sixty. Garuda with one claw seized the elephant, with the other the tortoise, and perched with them on a tree eight hundred miles high. The tree was unable to bear the ponderous weight, and unhappily, thousands of pigmy Brāhmans were then worshipping on one of its lower branches. Trembling lest he should destroy any of them he took the bough in his beak, and, continuing to hold the elephant and the tortoise in his claws, flew to an uninhabited country, where he finished his repast on the elephant and tortoise in peace.

"Garuda having surmounted astonishing dangers, at last seized the moon and concealed it under his wing. On his return he was attacked by Indra and the other gods for his crime in stealing the Amrita. He worsted Indra in the conflict and broke his thunderbolt. The other gods also were vanquished, excepting Vishnu. Even Vishnu was so sorely put to it in the contest that he came to terms with Garuda. His mother was released, Garuda was made immortal, and Vishnu promised him a higher seat than his own, while on his part Garuda became the *vāhan* or carrier of Vishnu. Since then Vishnu rides upon Garuda, while the latter, in the shape of a flag, sits at the top of Vishnu's car."

Garuda is worshipped at the great festivals before the different images of Vishnu, but he has no separate time of worship.[1] His image is placed in temples dedicated to various

[1] Abbé Dubois (p. 323) describes the actual homage paid to a species of Indian kite as the worship of Garuda. He says: "The Vaishnava Brāhmans every morning after ablution wait for the appear-

forms of Vishnu. To this day superstitious Hindus repeat the name of Garuda three times before going to sleep at night as a safeguard against snakes.

ance of one of these birds in order to pay it adoration. Sunday is the day particularly set apart for the worship of this sacred fowl. Troops of people are then seen uniting in their adoration and sacrifice ; after which they call the birds and throw bits of meat in the air, which they nimbly catch with their talons. It is a bird of prey seen everywhere about the villages. It is bigger than our falcon, but much smaller than the least of our eagles. Its plumage is handsome. The feathers of the head, neck, and breast are of a very bright and glossy white ; and those of the back, wings, and tail form a mantle of beautiful brown. But when it approaches near it becomes offensive from its unpleasant odour. Its ordinary cry is a kind of kree, kree ! uttered with a hoarse and croaking scream."

CHAPTER V

THE WORSHIP OF SACRED TREES AND STONES

> " Mark where yon tree rewards the stony shower
> With fruit nectareous, or the balmy flower.
> All nature calls aloud, ' Shall man do less
> Than heal the smiter and the railer bless ? ' "
>
> —HĀFIZ, a Persian Poet.

" Trees were temples of divinities, and in the old way the simple country folk to this day dedicate any remarkable tree to a god."— —PLINY, *Natural History*, xii. 3.

IN India, as already observed, all life is sacred. It might even be affirmed that Hindus were the first believers in the law of continuity, for in their creed the life of gods is connected with that of demons, the life of demons with men, the life of men with animals, the life of animals with that of trees and plants, the life of plants with a supposed life in rocks and stones, and the divine soul is thought to permeate all. There is no break anywhere, and tree and plant-worship follows as a necessary consequence on animal worship. In fact, according to the Hindu theory, all trees and plants are conscious beings, having distinct personalities and souls of their own as gods, demons, men, and animals (see Manu, i. 49). But it must be borne in mind that although trees may in their turn become the receptacles of the spirits of gods, men, and animals, they are peculiarly liable to be occupied by demons. That is to say, these beings may not only occupy a tree as its spirit or soul ; they may often resort to it as guests, or take up their abode in it as tenants. The idea seems to be that demons require protection from the weather like human beings, and occasionally betake themselves to trees as convenient and agreeable places of shelter. This explains the close connection between tree-worship, serpent-worship (for serpents often establish themselves in the roots of trees) and demon-worship.[1]

It is no unusual thing to find in certain localities a firm belief that certain trees are demon-haunted. A gaunt, solitary trunk is said to be the abode of a fierce, resentful spirit, or a dark grove or thicket hides some nameless, impalpable demon. The writer has experienced the annoyance of being taken considerably over half a mile out of his way in the dusk of the evening because his guide was afraid to pass a certain clump of trees. It is advisable, however, to make a clear distinction between trees and plants believed to be inherently sacred, and trees feared and revered as the home of spirit or demon. The tree-spirit is often conceived and represented as being able to detach itself from the tree and embody itself in living men and women, and this is the reason for the dread shown in passing certain trees at nightfall.

Another reason for the worship of trees is their wonderful utility in daily life. Their shade is grateful in a hot climate. Their wood is the source of fire, itself a god. Their fruits, juices, and bark are articles of food and have well-known medicinal and curative properties. The leaves supply many needs, amongst others roofing and thatch for houses. The Palmyra palm, so abundant in South India, has over fifty distinct uses to the people. What would the social life of the North Indian village be without the Pīpal-tree? Its shade and beauty are undeniable, and it naturally forms the Assembly Hall and Court House of the village community. And so highly reverenced is it that by an easy transition it becomes the abode of the village godling or guardian deity, and the centre for village worship.

When a Hindu plants a grove of mango-trees he will not take of the fruit of the grove, and it is considered a great disgrace for the trees to reach the fruit-bearing stage before they have been married to another kind of tree—usually a

[1] Monier Williams, *Religious Thought and Life in India*, p. 330.

tamarind, sometimes an acacia, or even a jasmine-tree which is planted in the grove. Often a costly ceremony takes place and many Brāhmans are feasted. In the same way the tank is often married to the plantain.[1]

Tree and plant-worship is of very ancient sanction and authority. As we have seen (in Part II, ch. viii.) the Soma-plant was revered in Vedic times not merely as the abode of divinity, but as itself a god. In Purānic times there arose, as the result of the churning of the sea of milk, a divine tree out of the ocean, named Pārijāta, which became the property of Indra and was transferred to his heaven. This tree was called Kalpadruma as granting all desires to those who did homage to its divinity. Tree-worship is undoubtedly a relic of the religions of aboriginal tribes (non-Aryan). In the Birbhum District of Bengal a great annual pilgrimage is still made to a shrine in the jungle to give offerings of rice and sacrifice animals to a certain ghost who dwells in a Bel tree.[2]

The custom, one so constantly notices in India, of hanging votive offerings or rags on the trees, perhaps as a receptacle for disease spirits, perhaps for recording vows, is of great antiquity. Ovid refers to it thus:

> "There stood a mighty oak of age-long strength
> Festooned with garlands, bearing on its trunk
> Memorial tablets, proofs of helpful vows."[3]

Names like Holyoake and Holywood recall our English worship of holy trees and groves.

Buddhism gives strong support to this custom of tree-worship, for Buddha in the course of his transmigrations was forty-three times a tree spirit. The famous Bo-tree at Gayā, under which Buddha received enlightenment, and its daughter Bo-tree, grown from the brand of the parent tree and sent by King Asoka in third century B.C. to Ceylon, receive the worship

[1] Sleeman, vol. i. p. 39.
[2] Hunter, *Rural Bengal*, pp. 131–94.
[3] See Ovid, *Metamorphoses*, viii. 741; also *Fasti*, iii. 267.

of pilgrims who come by thousands to these trees and offer prayer before them.

Classical analogies of tree deities are found in many places. We may instance—Daphne turned into a laurel that Apollo honours for her sake, and the sorrowing sisters of Phaethon changing into trees, yet still dropping blood and crying for mercy when their shoots are torn.[1]

The following are the trees and plants regarded as specially sacred by the Hindus:

(1) The Pīpal-tree (*Ficus religiosa*) is believed by some to be the abode of Brahmā and is consequently invested with the sacred thread by the regular Upanayana rite. Others say that in it abide Brahmā, Śiva, and Vishnu, but especially Vishnu in his incarnation as Krishna. Others again connect it with Vāsudeva, the father of Krishna. Devout Hindus consequently worship it, pour water at its roots, and smear the trunk with red ochre. Women make vows under it for the boon of male offspring and register their vows by tying cotton to its trunk or fastening strips of red material to its lower branches. A vessel of water for the comfort of the departing soul on its way to the land of the dead is hung from its branches, and beneath it are placed the rough stones which form the shrine of many a village godling. When a statement is made on oath the witness sometimes takes one of its leaves in his hand and invokes the gods above him to crush him, as he crushes the leaf, if he is guilty of falsehood.

One peculiarity remains to be noticed. This tree should only be touched on Sundays, when Lakshmī, the goddess of wealth, abides in it. On other days it is considered unlucky to touch it. Hindus on Sundays after bathing pour a vessel of water at its roots and walk round it four times. When the new moon appears on a Monday, pious Hindus walk one hundred and eight times round the Pīpal and wind cotton threads about its trunk.

This tree is very destructive to buildings. Its seeds are often dropped by birds into the interstices of the masonry of

[1] See Ovid, *Metamorphoses*, i. 452 ; ii. 345.

temples and shrines, and the tree grows and expands, forcing the stone or masonry asunder and often overturning or ruining the structure. A pious Hindu would sooner see the shrine of his deity destroyed than root out the tree and save the temple. A Pīpal shoot recently appeared in a crack in the plinth of the writer's house; the Hindu gardener, to test the prevalence of this belief, was ordered to remove it. He refused straightway and could not be induced to touch it.

Another instance of the reverence paid to this tree came under the writer's notice. We rested one day when on march under a tope of trees not far from the village well. While there, a respectable Hindu, wearing the thread of the twice-born, came to draw water. He drew his *lota* (a small brass drinking-vessel) brimful of water over the side of the well, and was about to wash his hands preparatory to drinking, when he was observed to pour the water deliberately back over the side of the well, repeating a prayer under his breath. He then drew for himself a fresh supply and quenched his thirst. On his departure we investigated the reason for his action, and found, some two or three feet from the surface, that a small Pīpal-tree was clinging to the side of the well. He had worshipped and honoured this diminutive shoot before satisfying his own needs.

(2) The Banyan-tree, also a variety of the fig (*Ficus Indica*), is of similar sanctity. It was under such a tree, the Bodhi-tree at Buddh Gayā, that Buddha obtained enlightenment. This tree is also sacred to Vishnu. When a Hindu plants one of these trees he uses the same rites as are customary at the consecration of an image of one of his gods. The tree once being planted continues to propagate itself by striking its branches into the soil by means of hanging tendrils which take root, and so the tree spreads and grows for centuries. The planter uses this prayer at the ceremony of consecration: "Oh Vishnu, grant that for planting this tree I may continue as many years in heaven as this tree shall remain growing on earth." He also expects, so great is the merit of planting such a tree, that he will not be

scorched by excessive heat on his journey to Yama, the regent of the dead.

(3) The Tulasī or Holy Basil shrub (*Ocymum sanctum*) is probably the holiest tree in India. It is a small shrub, not too big to permit of cultivation in a good-sized flower-pot. It has stem and leaves of a dull red and purple colour. Its leaves have an agreeable fragrance. It grows all over India and Persia. It is worshipped, often in conjunction with the Shālagrāma stone, a fossil ammonite, by all followers of Vishnu, and is most carefully tended as it is believed to contain the essence of the deity.

The Tulasī is a household god, and more particularly a women's divinity. The Hindu high-caste woman, debarred from outside temple-worship, offers to this little shrub peculiar devotion.

Manu's Laws (v. 155) exclude women from religious observances:

> "For women there is no separate sacrifice, no vow, nor even fast; if a woman obeys her husband by that she is exalted to heaven."

And in the Mahābhārata we read:

> "Women should always be honoured and treated with love, women have no sacrifices ordained for them. To serve their husbands with respect and willing obedience forms their only duty. Through the satisfaction of that duty they succeed in conquering heaven."

In other words, in Hinduism woman has no place.[1] Her husband has become her god. She is ranked with the Sūdras.[2] She cannot join her husband in his prayers, nor can she wear the sacred thread, even though of Brāhman birth. She must not read the Vedas nor hear them read. She has therefore developed a little religious life of her own: (1) "In the morning she sings a song which is intended to rouse up Krishna and Śiva, and she makes obeisances to the

[1] A prominent Hindu, speaking of the divisions in Hinduism, is reported to have said: "There are two points upon which we could all unite, the sanctity of the cow and the depravity of woman."

[2] The lowest of the four great groups into which the castes are divided.

rising sun; (2) after ablutions she puts on her caste mark (*tilak*) of red powder; (3) she has goddesses of her own: one room is often set apart for worship and contains the household idols. Her husband worships Vishnu, Śiva, and Ganesha. She worships their female counterparts, Lakshmī, Pārvatī, &c. She lights a lamp and says simple prayers to them and offers sweetmeats or fruit; but (4) her favourite worship gathers round the Tulasī-plant."[1] Every morning the ground round it is cleaned with cow-dung and water, and at night a lamp is hung near it. In the hottest months of the year a vessel of water, with a small hole perforated in the bottom, is hung over it so that it constantly receives moisture. The same honours are paid to it as to an idol, and worship is daily rendered to it. Salvation is assured to anyone who carefully tends it, and it is a common practice to place a sprig of Tulasī at the head of a dying person. To walk round this plant one hundred and eight times with the right shoulder always turned to it is considered a very meritorious action. Should the left shoulder be turned the efficacy would be lost! It is pitiful to think of the religious state of the women, shut out from the sources of enlightenment, dwelling in ignorance (of whom less than fifty in 10,000 can read or write), walking round the Tulasī-plant, caring for it, offering flowers and rice to it. and regarding it as the object of their prayers and hearts' devotion.

Several stories are told of the origin of Tulasī-worship. Ward relates that a woman named Tulasī engaged in religious austerities for a long time, and asked Vishnu that, as a reward, she might become his wife. Lakshmī, hearing of this, solemnly cursed the woman and changed her into the plant that bears her name. Vishnu, however, to comfort her gave her the assurance that he would assume the form of the Shālagrāma so as to continue to be near her. Hindus, therefore, continually keep one leaf of the Tulasī under, and another upon, the Shālagrāma (see p. 241).

Another legend is that Vishnu was fascinated with the

[1] *Arsenal*, p. 405.

THE SACRED PĪPAL TREE.

UNDER THE BANYAN TREE.

Photos by Messrs. Hands & Son, Jubblepore, C.P.

HINDU PRIEST WORSHIPPING THE TULASĪ.

The various articles in front are those used in Temple ceremonies, and in the central basket two black Shālagrāma stones are seen, and to the right in an egg-cup the white agate sacred to Śiva.

beauty of Vrindā, wife of Jalandhara, and to redeem him from this enthralment they applied to Lakshmī, Gaurī, and Swadhā. Each of these goddesses gave seeds to sow, from which grew trees with which Vishnu was enchanted. The first was the myrtle, the second the jasmine, and the third the Tulasī. Vishnu in this way was saved from the wiles of Vrindā.

Vishnu, in the representation of the Shālagrāma, is often married to the Tulasī-tree. The women in their houses marry him with full ceremonies on the eleventh day of the month Kārttik (October). The prayer of the Tulasī runs as follows:

"I adore that Tulasī, in whose roots are all the places of pilgrimage, in whose centre are all the deities, and in whose upper branches are all the Vedas."

(4) The Nīm or Nīmba-tree (*Azidirachta Indica*) is sacred in connection with the worship of the godlings of disease, who are supposed to reside in it. In particular it is occupied by Sītalā, the small-pox deity, and her six sisters. Hence during the rainy weather when epidemics prevail women bathe, dress themselves in clean clothes, and offer rice, sandalwood, flowers, and sometimes a burnt offering with incense at the foot of this tree. The Nīm is also connected with snake-worship, as its leaves repel snakes.

The leaves are used throughout North India for curative and medicinal purposes. Wounds and sores are bound up in Nīm leaves, and by mourners they are used as a means of avoiding death pollution, or as a mode of driving off the evil spirit which accompanies the mourners from the cremation ground. After the funeral they chew the leaves and some water is sprinkled over them with a branch of the tree. On the Hindu New Year's Day it is considered essential for every Hindu to worship the Nīm-tree, and to eat its leaves mixed with pepper and sugar, that he may not suffer from sickness or disease during the year. In practice very few worship the tree, but its leaves are generally eaten by most of them. At childbirth a branch of the Nīm-tree is often set at the door of the chamber. Nearly every northern Hindu cleans his teeth with a twig of the Nīm-tree. One more use remains to be given. It is a test of truth-speaking, and few Hindus would dare to speak a falsehood whilst under the shade of this tree. Among some tribes—the Banjaras for instance—a jealous husband throws a branch of the tree on the ground and says to his wife: "If thou be a true woman, lift that Nīm branch."[1]

Some few other trees are considered sacred. The Bel (*Aegle marmelos*), the Indian wood-apple with its triple leaf, is specially dedicated to Śiva with his threefold functions. Its leaves are laid on the linga to cool the heated deity. One of Śiva's many names is Bilvadanda, *i.e.* "he with the staff of Belwood."

The Babul-tree (*Acacia Arabica*) is used extensively in the exorcism of evil spirits. If you pour water for thirteen days successively on a Babul the evil spirits who inhabit it will come under your control. The ghost of a dead man burnt with this wood will not rest quietly, and anyone sleeping on a bed made of it has uneasy dreams. In the Panjāb a Hindu cannot legally be married a third time. He gets over the difficulty by marrying the Babul-tree, so that the wife he subsequently marries is counted as his fourth.[2]

Of grasses, the Kusa (*Pio cynosuroides*) is the holiest. It has been used since Vedic times in all religious ceremonies. It sanctifies the soil, forms the most sacred of seats, charms everything it touches, purifies the impure, and when wound round the fingers makes them fit to engage in the most solemn rites. In virtue it nearly equals the excreta of the cow.

Among plants, the Lotus (*Padma*) ought also to be mentioned. It is frequently alluded to in Indian poetry, and although not directly worshipped it has perhaps more sacred associations than any other flower. The Creator Brahmā was born from the lotus which sprung from the navel of Vishnu, and the goddess Lakshmī rose out of the ocean holding a lotus in her hand.

[1] Crooke, *Popular Religion and Folk-Lore*, ii. 104–5.
[2] *Ibid.*, p. 115.

Stone-worship

"This worship has been placed in the lowest class of Indian fetish-worship. The intelligence that argues that a stock or stone embodies divinity only because it has a queer unusual form is certainly not a high one. The original idea and motive of such practices as the worship of a stone oddly shaped, or of a jutting piece of rock, a huge boulder lying derelict in the midst of a plain, a circle of stones, a rudely carved pillar, fossils with their shell marks, an English milestone or telegraph-post set up where none was before, is simply the reverent attention paid to the Unaccountable Thing, the startling expression of an unknown power. Afterwards it is not difficult to perceive how this original adoration of strange-looking objects is modified by passing into the higher order of imaginative superstition. First the stone is the abode of some spirit; its strange situation or curious shape denotes *possession*. Next, this strange form or aspect argues *design*, the handiwork of supernatural beings, or is the vestige of their presence on earth; and one step further lands us in the world-wide regions of mythology or heroic legend, when the remarkable features of a hill, a cleft rock, a cave, or a fossil commemorate the miracles and feats of some saint, demigod, or full-blown deity."[1]

By the worshippers of Vishnu the Shālagrāma stone is regarded as a most sacred object. Images and idols of the gods have to be consecrated in a special ceremony by a Brāhman priest before they can be used, but this stone is inherently sacred and is worshipped as a part of the deity himself. It is a round black ammonite, and is found in Mount Gandakī in Nepāl. Ward says that popular belief is that insects perforated the masses of stone, so that they fall into the river Gandakī and are taken out by means of nets. Common ones are about the size of a watch, and they are valued according to their size, hollowness, and inside colour-

[1] *Asiatic Studies*, i. 13.

ing. For rarer kinds as much as Rs. 2000 are given. Hindus have a notion that whoever keeps this celebrated stone in his house can never become poor, but that the very day in which anyone parts with one of them he will begin to sink into poverty.

The reason why this stone is so sacred is given in the Bhāgavata Purāna : "Vishnu created nine planets to preside over the fates of men. Sani (the planet Saturn) commenced his reign by requesting Brahmā to become subject to him for twelve years. Brahmā referred him to Vishnu, who asked him to call on him next day. When he called he found that the god, dreading the influence of the inauspicious planet, had transformed himself into a mountain. Sani then became a worm, and ate into the vitals of the mountain for twelve years. At the expiration of that time Vishnu resumed his proper shape, and ordered that henceforth the stones of this mountain (Gandakī) should be worshipped as the representatives of himself."[1]

The Brāhmans usually worship this form of Vishnu in their homes. They first bathe or wash the stone, reading the formulas, and then offer flowers, incense, light sweetmeats, and water, repeating incantations. After worship the offerings are eaten by the family.

In the hot months, to cool the sacred stone, a vessel is suspended over it, as in the case of the Linga of Śiva, and a small hole is bored in the bottom and water poured into the vessel. The water which drips over the stone is carefully collected, and no orthodox Brāhman will eat his food in Western India until he has thrice sipped it. The marks of the stone are shown to dying men, in the belief that the concentration of the mind on this object will ensure the soul a safe passage to Vishnu's heaven.

A separate room or particular spot of the house is kept for the worship of this god. If the Shālagrāma should be touched by a low-caste man it is rendered impure, and has to be purified by rubbing over it cow-dung, cow's urine, milk,

[1] Wilkins, *Hindu Mythology*, p. 479.

butter, and curds—the five products of the cow. If a small part of this stone be broken off the broken part is always committed to the river.

Sleeman gives a curious story of a ceremony being performed to celebrate the marriage of a Shālagrāma stone to a Tulasī shrub.

"The Rajah of Orchha, in Central India, used to spend three lacs of rupees (about £20,000) on this marriage. The officiating priests told the writer that the procession consisted of 8 elephants, 1200 camels, 6000 horses, all mounted, and elephants caparisoned. On the leading elephant of this cortège was carried the pebble god (an ammonite, the only stone idol among the Hindus which is essentially sacred and entitled to divine honours without the ceremony of consecration). He was carried to pay his bridal visit to the little shrub goddess. All the ceremonies of a regular marriage were gone through, and when completed the bride and bridegroom were left to repose together in the temple of Ludhaura till the next year. Above 100,000 people were present, and they were feasted at the Rajah's expense."[1]

In addition to the black ammonite, Shālagrāma, white agates, typifying Śiva in his linga form, and red stones, as symbolising Ganesha with certain forms of coral, are also worshipped.

Shashthī, protectress of married women and of children, has no temples or idols, but her proper representation is a rough stone as big as a man's head, smeared with red paint and set up at the foot of the sacred banyan-tree. Even Śiva is worshipped by the well-known linga stone, as is that form of Śiva known as Panchānana, "the five-faced," who is the inflicter of epilepsy on children.

> "Among the smooth stones of the valley is thy portion ;
> They, they are thy lot ;
> Even to them hast thou poured a drink offering,
> Hast thou offered a meal offering."[2]

---

[1] Sleeman, vol. i. p. 148.

[2] Isaiah lvii. 6.

By a scarcely perceptible transition we pass from stone-worship to idolatry. A few chips on its surface or daubs of red paint suffice to convert the stone into an idol. The idol is then endowed with personal qualities, and among the ignorant passes from the stage when it is only regarded as a fetish to that when it becomes a powerful living being.

CHAPTER VI

WORSHIP OF THE GREAT MOTHERS

I. THE BENEVOLENT GODDESSES

"So, in particular churches at Munich and elsewhere, the shrines of the black Virgin are frequented by vast numbers of pilgrims, who hang votive offerings, often consisting of waxen arms and legs, around her altars, in the firm belief that they owe the restoration of broken limbs, and the recovery from various diseases, to her intervention."—MONIER WILLIAMS.

THE worship of Divine Motherhood prevails extensively in Eastern lands. Few great religions are without their deified, or highly reverenced women. Christianity has its Virgin Mary; Muhammadanism, Fatima and Ayesha; and Hinduism, its Śakti-worship—Kālī, Durgā, Rādhā, Sītā, and a host of others. In fact the worship of these Divine Mothers, often of mere local celebrity, but sometimes of well-known types, is one of the outstanding features of Hindu village life.

"In the first place, the living Mother is venerated by her children. Then every village has its own special guardian Mother, called Mātā in the North, and Amma in South India. Generally, also, there is a male deity, who protects, like the female, from all adverse influences, but the Mother is the favourite object of adoration. She possesses activity and force (called Śakti). She is more easily propitiated by prayer, flattery, and offerings, more ready to defend from evil, more sensitive to human need, more irritable and capricious in her temper and moods, more dangerously spiteful, and prone to inflict diseases, if offended by neglect.

"In point of fact the worship of the divine Mātris is a mere branch of Śaivism (Śiva-worship), and particularly that form of Śaivism called Śaktism.[1] Indeed one of the most remarkable features of the multiform and many-sided Hindu religion is the efficacy supposed to belong to this form of worship. Probably the idea of Mother-worship had its origin in the constitution of Aryan family life. Among the early Aryans the paternal and maternal tie, and indeed the whole family bond, was intensely strong. . . . If the father was venerated as the food-supplier and protector (Pitā), the mother was beloved as the meter out (Mātā) of daily nourishment—the arranger of the household, measuring and ordering its affairs as the Moon (also called Mātā) measured time. To the Aryan family the father and mother were present gods.

"Can we wonder that with the growth of devotional ideas, and the increasing sense of a higher superintending providence, the earliest religious creed was constructed on what may be called paternal and maternal lines? At first the sky (Dyaus, Zeus), bending over all, was personified as a Heavenly Father (Dyaus Pitar), and the Earth as the Mother of all Creatures. Then in the place of the Earth, Infinite Space (Aditi) was thought of as an Eternal Mother. Then Prakriti was the germinal productive principle, the Eternal Mother, capable of evolving all created things out of herself, but never so creating unless united with the eternal spiritual principle, called the Eternal Male, Purusha."[2]

With these ideas taking root in the earliest beginnings of Hinduism, it is not very astonishing to find that the ordinary Hindu has little difficulty in accepting Mother-worship as a part of his creed. It is impossible to exaggerate the prevalence of this idea. Village after village has its local Mother. Some of these are benevolent goddesses, who are worshipped because of the benefits they confer, but the great majority are, like the devils, inclined to cause harm, mischief, difficulties of all kinds, disease, and death, unless properly honoured and propitiated. Surely one of the chief functions of a mother should be the protection of her children from harm,

[1] See p. 179.

[2] Monier Williams, *Religious Thought and Life in India*, p. 223.

but the Hindu, while recognising this, adds the proviso that she only protects when her children have first cared for her well-being by making offerings at her shrine. Otherwise she can be painfully and dangerously destructive, and inclined to all sorts of mischief. Indeed many of these so-called Mothers are more dreaded than the demons themselves, so fierce and implacable are their natures.

Of the Benevolent "Mothers" examples have already been given of the Earth Mother (Dhartri Mai), already referred to [1] as a continuation of the worship of Prithivī, the Earth goddess of Vedic times, and Mā Gangā (Ganges), the great River deity.[2] There are one or two important Mothers who remain to be classified under this head.

I. Satī-worship

The word Satī (fem. of Sat = "virtuous") means "faithful wife"—the woman who by self-immolation on the funeral pyre accompanies her deceased lord to minister to him in the world of spirits is said to be the "faithful woman." Her resolve is set forth by Sir Edwin Arnold: [3]

> "But if death called Senani, I should mount
> The pile and lay that dear head in my lap,
> My daily way; rejoicing when the torch
> Lit the quick flame and rolled the choking smoke,
> For it is written if an Indian wife
> Die so, her love shall give her husband's soul
> For every hair upon her head a crore
> Of years in Swarga.[4] Therefore I fear not."

Is it strange that such a devoted woman after death was treated with exceptional honour? Her intercession was sought, and at the shrine erected over her ashes worship soon

[1] See footnote on p. 29.

[2] P. 213.

[3] *Light of Asia*, p. 161.

[4] Indra's heaven, situated on Mount Meru.

came to be paid.[1] She became the guardian Mother of every woman in the village, and was able to protect her worshippers and gratify their desires, having herself gained deification by her sacrifice.

In the sacred books of Hinduism there is sanction given to this terrible custom. In the Mahābhārata we read that when Pāndu died one of his wives, Kuntī, wished to ascend the funeral pyre, but she yielded her claim to Mādrī. "The bodies of Pāndu and Mādrī were burnt on the bank of the Ganges." When Krishna died his 16,000 wives set up a loud wail of sorrow, and four of them ascended the funeral pile. "The four wives of the heroic son of Shūra ascended the funeral pile, and were consumed with the body of their husband." [2]

We may sum up the chief motives which brought about the burning of Indian women on their husband's funeral pyre:

1. The perfectly natural wish of the wife to accompany her husband into the next world.
2. The implication of Hindu scripture that for a widow to die in this way is an act of the highest devotion.
3. The horrible yet strongly utilitarian motive of liberating a man's estate from the burden of the support of a number of widows.
4. Widow remarriage forbidden, and the consequent dread, failing the prospect of a comfortable provision being made for the widow among the husband's relations, of supporting life by the practice of immorality.
5. Strabo, according to Sir M. Williams, says it was done in order to prevent wives poisoning their husbands. (Strabo, xv. 30 and 62.)

[1] "Nor let the tomb of thy wife be accounted as a mound over the dead that perish, but let it be honoured equally with the gods, for travellers to worship, and someone going up the winding path shall say, 'She once died for her husband, and now is a blest divinity.'" —Euripides, *Alcestis*, l. 995.

[2] Mausala Parva, p. 24.

This rite was frequently practised by Hindu women from early times down to quite recently. Many thousands, if not millions, of women must have perished in this way. This practice, however, was prohibited by the British Government under Lord Wm. Bentinck in 1829, in spite of much opposition from the Brāhman priesthood. The Government remained firm, and the rite is now rarely practised. It still lingers, however, as the following extract from a Calcutta paper in the early part of 1911 will show :

"Bābu Surendrā Nāth Ghosh belonged to a respectable Kayastha family, and was aged thirty-two. He had been ill for some time past, and was confined to bed. On Monday last his wife, named Saibalinee Dassi, a woman of twenty-two years of age, was told by some inmates of the house that the doctors had pronounced her husband's condition hopeless. On Thursday, about one o'clock in the afternoon, the medical man in charge of Surendra told the inmates of the house that Surendra could not possibly live for more than half an hour. Surendra's wife understood what the doctor meant, and went up to her dying husband, who lay unconscious. She fetched some Ganges water and poured it into Surendra's mouth—the last thing she could do for him. She then crept downstairs and dressed herself in her best ornaments and sāri. She painted her forehead with vermilion and her feet with lac dye, as was the practice with the Satīs of old. She then bolted the door of the room, poured kerosene oil over her body, and set it on fire. The other inmates of the house took no notice of her, as they thought she was overcome with grief and could not bear to be present at the death of her husband. A relation of Surendra, named Kshirod, however, noticed the smell of something burning in the room where the wife was. He broke open the door, and saw the woman in flames, standing with hands folded and lifted in prayer. He raised an alarm, and managed to secure a bucketful of water, which he dashed against the burning body. Saibalinee motioned to him to desist, but he poured another bucketful of water on her, on which she fell down and expired in ten minutes. She died five minutes before her husband. The occurrence caused a great sensation in the neighbourhood, and a large number of Hindu ladies of all castes appeared in order to secure a little of the vermilion or lac dye, which is considered holy by every orthodox Hindu wife."

In Nepāl, and in semi-independent Native States, this revolting practice is still carried on. The dead husband

and the Satī are made to lie side by side on the pyre. The woman's right hand is placed under the husband's head, and inflammable materials are placed round her. Men with long poles wait to see if the woman in the agony of burning tries to escape, and in that case they thrust her back into the fire.

II. Shashthī, the Goddess of the Married Woman

Married life is the only possible existence for a respectable woman in India. The state of spinsterhood, as understood in Western lands, would be considered a shameful existence in the East. As women are allowed no formal initiation into the Hindu faith, no investiture with the sacred thread, marriage is to them their regeneration, their only hope of salvation. Henceforth they belong to their husbands, the husband becomes their god, into whose service they gladly merge their personalities, their hopes, their whole future.[1]

They are not unhappy, are rarely ill-treated (except perhaps by the mother-in-law while they are young), and are often deeply loved by their husbands. As separate units or members of society they simply do not exist—they have no status, and it is exceedingly bad form when paying a call or a friendly visit to a Hindu to allude to them by name or inquire after their health, unless under a general term, such as " the house," " the pillars of the house," &c. In spite of the low position of women in social life to-day, there is reason to believe that in ancient times women were greatly honoured. There is a remarkable definition of a wife in the Mahābhārata which it would be difficult to parallel in English literature. This is the literal translation :

> " A wife is half the man, his truest friend—
> A loving wife is a perpetual spring
> Of virtue, pleasure, wealth ; a faithful wife
> Is his best aid in seeking heavenly bliss ;

---

1 " Even though he be destitute of virtue, or void of all good qualities, or seeks pleasure elsewhere, yet a husband must be constantly worshipped as a god by a faithful wife."—Manu, v. 155.

A sweetly-speaking wife is a companion
In solitude, a father in advice,
A mother in all seasons of distress,
A rest in passing through life's wilderness." [1]

The guardian goddess of the home, the presiding deity at childbirth, the giver of children, the friend and helper of married women is Shashthī. She is represented as a yellow woman sitting on a cat, and nursing a child.

Ward describes her worship: "She is worshipped six times a year, but women who have lost their children worship her monthly. At the time of worship every mother in the village, dressed in her best clothes, with her face shining with oil and vermilion, and with all her ornaments on, goes to the place of worship under the banyan-tree, where she is usually represented by a stone about the size of a man's head. They, one and all, bring offerings, which the officiating Brāhman blesses, and which are afterwards sent to his house, or given to the female bystanders whom Shashthī has not so far favoured. These women eagerly open the end of their garments to receive what the assembled mothers bestow. When the giver says, "May the blessing of Shashthī be upon you, and next year may you bring offerings *with a child in your arms!*" the receiver adds with eagerness, "Ah! if she bestow this blessing I will celebrate her worship; I will keep my vows, and will bring offerings every year."

On the birth of the child Shashthī is, of course, specially honoured. Infantile lock-jaw is a most fatal disease in India for newly-born children, and is due to the use of filthy methods and dirty instruments at childbirth. Hence when the child is six days old every father performs "pūjā" to the goddess. From the sixth to the twelfth day is the danger period, and, if all goes well, on the twenty-first day the mother makes thank-offerings to the goddess, and garlands the stone which represents her. These homely ceremonies take place in the

[1] Mahābhārata, i. 3038, translated by Monier Williams.

evening, and if the mother is unable to go to the shrine a branch of the banyan-tree is fastened to the floor, and the ceremonies are performed before it.

II. The Malevolent Goddesses

It is difficult to say where demon-worship ends, and Mother-worship begins, in considering the malevolent Mothers, the goddesses of disease, of cruelty, of hate, of malice, and revenge. These goddesses, euphemistically called "Mothers," are replete with every characteristic of demonology. Goddesses of this type in the higher forms of such worship are usually called "Devī," or named after one of the numerous representations of Śiva's female counterpart—Kālī, Tārā, Durgā, &c. In the lower forms they are mere village godlings, spiteful, irritable, and uncertain in temper; fierce and terrible by nature.

"In Gujerāt, besides numerous varieties of the more popular forms, there are about 140 distinct Mothers. Some are rudely carved images, others mere symbols, and others only empty shrines without any visible representation. One of these Mothers was named Khodiyar, 'Mischief.' Her character appeared to be anything but maternal! So hurtful and mischievous was she that any outbreak of sickness in the village was entirely attributed to a temporary slackness in supplying her with nutriment. Extraordinary offerings therefore had to be offered—animals killed, and blood poured out—before the 'Mother's wrath was appeased and the disease abated.'

"All these Mothers delight in blood, and drink it. Hence the blood of swine, goats, and cocks, beside all kinds of cooked grain, is offered to them. One particular Mother is said to have a special fancy for black kids, and can only be prevented from causing sickness and death if the blood of at least three or four thousand such kids is presented to her every year. One of the most malicious of Mothers is the spirit of any woman who dies unpurified within fifteen days of childbirth. She becomes a demon, called Churel, and is always on the watch to attack other young mothers."[1]

I. Sītalā, the Smallpox Deity

It is quite a commonplace of Indian rustic belief that sickness and disease is not the result of natural causes, but the work of Mother-demons and devils, witchcraft, the evil eye, and so on. The basis on which this belief rests is very easy to understand. Certain varieties of disease, such as the delirium of fever, epilepsy, convulsions, hysteria, &c., appear to bear outward evidence of demon possession. Others, such as cholera, which comes suddenly and with such severity, and smallpox, so disfiguring and dangerous a disease, are ascribed to the agency of a god or goddess.

The diseases of mankind are said to be classed under three heads:

1. Those suffered for sins in a previous birth or births.
2. Those for sins committed in this birth.
3. Those purely accidental. Only these can be cured by a doctor.

Epidemics are classed by Hindus under second head, and demand divine propitiation.

The Indian custom of giving euphemistic names to things that are dreaded, in the hope of conciliating them and warding off their evil designs, is typically illustrated by the names given to Sītalā, the smallpox deity. The word means "she that makes cool," whereas the customary symptom of smallpox is high fever. Mātā, the common word for smallpox, means "the Mother," and it is almost invariably used with the respectful affix Mātāji, or "the Honourable Mother." Sometimes the people go still further, and call her Mahā Mai, "the Great Mother." "'The Great Mother' has come out in the village, and a child has died." In South India she is known by the name of Māri Amma.

[1] Monier Williams, *Religious Thought and Life in India*, pp. 223–225.

This goddess may either avert smallpox, of which there are three different kinds, or cause smallpox, or be herself smallpox. In some parts of the country persons who die of smallpox are not burnt lest the goddess should be burnt too. She is represented as a yellow woman, sitting on a water-lily, dressed in red, and suckling an infant. Her shrines are usually found outside villages, under trees, or in groves. She has little or no respect paid to her by men, except during epidemics, but thousands of women and children regularly worship her. Usually a few fetish stones, as befits an aboriginal deity, attended to by some low-caste menial, constitute her shrine, but occasionally she is promoted to a regular building, and comes in that case to be regarded as a form of Kālī Devī.

The attitude of the people towards the disease seems to be as inconsistent as the names given to it are inappropriate. They dread its coming, and pray and sacrifice to it in their temples and before the shrines of "the Mother goddess" in order to avert it; but when it comes, the family in which it appears, profess to be honoured by its presence in their midst, and hold in special regard one of the number who has survived an attack, but is badly marked. Smallpox often leaves its victims wholly or partly blind, and even when it is possible to restore or increase the sight, the operation is often refused on the ground that it would be disrespectful to the goddess.

"In Bengal she is worshipped on a piece of ground marked out and smeared with cow-dung. A fire is then lit, and clarified butter and spirits are thrown upon it, and the worshipper makes his obeisance, bowing his forehead to the ground and muttering incantations. In the spring of the year the Hindus inoculate their children of two years of age against smallpox, and the Brāhman who officiates and performs the operation makes presents to render Sītalā propitious, and promises, if the inoculation is successful, to give her still greater gifts. At the close of the operation the Brāhman places the flowers which have been offered to the goddess in the hair of the child as a charm. When smallpox breaks out in any locality prayers are offered daily to Sītalā, and if a patient becomes dangerously ill he is placed in front of the image of Sītalā, and bathed in the water which has been offered to the goddess, some of which is given him to drink."[1]

The divine force antagonistic to Sītalā is Shashthī, who, as already mentioned, is the guardian goddess of women and children. She is often specially worshipped in outbreaks of cholera.

Beggars often go about with a gilded stone, which they teach is sacred to Sītalā, and terrorise the unfortunate villagers by calling down the wrath of the goddess on villages who have not yielded the expected largess.

There is a darker side still to Sītalā worship. In times of smallpox epidemics of unusual severity human sacrifices have been known to be offered to stay the ravages of the disease.

One or two other methods of protection from the disease are noteworthy. Children are dressed in rags, and given opprobrious names. The Nīm tree is supposed to have influence over the disease, hence branches of it are hung in the doorways. Thunder disturbs the goddess, so the family flour-mill is rattled. Another device is to feed a donkey, which is the animal on which Sītalā rides.

II. The Cholera Mothers and Godling

Cholera is very prevalent at certain seasons of the year, and greatly dreaded. There are several presiding deities over this disease, and in different parts of the country different deities are propitiated. In the western districts of the United Provinces Kālī Devī[2] is worshipped, and a magic circle of milk and spirits is drawn round the village over which the cholera fiend will not dare to step. The Sāstras

[1] Ward, *Hindoos*, p 108.

[2] See p. 184.

which are written in praise of Kālī are also read, and the villagers worship at a Satī shrine if there be one in the village. The next stage is the loosing of a scape-goat. Sometimes a bull buffalo is used for the purpose. It is painted red, and led through an affected town in procession, and then driven out of the place into the jungle, and it carries the cholera wherever it goes. Animal sacrifices to Kālī are often made during cholera epidemics, and there is a well-authenticated case of an English official finding a living human victim tied up before a shrine in a time of cholera. We are reluctantly compelled to come to the conclusion that human sacrifice has been occasionally practised for centuries in India as a last resort for propitiating divine wrath when manifested in strange and inexplicable ways. In outlying districts it is still suspected to be the motive of mysterious murders. A good deal of pure savagery, with many rough and barbarous rites, lingers side by side with lofty and highly-organised ceremonial in this land of many contrasts. Brāhmans may do their best to discourage and refine these hideous practices, but they are not sufficiently strong to altogether suppress them.

Other cholera goddesses are Hulkā Dēvī, the impersonisation of vomiting, and the dread Mārī Mai, or "Mother Death," who is said to be Sītalā's sister.

Brief mention should here be made of the Cholera Godling, Hardaul or Hardaur. Contrary to most of the godlings of rural India he is a distinct historical personage. "Hardaur Lāla was the second son of Bir Sinha Deva, the miscreant Rājā of Orchha in Bundelkhand, who, at the instigation of Prince Jahangīr, assassinated the accomplished Abul Fazl, the litterateur of the court of Akbār. His brother, Jhajhar, succeeded to the throne on the death of his father, and after some time, suspecting Hardaur of undue intimacy with his wife, he compelled her to poison her lover, with all his companions, at a feast in A.D. 1627.

"After this tragedy the Princess Kanjavatī, sister of Jhajhar, and Hardaur were about to be married, and when

HANDPRINTS OF SATĪ WOMEN.

Each print commemorates a Satī, and the tablet is to be found at the Main Gate Jodhpore, Rājputāna.

Photo by Messrs. Hunds & Son, Jubblepore, C.P.

AT THE SHRINE OF THE DEMON GODDESS.

South Indian devotees propitiating the local Mother by rolling round her shrine. These goddesses called "Mothers" are replete with every characteristic of demonology.

By kind permission of Editor, "Foreign Field."

the mother issued the wedding invitations the Rājā Jhajhar mockingly suggested that one should be sent to Hardaur. Thereupon she in despair went to his tomb and lamented his wretched end. To her surprise Hardaur from below answered her, and promised to attend the wedding, and make all the necessary arrangements. The ghost kept his promise, and the marriage ceremony was performed as befitted the honour of his house. Subsequently he visited the bedside of the Emperor Akbār at midnight, and besought him to issue an order that platforms should be erected in his name, and honour paid to him in every village of the Empire, promising that if he were duly propitiated no wedding should ever be marred by storm or rain, and no one who, before eating, presented a share of the meal to him should ever want bread. Akbār, it is said, complied with his requests, and since then the ghost of Hardaur has been worshipped in nearly every village in North India. Alas, for the authenticity of this story, the chronology is hopeless! Akbār died in A.D. 1605, and Hardaur was murdered in 1627.

"In his native land of Bundelkhand Hardaur is a wedding godling of about the same rank as Dulhā Deo, but to the north of the Jumna his reputation rests on his power to stay the ravages of cholera. The terrible epidemic of cholera, which broke out in the camp of the Governor-General, the Marquess Hastings, during the Pindāri war, is generally attributed by the people to the killing of beef for the use of the British troops in the grove where the ashes of Hardaur repose.

"The expulsion of this godling from a village takes many forms, and is often provocative of quarrels and riots. In one district he was enticed into an earthen pot by magical rites, and the lid having been fixed on the pot was carried at dead of night to a neighbouring village, the inhabitants of which were at daggers drawn with those of the first village. The villagers tried to bury the pot secretly in the midst of their enemies, but the other villagers were on the watch, and a serious riot ensued. In the Bombay Presidency the village potter is sometimes asked to make an image of the Cholera Demon, and when ready the villagers form in procession and take the image to a spot outside their village, and there they worship it."[1]

III. Manasā, the Snake Mother, and Snake-worship

> "Terrific poison next issued from the waters;
> This the snake-gods claimed as their own."
>
> —*The mythical churning of the Ocean.*

The snake is dreaded, and, in consequence, propitiated and worshipped, largely on account of the fear associated with its mysterious habits and deadly poison. Its stealthy approach, fascinating sinuous movements, the cold fixity of its eye, the protrusion of its forked tongue, the suddenness and deadliness of its attacks, make it particularly dreaded by women whose habits of walking barefoot in the fields in early dawn, and groping in dark corners of the house, render them especially exposed to their bites. One of the great reasons why so few Indians will stir out of the house at night is for fear of the snake. Nor is this to be wondered at, for over 20,000 die annually in India from snake-bite.

On the other hand, it is certain that to some minds the beautiful markings, spiral movements, and generally striking aspect of many species of innocuous snakes, are suggestive of only pleasant ideas. To such persons serpents are typical of divine beauty and beneficence, while the coiling of their bodies into rings and circles, and their annual rejuvenescence by the renewal of their skins, symbolise immortality, and the never-ending cycles of Eternal Time.

Snake-worship prevails largely in certain districts of India, and some tribes, notably the Nāgas, claim snake origin. The race of Nāgas, who are supposed to be half human and half serpent, is fabled to have sprung from Kadru, one of the wives of Kasyapa (see Garuda, p. 228), who gave birth

[1] Crooke, *Popular Religion and Folk-Lore in N. India*, ii. pp. 135–146.

VILLAGE SHRINE OF SĪTALĀ (MĀTĀ) THE SMALLPOX GODDESS.
(Note flag, and marks made by suppliants over doorway.)

Photo by Miss Florence E. Walker.

THE THOUSAND-HEADED SNAKE, SESHA,
coiled in the form of the syllable O.M.

In this picture the Hindu Triad is seen. Śiva is seated on the half-moon above the serpent, and in the lower coil reclines Vishnu, attended by Lakshmī, while Brahmā springs from the lotus in the centre.

to 1000 Nāgas, who became the progenitors of the whole serpent race. Some of the females among them married human beings, and originated the present race of Nāgas. The hero, Bhīma (see p. 271), was nourished by the Nāgas, who freed him from the poison he had swallowed, and gave him an elixir to drink which endowed him with the strength of 10,000 Nāgas.

The thousand-headed snake, Sesha, one of the Nāga kings, is sometimes represented as forming the couch and canopy of Vishnu, while asleep during the intervals of creation. He is the emblem of infinity. According to popular belief earthquakes are caused by his shaking one of his thousand heads. The great Nāga festival is held about the end of July, and in districts where snake-worship is rife thousands flock to the Nāga shrines on that particular day. In some parts childless women go to snake-holes, and place there offerings of milk and eggs, making invocations and prayers. In fact, throughout India the worship of serpents and the worship of Nāgas is inextricably blended.[1]

There are many minor snake deities in different parts of India, as, for instance, Nāgeswar, the serpent deity of Benares, but the great legendary king of snakes is Vāsuki, who reigns, together with Sesha (Ananta) and Takshaka, over a portion of Pātāla (the lower regions) where the Nāgas are supposed to dwell, called Nāga-loka. Vāsuki, also, was the fabled rope used by the gods and demons at the churning of the Sea of Milk.

Manasā

Manasā is Vāsuki's sister, and was wife to a sage named Jaratkāru. She is queen of the snakes, and is worshipped as the protectress of men and women from these dangerous reptiles. One of her best-known names is Vishaharī, which means "the destroyer of poison."[2] Like all "Mothers,"

[1] Condensed from Monier Williams, *Religious Thought and Life in India*, pp. 321–323.

[2] Wilkins, *Hindu Mythology*, p. 474.

Manasā is of a jealous disposition, and unless constantly propitiated is liable to wreak her revenge by sending the deadliest of snakes to the houses of the people.

The great snake festival is the Nāgapanchamī, held on the fifth day of February. On that day people paint figures of serpents and birds on the walls of their houses. Generally speaking, no image is made of the goddess, a branch of a tree, a pan of water, and an earthen snake being representative of her. A song founded on the following story concludes the worship of this deity.

"A merchant, named Chanda, not only refused to worship Manasā, but professed the profoundest contempt for her. In process of time six of his sons died from snake-bites. To avoid a similar fate his eldest son dwelt in an iron house; but Manasā caused a snake to enter through a crevice, which bit him on his wedding day, and caused his death also. His widow, however, escaped, and went weeping to her mother-in-law, who, with the neighbours, vainly tried to induce Chanda to propitiate the goddess. Manasā herself urged his friends to prevail upon him not to remain so hostile to her. At last he so far yielded to their wishes as to throw a single flower with his left hand towards her image, which so delighted her that she restored all his sons to life, and from that time, since men came to know of her power, her worship has become celebrated, and she takes rank as one of the great mothers."[1]

[1] Ward, *Hindoos*, p. 109.

CHAPTER VII

HERO AND SAINT WORSHIP

" That holy man who stands immovable,
As if erect upon a pinnacle,
His appetites and organs all subdued,
Sated with knowledge, secular and sacred,
To whom a lump of earth, a stone, or gold,
To whom friends, relatives, acquaintances,
Neutrals and enemies, the good and bad,
Are all alike—is called ' one yoked with God.' "

—*Extract from Bhagavad Gītā*
(set in verse by Monier Williams).

" Where stands yon anchorite towards the orb
Of the meridian sun, immovable
As a tree's stem, his body half concealed
By a huge ant-hill. Round about his breast
No sacred cord is twined, but in its stead
A hideous serpent's skin. In place of necklace,
The tendrils of a withered creeper chafe
His wasted neck. His matted hair depends
In thick entanglement about his shoulders,
And birds construct their nests within its folds."

—KĀLIDĀSA, *Sakuntala*
(translated by Monier Williams).

ACCORDING to the Pantheistic creed of Hinduism, God and His Universe are one. His presence pervades all things, animate and inanimate, but He is believed to be specially present in great and good men. Such men are therefore held to be entitled to reverence and worship from their fellow-creatures, because they are embodiments of His essence in varying degrees and forms. The homage they receive during life is not always that of actual worship, but after death their claim is usually recognised.

"In India," says Sir Alfred Lyall,[1] "whatever be the original reason for venerating a deceased man, his upward course towards deification is the same. At first we have the grave of one whose name, birthplace, and parentage are well known in the district; if he died at home his family often set up a shrine, instal themselves in possession, and realise a handsome income out of the offerings; they became hereditary keepers of the sanctuary, if the shrine prospers and its virtues stand test. Or if the man wandered abroad, settled near some village or sacred spot, became renowned for his austerity or his afflictions, and there died, the neighbours think it great luck to have the tomb of a holy man within their borders, and the landholders administer the shrine by manorial right. In the course of a very few years, as the recollection of the man's personality becomes misty, his origin grows mysterious, his career takes a legendary hue, his birth and death were both supernatural; in the next generation the names of the elder gods get introduced into the story, and so the marvellous tradition works itself into a myth, until nothing but a personal incarnation can account for such a series of prodigies. The man was an Avatār of Vishnu or Śiva; his supreme apotheosis is now complete, and the Brāhmans feel warranted in providing for him a niche in the orthodox Pantheon.

"The earliest start of even a first-rate god may have been exceedingly obscure; but if he or his shrine make a few good cures at the outset (especially among women and valuable cattle) his reputation goes rolling up like a snowball. This is the kind of success which has made the fortune of some of the most popular, the richest, and the most widely-known gods in Berar, who do all the leading business."

There is no limit to this kind of deification in India. Volumes might be written describing instances that have occurred, or are constantly occurring, in all parts of the country. Let a man show any heroism, any extraordinary sanctity, any act of great self-sacrifice, or any so-called

[1] *Asiatic Studies.*

miracle, a niche is sure to be allotted him amongst the 330,000,000 gods of the Hindu Pantheon. Still it is important to note that the granting of divinity is usually associated with four classes of people—kings, warriors, Brāhmans, saints and sages—these enjoying a kind of *a priori* claim.

First, with regard to *kings*. In Manu's law book a king is said to be created by drawing eternal particles from the essence of the eight guardian deities of the world. Again, he says, " A king, even though a mere child, must not be treated with contempt, as if he were a mortal; he is a great divinity in human shape." Instances of such worship recently came under the writer's notice. At Ajodhya, near Fyzābād, a new marble statue has recently been erected in memory of Queen Victoria, and within a few weeks of the erection of the statue a constant stream of pilgrims were offering worship, pouring sacred water and scattering flowers on the pedestal of the good Queen's statue.

At the recent Durbar at Delhi, when King George and Queen Mary amid scenes of unparalleled magnificence had received the homage of all India and taken their departure, crowds of Hindus swarmed over the arena and, prostrating themselves before the empty thrones, offered " pūjā " or worship—as a mark of their extreme veneration. After which they carried away to their homes handfuls of dust from the place where their Majesties had stood. The same occurred after the gorgeous Pageant in Calcutta. There is a striking parallel in *Wisdom of Solomon*, xiv., v. 20, " And so the multitude, allured by the grace of the work, took him now for a god, which a little before was but honoured as a man."

The transition from the worship of kings to that of *military heroes* and warriors is easy. The great heroes of the Rāmāyana and Mahābhārata were firstly, warriors who were ultimately deified, and, in the case of Rāma and Krishna, became incarnations of Vishnu. An example will be given in this chapter of a Muhammadan warrior, Ghāzi Miyān, who, with the wonderful catholicity of Hinduism, is probably more reverenced to-day by Hindus than by Muhammadans.

A still more remarkable case occurred in the Panjāb, where a body of fakīrs became "Nikkal Sen" worshippers. General Nicholson, the Mutiny hero, who met his death at the assault of Delhi, was a horseman of unexampled bravery. He frequently made night journeys of wonderful speed, and confounded his enemies by appearing suddenly before them. His followers, the hardy Northern tribesmen, from adoration rose to worship of their hero. Nicholson was much annoyed, and tried to stop the progress of deification by administering corporal punishment, but this made them persist in their "pūjā" with even greater determination, as the chastisement was regarded as an additional proof of his divinity. On hearing of Nicholson's death, the head of the sect committed suicide.

Coming next to the *Brāhmans,* Manu affirms that a "Brāhman is a mighty god, a supreme divinity, whether he be learned, or unlearned, or even employed in inferior occupations" (ix, 317, 319). "From his birth alone a Brāhman is regarded as a divinity even by the gods" (xi. 84). Especially are religious teachers, Gurus, objects of worship among Hindus. A spiritual guide in the estimation of his disciple is literally a god. Whenever he approaches, the disciple prostrates himself in the dust before him, and never sits in his presence without leave. He drinks the water with which he has washed the Guru's feet, and relies entirely on his blessing for final happiness. It matters little if the character of the Brāhman priest be none too spotless, he in his nature, and by reason of his office, is considered holy.

The last group of deified beings is the most important because the most numerous. Nothing is easier for a *saint or sage,* who has become a Sannyāsi, *i.e.* has renounced family ties, and lives and practises a life of asceticism, than to be deified. When he dies his body is not burnt, because he is supposed not to have died at all. He is believed to be in a trance, sanctity exhales from his body like perfume from a rose, and his tomb becomes a noted place of pilgrimage.[1]

[1] Monier Williams, *Religious Thought and Life in India*, pp. 257–260.

The Hindu Saint

The worship of the sainted men of India, the Sādhu and Sannyāsi, is so common throughout India that a special place must be given to it, and a description given of the type of man worshipped.

The word Sādhu literally means "a perfect one." He is regarded as "the great power of God"—the visible manifestation of the divine energy he has acquired by his exemplary piety and devotion. Alas! the actual so rarely reaches the ideal. There are both good and bad Sādhus amongst the 5,500,000 men shown in the Census of 1911, as "Sādhus, mendicants, and professional beggars," but the good—few in proportion at any time—are getting fewer and men of idle, dissolute lives predominate. In fact idleness, gluttony, and ignorance are the characteristic marks of this class to-day. The testimony of one of the most prominent Indians of the day, H.H. the Mahārāja Dhirāj of Burdwān, published in the *Calcutta Review*, may here be quoted: "I think no other country is so full of Sannyāsis and Fakīrs, Param Hansas and Sūfis, Sādhus and Mollas of all sorts and denominations as India. The reason why these people flourish is a very simple one. The life of a tramp is easy in this country; a thief, as well as an honest man, is likely to get alms from any house in India by appearing as a Sannyāsi or Fakīr, for the people are mightily afraid of being cursed by a beggar if he is turned out without alms. So, many idlers, not caring to earn a living by honest industry, put on the garb of a Sādhu and easily maintain themselves by begging. Hence, amongst Sannyāsis and Sādhus in this country nowadays, only a few true and respectable men, who have really relinquished all worldly desires and subdued their passions, are to be found. The majority of them are simply beggars, thieves, bad characters, and even criminals evading the clutches of justice."

Not all can be so classed. Visiting Akbarpur in 1912 was

a well-known Sādhu whose profession of religion is sincere beyond question. This gentleman is a graduate of the Allāhabād University and comes of a wealthy and respectable Hindu family of Allāhabād. Shortly after taking his degree he heard the call to the religious life and abandoned his wealth and prospects, his ease and domestic claims, for the life of a wandering ascetic. It is a relief to record his evident sincerity and zeal when so many of his order pass their lives with no possible good to themselves or to the community which maintains them. Some of these "knights of the road" are very wealthy. They have numbers of *chelas* (disciples) who contribute to their support. They belong to the aristocracy of the Sādhu world, own costly equipages, elephants, &c., and feed on sumptuous dishes a prince might well envy. From their *gaddis* or seats of office they control their affairs and rule over their bands of followers—disciples and retainers.

No reformation is possible among them until the Hindu community exercises better discrimination in the bestowal of charity. We constantly hear of the poverty of India, but imagine the drain to the community that the maintenance of 5,500,000 of such people entails. The Sādhus regard it as their right to be fed by the community, and some of them go to the length of extorting charity by threats of personal violence.

Of a different type to the ordinary "Saint" is the man who works miracles. It is said of him in India what in Samaria they said of Simon Magus: "This man is the great power of God." Sooner or later, in life or after death, he is canonised. And we must remember that a miracle in India is not an interposition of the divine in the natural course of events, because no villager knows the laws that govern nature, but a miracle only means anything that may pass the peasant's simple understanding, which occurrence is rapidly enlarged by repetition or report to formidable dimensions.

There is keen rivalry between the followers of various saints on the death of their leaders, especially if expense has been incurred by erecting shrines and tombs with the hope of attracting worshippers. A process of canonisation is constantly going on. Holy men are often canonised on grounds considered insufficient, and the disciples of prominent Sādhus compete with each other on the death of their masters, as if universally acknowledged, his shrine will become a valuable source of income. Unfortunately indiscriminate and ill-regulated canonisation is often given. This is one of the main weaknesses of modern Hinduism. A Government official writes : " Hinduism lies in urgent need of a Pope, or acknowledged orthodox head, to control its wonderful elasticity and receptivity, to keep up the standard of its deities and saints, and generally to prevent superstitions running wild into a tangle of polytheism."

An unforgettable sight was witnessed one winter morning at the great Kumbh Mēla at Allāhabād. Thousands of people thronged the banks of the Ganges and the Jumna. Suddenly the crowd parted and down the opening lane swept some half a dozen elephants gorgeously caparisoned, following these, a band of native musicians, after which a few tattered banners were borne along, and then some two hundred Sādhus, stark naked, their bodies covered with smears of sacred ashes and ochre, their matted hair falling over their shoulders, and revealing glimpses of drink and drug-sodden eyes—so lurched forward these holy men of India! . . . The people bent in worship as they passed, and, when the procession was over, rushed to the place where their sacred feet had trod, and, seizing the mud, pressed it to their foreheads, eyes, and lips.

A very horrible sect of Sādhus exist and are sometimes met with, called the Aghorīs. These are eaters of offal, dead bodies, and even ordure. They do this to prove that they are indifferent to worldly objects and have reached a state of absolute passivity. They smear their bodies with excrement, and carry it about with them in a skull or a wooden cup, either to swallow it if a few *pice* (farthings) be given, or to throw it on persons who refuse their demands. They also inflict gashes on their bodies so that the crime of blood may rest on the householder who denies their extortionate demands.

To sum up. There are a few saintly men of genuine piety, but the great majority of these mendicants, of whatever order or class, live unchaste lives, often addicted to the use of intoxicating drugs, and total strangers to real purity of heart.

Two or three examples of Hero and Saint worship may be of interest. They are chosen from well-known and historical characters, as it is only possible to collect reliable information about such characters.

I. Ghāzi Miyān

The extraordinary catholicity of Hinduism was never better illustrated than in the case of Ghāzi Miyān, or Sayyid Salār Masaud to give him his real name. Muhammadan though he was, and nephew of the ruthless Muslim conqueror, the Sultān Mahmud of Ghaznī, whose career is written in blood on the pages of Indian history, all is forgotten in the sanctity that has lingered round his name, and he is worshipped to-day by more Hindus than Muhammadans at his famous shrine near Bahraich, in the United Provinces.

Ghāzi Miyān was born in A.D. 1015 and led one of the early invasions into Oudh, and was slain in a battle with the Hindus at Bahraich in A.D. 1034. Close to the battlefield where he met his death is a tank with the image of the sun god on a stone slab on its banks. Masaud, whenever he passed it, was wont to say that he wished to have this spot for a dwelling-place and would, if it so pleased God, through the power of the spiritual sun, destroy the worship of the material. He was therefore buried by his followers in this chosen resting-place, and tradition avers that his head rests on the image of the sun he had given his life to destroy.

Some believe that the worship of Masaud merely succeeded some primitive local worship such as that of the sun, and it is significant that the great ceremony in honour of the martyr is called the *Byāh*, or marriage of the saint, which may also be a continuation of the ancient marriage of the Earth and the Sun celebrated to promote fertility of the crops.

It is this marriage festivity which is the occasion for the great *Mēla* held yearly at Bahraich. One day in May a long procession of pilgrims may be seen wending its way on the highroad that runs westward from Benares and Jaunpur to Fyzābād and over the Ghagrā River to Bahraich. On the top of each pilgrim's bundle of clothes, cooking pots, and foodstuffs, rising high above the heads of the people as they march, is a miniature toy bed, a representation of the marriage bed of the saint they are marching so many leagues to honour. Bands of pilgrims similarly equipped gather from all quarters and meet under a gigantic tree which stands in the heart of the town. The standard is then set up and the celebration, which occupies over a month, begins. When ten days are left for the nuptials a procession is formed, headed by Ghāzi Miyān's standard, his bed, and kettledrum—the latter the insignia of royalty in the East. Vows are made at his shrine, offerings of beds, stools, bed-sheets, and flowers, fruit, sugar, and other things are made. And the nuptial rite itself takes place at midnight, on the first Sunday of June, when several female singers and dancers enter the shrine, when, after performing music and dancing, they pour out the contents of the water jars kept there, and leave the place after closing the doors behind them. The water so poured out is received into a reservoir outside, and numbers of blind and diseased persons bathe their foreheads and eyes with it, while lepers dip their whole persons in the reservoir and, doing so, cry out: "Saint, send the wave to us." The *Mēla* (or religious festal procession) then returns to the town. The belief in Ghāzi Miyān's mediation is firm and widely spread, and although as a rule only the lower classes attend the actual ceremonies, the wealthy classes observe his marriage feast by distributing sugar, fruit, and melons among the poor.

The land has many such shrines, and Hindu and Muhammadan alike, unite in honouring any man who in life showed unusual bravery or peculiar sanctity or self-denial. There is a similar and less widely known shrine in the Fyzābād District sacred to a Muhammadan saint, Makdūm Sāhib, who, it is said, vanquished his Hindu opponent (a saint noted for learning as for holiness) not by an appeal to the arbitrament of the sword, but by argument. However that may be, Hindus again are in a decided majority amongst those who frequent his tomb. This saint is said to have wonderful powers of exorcism, especially in the case of mental complaints, and numbers of feeble-witted and mentally-afflicted women resort to his shrine. These, when seated in rows in front of the tomb, are ministered to by a number of priests who set their heads moving forwards and backwards (often striking their foreheads on the ground in front of them) with an ever-increasing momentum. At intervals the women are stopped, and through the din of the drums which resound to stimulate the excitement of these mental sufferers (!) the evil spirit inside the brain is asked when he will depart. At last, through sheer fatigue and the maddening unaccustomed excitement, the women sink exhausted and fainting to the ground. A shout is raised: "Bhūt jal gaya"—"The spirit is burnt out"—and another victory is ascribed to the holiness and power of Makdūm Sāhib.

The worship of Muhammadan saints is, as we have said, a wonderful instance of Hindu receptivity. It also shows with remarkable clearness the curious trait of resignation to whatever is the will of the gods which is ingrained in the mind of the people. Because such vandalism was permitted by the gods, it follows that these persecutors of the faith, who slaughtered Brāhmans and desecrated shrines, were semi-divine, and so are worthy of worship. The recent Census returns 2,500,000 Hindus as worshippers at such shrines in the United Provinces, which have a population of 47,000,000.

II. Bhīma, the Hindu Hercules

Bhīma was one of the five heroes of the Mahābhārata, the Pāndu princes, and is the type of great strength and brute courage, and for this reason is installed as one of the guardian deities or wardens of the Hindu temples, with Hanumān, his half-brother, both sons of Vāyu the wind. He combined with vast strength an irascible temper, vindictive and cruel, making him " terrible " as his name implies. His strength required replenishing by huge supplies of food, and half the food of the family was allotted to him, the other half being divided between his four brothers and Draupadī. He therefore well earned his second name of Vrikodara—" wolf's belly."

The weapon he generally used was the club which, to suit his great strength, was of gigantic size. The explanation given of his strength is that he was poisoned by his cousin, Duryodhana, who threw his body into the Ganges. It sank to the realm of serpents, and in the underworld assimilated the power of the serpents, and rose ten thousand times endued with health and vigour. His conflicts were numerous and ferocious. He waged war against the Asuras—the demons—tore them asunder, and made them promise to cease molesting mankind.

In the wars that the Pāndu princes waged with the Kurus Bhīma took a very prominent part. On the first day he fought against Bhīshma, on the second he slew the two sons of the Rājā of Magadha, and, after them, their father, killing him and his elephant with one mighty blow of his club. In the night between the fourteenth and fifteenth day of the battle Bhīma fought with Drona from the setting to the rising of the sun. On the seventeenth day he killed Duhsāsana and drank his blood as he had vowed to do ; on the eighteenth and last day of the fight Duryodhana met Bhīma in single conflict, and Bhīma was getting the worst of it when he struck an unfair blow which smashed Duryodhana's thigh and brought him to the ground. In his fury Bhīma kicked his prostrate foe and behaved so disgracefully that his brother, Yudhishthira, struck him in the face with his fist and directed Arjuna to take him away.

To enlarge further upon his career is not necessary. He amply vindicated his title of the Hindu Hercules and is reverenced to-day together with Bhīmsen, Bhairon, and many others as heroes, of extraordinary valour and prowess.

III. Dulhā Deo, the Bridegroom Godling

This is one of the great godlings of the Central and North Indian aboriginal races. In his worship there is the echo of a great tragedy which still exercises a profound influence over the minds of the people.

The bridegroom on the way to fetch the bride is always treated with special reverence. He rides in state in a palanquin and is clothed in great splendour. It is said that Dulhā Deo was an unfortunate bridegroom who was killed by lightning in the midst of his marriage rejoicings, and he and his horse were turned into stone, and from that time forward he has been an object of worship.

General Sleeman gives the legend in another form: "In the valley of the Nerbudda, near Bhopāl, one may see on the side of the road, upon a spur of the hill, a singular pillar of sandstone rising in two spires. On the spur of a hill half a mile distant is another sandstone pillar not quite so high. The tradition is that the smaller pillar was the affianced bride of the larger one, who was a youth of great eminence in those parts. Coming to his uncle to pay his first visit to his bride, he grew more and more impatient as he approached nearer and nearer, and she also shared the feeling. At last he was unable to restrain himself and looked with all his might towards the place where his bride was said to be seated. Unhappily she felt the same inclination, and so they saw each other at the same moment. At that moment the bride and

NAKED HOLY MEN AND THEIR WORSHIPPERS.
(Note the reverential attitude of the men at the back.)

Photo by Gangi Sāh, Naini Tāl.

BHÎMA, THE HINDU HERCULES.
(One of the five Pāndu Princes.)

bridegroom and uncle were all three converted into stone pillars, the two former because, like Lot's wife, they indulged in the sin of curiosity, the latter because he did not restrain them. Nowadays as a singular fact bearing out the truth of this legend, contrary to Hindu custom, the bride of those parts always goes in procession to the bridegroom to prevent an occurrence of this calamity." [1]

"This deity is one of the chief household gods of the primitive hill-people. Flowers are offered to him on the last day of February, and a goat at marriages. In some places even Brāhmans worship him, and his symbol or fetish is a battle-axe, the national weapon, fastened to a tree. In Mīrzapur he is worshipped in the family cook-room, where oil and turmeric are offered to him; when two or three marriages take place at the same time there is a combined offering of a goat and cakes. A goat is fed on rice and pulse, and its head is cut off with an axe, the worshipper folding his hands and saying: 'Take it, Dulhā Deo.'" [2]

It is probable that the origin of his deification is the grief of his relatives at his sudden and untimely death, carried away as he was in the midst of his wedding celebrations. Such a motive is seen in the *Wisdom of Solomon*, xiv. 15: "For a father afflicted with untimely mourning, when he hath made an image of his child soon taken away, now honoured him as a god which was then a dead man. . . . Thus in process of time an ungodly custom grown strong was kept as law."

[1] *Rambles and Recollections*, i. p. 123.
[2] Crooke, *Popular Religion and Folk-Lore of N. India*, i. 120.

CHAPTER VIII

ANCESTOR-WORSHIP

" We living men, survivors, now return
And leave the dead ; may our oblations please
The gods and bring us blessings ! Now we go
To dance and jest and hope for longer life."
—*Rig-Veda*, x. 18, 3.

" Little the Manes ask, the pious thought stands instead of the rich gift, for Styx holds no greedy gods."—OVID, *Fasti*, ii. 353.

" THE worship of ancestors in some form or another is the beginning, the middle, and the end of religion among the Indian peoples," says Professor Bhattacharjya. Its principles are not difficult to understand, for they plainly keep up the arrangements of the living world. The dead ancestor now passed into the deity, simply goes on protecting his own family and receiving suit and service from them as of old ;[1] the dead chief still watches over his own tribe,[2] still keeps his

[1] Hymn addressed to the *Pitris* or *Pathus* (departed ancestors) by which their powers and prerogatives may be seen :

" Let the lower, the upper, and the middle Fathers, the offerers of Soma, arise. May these Fathers innocuous, and versed in righteousness, who have attained to (higher) life, protect us in the invocations. Let this reverence be to-day paid to the Fathers who departed first, and who (departed) last, who are situated in the terrestrial sphere, or who are now among the powerful races (gods). . . . Invited to these favourite oblations placed on the grass, may the Fathers, the offerers of Soma, come ; may they hear us, may they intercede for us and preserve us. Bending the knee, and sitting to the south, do ye all accept this sacrifice. Do us no injury, O Fathers, on account of any offence which we, after the manner of men, may commit against you."—*Rig-Veda*, x. 15, 1.

[2] Villages are believed to be haunted by the spirit of the *patel* (the old proprietor). In some cases the ghost was so forward that

authority intact by helping friends and harming enemies; still rewards the right and sharply punishes the wrong.

Amongst the early Aryans ancestor-worship was commonly practised, indeed the whole Vedic burial rites are instinct with reverence for the dead. The burial ceremony pictured in the hymn in the Rig-Veda, quoted above, so clearly depicts the deep regard for the dead, from which ancestral-worship sprung, that we give it in full. "The friends and relatives stand about the corpse of the dead man. By the side of the corpse sits the widow. The hymn begins:

> 'Depart, O Death, upon some other pathway, upon thy path, which differs from the path of gods . . . harm not our children, nor our heroes . . . These living ones are separated from the dead; this man is dead, but we go back to dancing and laughter, extending further our still lengthened lives.'"

The priest then puts a stone between the dead and the living and says:

> "I set up a wall for the living, may no one of these come to this goal; may they live a hundred full harvests and hide death with this stone."

The matrons assembled are now bid to advance without tears and make their offerings to the fire, while the widow is separated from the corpse of her husband and told to enter again into the world of the living. The priest then removes the dead warrior's bow from his hand:

> "Let the women, not widows, advance with the ointment and holy butter; and without tears, happy, adorned, let them mount the

---

the head of the village found it impossible to keep it in order. Their children and cattle were in consequence liable to serious accidents of one kind and another. Sometimes they were bitten by snakes, and at others thrown down and beaten most unmercifully. Any person who falls down in an epileptic fit is supposed to be thrown down by a ghost or possessed by a devil. Sometimes the ghost of the old proprietor is a friendly spirit who if the cultivators treat him properly will not allow the people of other villages to encroach upon his village boundary with impunity.—Sleeman, vol. i. p. 269.

altar." (Turning to the widow) "Raise thyself woman, to the world of the living; his breath is gone by whom thou liest; come hither . . . I take the bow from the hand of the dead for our (own) lordship, glory, and strength."

Then he addresses the dead:

"Thou art there, and we here; we will stay every foe and every attacker with power got from thee. Go thou now to Mother Earth, who is wide-opened, favourable, a wool-soft maiden to the good man; may she guard thee from the lap of destruction. Open, O Earth, be not oppressive to him; let him enter easily. Cover him like a mother, who wraps her child in her garment. Roomy and firm be the earth about thee; from this time thou, O man, hast thy happiness and home yonder; may a sure place remain to thee for ever. I make firm the earth about thee; may I not be harmed in laying the clod here; may the fathers hold this pillar for thee, and may Yama make thee a home yonder."

"In Brāhmanistic times, when the burning of the dead was practised, the text, as quoted, of the Aryan rite was retained, but twisted and altered into a crematory rite. There are, however, several additions to the earlier ceremonial. The body is shaved, bathed, and decorated with garlands and flowers. It is covered reverently with a new white sheet and placed on a litter, an oblation (Pinda) being offered to the guardian deities of the soil who protect the road to the burning-ground from evil spirits. The name and family of the deceased man are pronounced by his son and the son's wife, and other women of the household reverently circumambulate the corpse and utter lamentations. The body is then borne to the place of cremation, which is near a river if possible. A proper place is chosen for the erection of the funeral pile and well purified by the sprinkling of holy water. A kind of altar is then made and consecrated. The funeral pyre is constructed, Tulasī, Palāsa, and sandal wood being used in addition to the ordinary fuel. Five Pindas, or balls of rice, are placed on the deceased man's body, and his eldest son or representative applies the fire to the wood, reciting from the text already given. When the body is half-burnt the skull ought to be cracked with a blow from a piece of sacred wood. The idea is that the soul may not have been able to escape [1] through the aperture at the top of the head, called the crevice of Brahmā, and that the cracking of the skull may make an outlet and facilitate its exit. During the cremation an oblation of clarified butter ought to be offered in the fire and a Mantra recited entreating the god of fire to convey the deceased man to heaven. When the body has been consumed, all present at the funeral purify themselves with ablutions. Sesamum and water are then offered as an oblation, while the name and family of the deceased are again repeated. Finally, a few leaves of the Nīm tree are chewed by all, and the funeral procession returns home." [2]

The Srāddha ceremonies follow on after the burial rites are completed. It is well known that these practices are common amongst all Hindus who have come under the influence of Brāhmanical teaching, but not so generally known that amongst the aboriginal tribes of India they are widespread. Crooke tells us that the Ghasiyas of Mīrzapur

[1] The early Aryan belief in immortality and in the enjoyment of the future state are described in the Rig-Veda, ix. 113, 7 ff. :—

" Place me, O purified (Soma) in that imperishable and unchanging world, where perpetual light and glory are found. Make me immortal (in the realm) where king Yama dwells, where the sanctuary of the sky exists and those great waters (flow). Make me immortal in the third heaven, in the third sky, where action is unrestrained and the regions are luminous. Make me immortal in the world where there are pleasures and enjoyments—in the sphere of the sun—where ambrosia and satisfaction are found. Make me immortal in the world where are joys and delights and pleasures, and gratifications, where the objects of desire are attained."

That these pleasures were sensual ones is proved by many passages. The *Katha Upanishad*, i. 25, referring to the Apsaras, the courtesans of the gods, says :

" Ask at thy will, says Yama to Nachiketas, all those pleasures which are difficult to be had in the world of mortals, those fair ones with their cars and instruments of music—for such as they are not obtained by men ; receive them from me, and allow thyself to be waited on by them."

[2] Monier Williams, *Religious Thought and Life in India*, pp. 298–300.

prepare a feast on the tenth day after the death of one of their number, and when they have gathered the brotherhood together, the son of the dead man goes in the direction the dead man's body was carried and calls out his name two or three times, and invites him to consume the offerings they are ready to present. The Kharwars set aside the south room, the holiest part of the house for the sainted dead. They worship the spirits of the dead in the month of August near the house fire, and the master of the house sacrifices one or two black fowls and offers cakes and balls of rice boiled in milk. He then calls out:

> "Whatever ghosts of the holy dead or evil spirits may be in my family, accept this offering and keep the field and the house free from trouble."

The Korwas worship their dead in February with an offering of goats slaughtered by the eldest son. The Khariyas put the ashes of the dead in an earthen pot and throw the pot in the river. They afterwards set up in the vicinity slabs of stone as a resting-place for them, and to these they offer daily oblations. These instances will serve to show how widespread is ancestor-worship.[1] Other similar rites might be cited.

These are some of the customs of Ancestor-worship prevalent amongst the aboriginal tribes of Central and North India. Needless to say, they differ in detail in various localities. Orthodox and caste Hindus observe the regular Srāddha ceremonies, held for ten days or a fortnight after the death of their relatives. The spirits of departed ancestors are believed to attend upon the Brāhman priests invited to the Srāddha, "hovering around them like pure spirits and sitting by them when they are seated." Great reverence and honour is, therefore, paid to the Brāhmans.

[1] Sir Alfred Lyall relates that in one of the recent Indian censuses a Hindu householder filled up his schedule by returning as Head of the Family his deified ancestor whose profession he described as "subsistence on an endowment," while the question whether the divine personage was literate or not was somewhat indirectly answered by entering him as "Omniscient."

ANCESTOR WORSHIP.

Brāhman Priest (seated in front) instructing deceased man's relatives how to offer Pindas (balls of rice) to the spirit of the departed.

Photo by Rev. Geo. Spooner, M.A.

"The main object of the ceremony is nothing less than to provide the departed spirit with an intermediate body. Were it not for this body, believed to be created by the offerings made during the funeral ceremonies, the spirit of the departed would remain an impure and unquiet ghost (Preta), wandering about on the earth or in the air among demons, and condemned to become an evil spirit.[1] The intermediate body, once assumed, converts it from a *Preta* (a ghost) into a *Pitri* (or ancestor). The ball of rice (*Pinda*) offered on the first day after death nourishes the spirit in such a way as to furnish it with a head; on the second day the Pinda gives it a neck and shoulders, on the third a heart, and so on. By the tenth day the intermediate body is sufficiently formed to feel the sensation of hunger. It has now become a Pitri or ancestor. On the eleventh and twelfth day it feeds voraciously on the offerings, and so gains strength on the thirteenth day for its terrible journey to Yama, who is regent or president of the dead.

"According to the Garuda Purāna, the book in which Vishnu, questioned by Garuda, reveals the secrets of the future world and the punishment of the wicked, the man who dies without proper funeral ceremonies has to travel to the regions of torment, a journey of 86,000 leagues. The sensitive soul travels at the rate of 200 leagues a day, finding no resting-place; at one time scorched by the burning heat, at another time pierced by icy cold winds; now rent by thorns, now

[1] "The popular belief is that the better the man the more mischievous his ghost if means are not taken to put him to rest. Man-eating tigers are thus accounted for. Popular opinion is that the only sure way of destroying a tiger who has killed many people is to begin by making offerings to the spirits of his victim, thereby depriving him of their valuable services, as these spirits are supposed to guide the tiger from all danger. The human tiger is said to have no tail, and this forms the difference between it and the ordinary species. The Gonds, a wild jungle tribe, raise to its honour a small shrine and sacrifice to these spirits. They will tell you that if regular worship is performed on their shrine and good sacrifices of fowls, goats, sheep, &c., take place, the ghosts of the departed will relinquish their offices with the tigers and be quiet."—Sleeman, vol. i. p. 155.

attacked by fierce animals, venomous serpents and scorpions. It falls into deep pits, has to walk the edge of razors, stumbles about helplessly in profound darkness; here it struggles through loathsome mud swarming with leeches; there it toils through burning sand. Midway is the awful river Vaitarani, 100 leagues in breadth of unfathomable depth, filled with blood, infested by large sharks, crocodiles, and sea monsters; darkened by clouds of hideous vultures. Thousands of condemned spirits stand trembling on its banks. Consumed by a raging thirst, it (the Preta, or evil spirit) drinks the blood which flows at its feet, then, falling headlong into the torrent, is overwhelmed by the rushing waves. Finally, it is hurried down to the lowest depths of hell, and there it undergoes inconceivable tortures inflicted by Yama's officers."[1]

This description has been given to show the belief the Hindu holds with regard to a future state of punishment. On the other hand, he is taught that by performing the funeral ceremonies, and by offering nutriment to the souls of the departed in the shape of balls of rice, cakes of meal, water to bathe in, and milk for them to drink, &c., he not only accelerates their progress through the dread journey and lessens its terrors, but hastens the processes of its future births, and ultimate union with the Supreme Being. This can best be done by feasting and feeing royally the attendant Brāhmans, who for the time being are the earthly representatives of the departed ancestor. He who nourishes and benefits the Brāhmans, nourishes and benefits the Pitris (ancestors).

The place where the Srāddha is made always faces the South, the land where Yama rules over departed spirits, and the ground is smeared with cow-dung. The chief agent in the ceremony is the eldest son, and the man who dies without having a son to perform these ceremonies is considered very unfortunate, and goes to a Hindu hell called Put. So that

[1] Monier Williams, *Religious Life and Thought in India*, vol. i. pp. 293–4.

conversion to Christianity meets with the old objection: "Suffer me first to go and bury my father" (Luke ix. 59), or, as the Hindu puts it, "Who will perform my father's Srāddha if I become a Christian?"[1]

The Srāddha observances differ amongst different castes and in various localities. Gayā, in Bengal, is the great place for the performance of the Srāddha, where the ceremonies have the greatest efficacy. Large sums of money are spent by pious Hindus in travelling there, performing the various ceremonies, and in fees to the officiating priests.

The Srāddha in a modified form is repeated every month during the first year and afterwards is a yearly rite. In conclusion, it ought to be said that Hindus all believe that the observance of the Srāddha confers great reflex benefits on all relatives who join in presenting to their deceased kinsmen the balls of rice and libations of water. He who does so stores up merit, and procures future advantages for himself and his family; and the soul of the departed from being a Preta, a malevolent and unquiet spirit, a source of trouble and evil to him, becomes, thus propitiated and benefited, a Pitri, a kindly and beneficent guardian spirit.

[1] The Mahābhārata, citing a verse from Manu, says: "Since a son delivers his ancestors from the hell called 'Put,' the son was therefore called 'Putra' (deliverer from hell) by the self-existent (Brahma) himself" (*Adi parva*, 74, 37).

CHAPTER IX

DEMON AND DEVIL WORSHIP

> " Armed for the conflict, see ! the demons come—
> Ahi and Vritra, and a long array
> Of darksome spirits."
>
> —*Rig-Veda.*

NEVER very far absent from the thought of the Hindu is the fear of demons and devils, who are powerful because of their vast influence and their terrible malignity, and who constantly overshadow, thwart, or ruin his best endeavours. This dread has haunted for centuries Hindus of all ranks and castes, from the highest to the lowest, and may now be said to be ingrained in their very being. Going back to early days, the Aryans of the Rig-Veda—which itself contains a strong element of demonolatry—believed firmly in demons, although demonology was not then so fully developed as now. Indra is represented as a slayer of demons, the Asuras ; Soma and Indra were slayers of the demon of drought, Vritra. In one of the Vedic hymns we read :

> " I balm with oil the mighty Rākshasa Slayer (Agni) ; to the most famous friend I come for shelter. Roam also, in the air, O King, around us, and with thy jaws assail the wicked spirits, with fervent heat exterminate the demons."

With the lapse of centuries demon and devil worship has steadily increased in power and influence, and at the present time is universally prevalent and all-controlling. No thoughtful person can live in India for any length of time without coming to the conclusion that, whatever may be their outward beliefs, fully 90 per cent. of Hindus live in the thraldom of evil spirits.[1]

In some proof of this statement (which has behind it the great authority of Monier Williams, and is made with a due sense of its gravity), the reader of these pages will have noted that the goddesses of the Hindu Pantheon most worshipped are not the mild and gentle Pārvatī, but the fierce blood-thirsty Kālī, with other terrible manifestations of the Śakti of Śiva. Turning to the gods, we find that practically all the Avatāras of Vishnu have as their object the slaying of demons and tyrants, and Ganesha is reverenced as the remover of obstacles and the counteracter of evil influences. Hindus greatly dread and worship Śiva, the terrible agent of destruction. In all important occasions they consult the movement of the planets and fear the destructive and malevolent planets, Sani, Rāhu, &c. They avoid the evil influences of certain months, days, hours, and seasons, the power of the evil eye, of omens, and of the repetition by an enemy of certain mantras and curses; above all, they dread evil spirits, and perform many ceremonies to drive them away. Countless in fact are the offerings, sacrifices, purificatory ceremonies used to counteract the evil influences of the numerous hostile forces that encircle a man's life. Even the great gods of Hinduism are themselves subject to these malign spirits and fear their approach. There is no limit to these

[1] Sir Alfred Lyall declares that every mysterious, gruesome-looking dell, cavern, steep pass and wild, desolate hill-top or ridge in Central India has its Deo (god), never seen of man but felt by those who visit the spot—by shepherds and herdsmen camping out far amid the melancholy wolds, or by travellers along the lonely tracks. . . . The whereabouts of the spirit is sometimes marked by a heap of stones, sometimes by rags tied to a bush, occasionally by chains suspended mystically from a cliff or a tree; or the spirit wanders round a huge Banyan tree or ruined temple. Mr. Bowring, in his *Eastern Experiences* (1871), describes the Spirit-houses found in the Mysore forests—little sheds built over the white ant-hills and dedicated to the wood demons. Captain Forsyth, writing about Berar, mentions that when Gonds fell the wood on a hillside, they leave a little clump of trees to serve as a refuge for the spirit whom they have dislodged.

demon agencies. The land groans under the burden of them.

"Evils of all kinds, difficulties, dangers, disasters, famines, diseases, pestilences, and death are thought by the ordinary Hindu to proceed from demons, or, more properly speaking, from devils and devils alone. These malignant beings are held to possess varying degrees of rank, power, and malevolence. Some aim at destroying the whole world, and threaten the sovereignty of the gods themselves. Some delight in killing men, women, and children out of a mere thirst for human blood. Some take a mischievous pleasure in tormenting, or revel in the infliction of sickness, injury, and misfortune. All make it their business to mar and impede the progress of good works and useful undertakings."[1]

It must not be thought that the existence of good deities and benevolent demoniacal powers is denied, but these awaken no instincts of fear or even apprehension in the Hindu's breast, and therefore are not in need of constant propitiation. "The more feared the more worshipped" is a good axiom with which to measure the force of religious feeling in India. The demons and devils are regarded with more awe than the gods who defend men from their malice.

The classical name of demons is Asura (from *Asu*—"breath," "spiritual," "divine"), and this name was originally restricted to beings of malevolent intent with a semi-godlike nature who had access to the heavens of the gods. In the sense of "god" it was applied to some of the Vedic deities—Indra, Agni, and Varuna—but in later literature it came to have quite a different meaning, being used as a general term for all demons and evil spirits. Śiva is called the "lord of demons," and he has armies of beings called Pramathas, who do his will. There are also the Daityas, the supposed children of the goddess Diti by Kasyapa, who occupy one of the seven lower regions or hells which are peculiarly the abode of demons. Associated with these semi-divine demon hosts, though of different descent, are the

[1] Monier Williams, *Religious Thought and Life in India*, p. 231.

Rākshasas, with their chief Rāvana. These are ever hostile to men and gods, and are engaged in unending conflict with them. As they occupy so important a place in Hindu mythology, a separate section of this chapter is devoted to them.

" There is one demon king specially feared by the Hindus, Kali of the Kaliyuga. He is not to be confounded with Kālī, the wife of Śiva. No human being is believed to be able to withstand him. In the Bḥāgavata Purāna he is said to have cut off the three legs of Dharma (Religion), *i.e.* contemplation of god, purity of life, and mercy toward living beings, and to now be aiming at the destruction of the fourth leg—the truth of the Vedas. The legend is that when Parīkshit, the king of Kaliyuga, saw Kali in the disguise of a Śūdra torturing an ox he was horrified and sought to kill him, but as Kali begged for his life he permitted him to find his abode in gambling-houses, taverns, in women of unchaste lives, in slaughtering-places, and in gold. Kali agreed to do so, but after the monarch's death he disregarded his limitations and spread himself throughout the length and breadth of the wide world. In our days every vice, every crime is set down to the ascending power of Kali, who now reigns in Kaliyuga. " It is the ripening of Kali " is the melancholy explanation of any violation of moral and social rules.[1]

There is a secondary type of demons, namely, those which owe their creation to man. These are called Bhūts (Sanskrit *Bhūta*, " formed," " created "), and are by far the more important class, as it is chiefly to these evil spirits that propitiation and worship is given. The aboriginal tribes and primitive peoples live in grievous bondage to them, and Hindus generally believe that the vast majority of malignant devils were originally human beings. They are the spirits of those who were murdered, or who died under unexpected or tragical circumstances, as, for instance, those killed by tigers, or from snake-bite ; those who met their death away from their relations, and therefore out of reach of the proper

[1] *Arsenal*, p. 410.

funeral rites, are all specially to be feared. "Unsepulchred they roamed and shrieked, each wandering ghost." [1]

Sir Monier Williams relates how in one part of India he found the people worshipping the ghost of a milkman who was killed by a tiger and became a devil. In another place the ghost of a potter became a devil and a terror to the whole neighbourhood. The priests of these devils were milkmen and potters respectively. A robber who was hanged at Trichinopoly became so popular a demon that mothers named their children after him.

One out of the four bastions of nearly every fort in the Deccan has on it the shrine of a demon called Chand Khān, whom, tradition says, was originally a workman who perished, or was sacrificed, in the erection of one of the earliest forts. Possibly a human sacrifice to ensure the stability of the building. A number of other instances might be given, especially from South Indian demonology. Śaivism prevails in the South, and Śiva represents the ascetic, dark, awful, bloody side of Hinduism, and it is undoubtedly due to this fact that "the whole Southern population is almost hopelessly and incurably afflicted with demonophobia." [2]

A remarkable doctrine is common in India, but especially in South India—that, when men or women, notorious for any particular vices, die, they themselves may become extinct, but their evil natures never die. Their crimes live after them in the shape of malignant demons, and every one of their vices assumes its corresponding personality. And thus we have legion after legion of foul fiends and unclean spirits, bearing names corresponding to such expressions as deceit-devils, gambling-devils, cruelty-devils, lust-devils, blasphemy-devils, murder-devils, &c., all of these on the look out for weak-minded victims, and ready to instigate them to commit similar crimes.

It is a terrible thought that year after year, and even day by day, men and women, through their sinful habits, are

[1] *King Lear.*

[2] Monier Williams, *Religious Life and Thought*, p. 244.

adding to the number of the demon host, but it must not also be forgotten that the ranks of good spirits are constantly being recruited by the deaths of righteous men, saints and sages, who are for ever contending against the fiends.

These devils are mostly feared by women and children and by people in any serious crisis of their lives, such as marriage or childbirth. It is a very common thing to see women and children wearing an amulet, sometimes roughly engraved with the image of a Devī, to ward off the attacks of demons.

According to some authorities these devils may be grouped under three classes, each class having a distinct origin :—

A Bhūt is a spirit emanating from one who has died a violent death either by accident, suicide, or capital punishment, and has not had his proper funeral ceremonies performed afterwards.

A Preta is the spirit of a deformed or crippled person, or of one defective in some limb or organ, or of a child that was born prematurely. This class is not necessarily evil-disposed to men.

A Pisācha is a demon created by men's vices. It is the ghost of a murderer, drunkard, liar, adulterer, or criminal of any kind, or of one who died insane.

Monier Williams,[1] while giving this classification, goes on to say that it is never consistently maintained, and that his own inquiries led him to the conclusion that the terms Bhūt and Preta were, as a general rule, applied to all demons and ghosts indifferently, and the term Pisācha to mischievous and malicious imps and fiends. Such demons haunt burial grounds and take up their abode in trees, and are addicted to midnight roaming. They take either hideous or beautiful shapes, and even the form of men. They require the support of food, and delight in the blood of living animals. But according to popular belief they may, also, feed on corpses, ordure, and carrion, and may even occupy and vivify dead bodies.

[1] Monier Williams, *Religious Life and Thought*, p. 242.

Worse still, an evil spirit may enter the bodies of living people through one of its openings, and to dislodge it when once it has taken up its abode in the interior is very difficult. Once in possession, they cause all kinds of unpleasantness and misery. They agitate the limbs or face as in the case of epilepsy and nervous twitchings, and impel the sufferer to frantic movements, in which all devils take particular delight. They may take the character of a dog, cat, serpent, or other animal. It is fully believed that if a person is possessed by a dog-demon that he will take to barking like a dog, &c.

The subject of spirit-entries is, therefore, of great and vital importance to a Hindu. "They can enter and leave the body in various ways; often they use the crown of the head and enter through one of the crevices of the skull known as the "crevice of Brahmā." Bhūts are especially fond of entering by the mouth, and elaborate precautions are taken at meals, and frequent mouth-washing forms part of the daily ritual of the Hindu. Yawning is rigidly discouraged, for either at such a time the Bhūt may go down your throat, or part of your own soul may escape up it. So when yawning you must snap your fingers and scare the demon, repeat the name of your favourite god—Nārāyan, Rāma, &c.—and put your hand to your mouth. Sneezing also is due to a Bhūt entering and leaving the nose, and is to be avoided if possible. Hands and feet are also spirit-entries, and are, therefore, carefully washed before meals and prayers. The ears are believed to communicate direct with the brain, and are carefully guarded by the villager, whose apparent deafness is often due to the way his ears are closed lest they should prove a spirit-entry.[1]

"With regard to so-called worship, I need hardly repeat that there is no real worship of Bhūts. Nor has any demon—not even one of the highest class—any imposing temple-like structure erected in his honour. Often a mere heap of earth piled up in pyramidal shape near some tree, or a similar erection formed with bricks, and painted with streaks of

[1] Crooke, *Popular Religion and Folk-Lore*, i. 230–43.

white, constitutes the only shrine, while another heap in front with a flat surface does duty for an altar. There is rarely any idol; though sometimes, if the demon's origin be traceable to some high personage, he may be represented by a rude image of some one of the terrible forms of Śiva. No real prayers are said at such shrines, though incantations may be recited. The propitiation consists in offerings of food, and in various ceremonies which differ in different localities."[1]

We must now deal specifically with two or three of the more important demons.

I. Rāvana and the Rākshasas

In the great mass of the legends of the Hindu Pantheon, in its wars and conflicts, the gods are constantly represented as waging bitter strife, with varying fortunes, against these demon gods, the Asuras. This is surely symbolical of the eternal battle that knows no quarter or compromise between good and evil.

It is not, therefore, very astonishing that the pure and gentle Rāma should have to fight a long and terrible war with Rāvana, the demon king of Ceylon, and his dread allies, the Rākshasas; or that lovely Sītā, pearl of stainless beauty, should be abducted by Rāvana, and for many years remain in his power. The conflict so graphically described in the Rāmāyana is true in its main aspects to human life itself. Perhaps for this very reason it holds to-day so unique a place in the life and thought of India.

One most remarkable thing is that the power wielded by the archdemon, Rāvana, is supposed to be acquired by the practice of fearful penances and religious austerities. It is said that he underwent severe austerities, standing on his

[1] Monier Williams, *Religious Life and Thought*, p. 243.

hands in the midst of five fires, with his feet in the air for 10,000 years, and so was made invulnerable by Brahmā, the Creator, against gods and demons. He also obtained the boon of being able to assume any form he chose, but Brahmā stipulated that he should die in the end through a woman.

The word Rākshasa means "harmer" or "destroyer," and all the Rākshasas are malignant and terrible beings. They travel at night, haunt burning grounds, disturb devout people, devour human beings, and are cannibals, and, even filthy carrion eaters, but Rāvana, their chief, was the very incarnation of evil. He is described as having ten heads, twenty arms, copper-coloured eyes, and bright teeth like the young moon. His form is thick as a mountain. His strength so great that he could agitate the seas and split open the tops of hills:

> "The sun itself withholds his glow
> The wind, in fear forbears to blow;
> The fire restrains his wonted heat
> Where stands the dreaded Rāvan's feet."[1]

Added to this, he was utterly immoral, a breaker of all laws, and a ravisher of other men's wives. His physical strength, his austerities, and Brahmā's promise made him invincible, and he enjoyed undisputed empire, which he used for his evil purposes.

Moor[2] gives an explicit account of the vast dominion and authority acquired by Rāvana. All the gods and demigods were forced to perform menial offices about his person and household. Indra made garlands of flowers to adorn him, Agni was his cook, Sūrya (Sun) supplied light by day and Chandra (Moon) by night. Varuna purveyed water for the palace, Kuvera furnished him with money. The Nine Planets used to arrange themselves into a ladder by means

[1] Griffith, *Rāmāyana*, i. 83.
[2] *Hindu Pantheon*, p. 333.

of which Rāvana ascended his throne. Brahmā became his herald, proclaiming his titles. Śiva was his barber and trimmed the giant's locks. Vishnu had the honourable occupation of training his dancing girls. Ganesha had care of his cows, goats, and herds. Vāyu (the Wind) swept the house. Yama washed the linen. Nor were the female divinities exempted. Pārvatī was Ayah, or head nurse to his children, Lakshmī and Sarasvatī were also nurse-maids. Earthy beings and queens, too, were forced to enter Rāvana's service, and no less than ninety-six royal families were represented on his palace staff.

The insulted gods whose power he had usurped, and his many evil deeds, cried out to heaven for vengeance. The cry was answered. Vishnu himself became incarnate for the express purpose of destroying Rāvana, and took the name of Rāma. The abduction of Sītā, Rāma's wife, an incarnation of Lakshmī, marked the last stage in Rāvana's career of lust and cruelty. She was the woman by whom he was destined to be destroyed. Rāma called to his aid vast hosts of monkeys and bears under the leadership of Hanumān and Sugrīva. After repeated attacks and skirmishes a final engagement was fought between the Rākshasas and the composite army under Rāma and Hanumān. This was of seven days duration. Rāma singled out his great enemy and cut off his head a hundred times, but it was always miraculously restored. Now Rāma owned an arrow which had this wonderful property, that, if it went into the air, it became a thousand, and if it entered the body of an enemy it became an innumerable multitude. Rāvana, at the sight of this arrow, trembled with fear, and would have fled, but he recollected that Śiva had given him an arrow also that would rescue him in time of extreme peril. He discharged it at Rāma, and it destroyed Rāma's arrow, splitting it into fragments. Still, however, he was full of fear, for, whichever way he turned, he saw Rāma. If he shut his eyes he still saw him in his mind. At length, perceiving no way of escape, he began to flatter Rāma ; his flattery succeeded when his might could not prevail, and Rāma was so softened that he declared he would never destroy Rāvana. The gods, alarmed lest, after all, Rāvana should be spared, excited him to reproach Rāma, at which Rāma, indignant at such conduct, let fly the arrow which pierced Rāvana's body, proceeded through earth to the regions below, and, having bathed there, returned in the form of a goose, and again entered the quiver in its original shape. When the gods heard of Rāvana's death they could not believe the news, and in whispers asked each other "Is he dead?" "Is he really dead?" and when it was known that in truth he was dead, Rāma, the gods, and the monkeys began to dance together.

Rāvana's chief wife, Mandodarī, after his death, came to Rāma weeping; and Rāma, not knowing who she was, gave her this blessing that she should never become a widow. On finding out his mistake he was greatly perplexed, as he could not withdraw his word. So he ordered Hanumān to keep continually throwing wood on Rāvana's funeral pyre, as, according to the Hindu saying, "So long as the body of her husband is burning, a woman is not called a widow." To this day, therefore, Hanumān keeps laying logs on the fire; and every time a Hindu hears strange buzzings in his ears he says he hears the bones of Rāvana burning.

Nowadays the Rākshasas are supposed to live in trees and cause trouble to those who pass their way at night. They always were gross feeders, and their reputation for greediness in food still lingers. If a Hindu is eating by lamplight and the lamp goes out, he will instantly cover his dish with his hands to preserve the food from the Rākshasas. The finger nails of the Rākshasas, according to popular belief, contain a deadly poison, and their touch produces insensibility and even death.

II. Kuvera, the God of Wealth

"The Regent of the North,
Environed by his Yakshas, all in gold,
On yellow horses, bearing shields of gold."
—Arnold's *Light of Asia*, p. 24.

It is strange that the Hindu Pluto, the lord of gold and riches, should be classed as a demon, but such, in fact, he is. Kuvera is Rāvana's half-brother, and at one time he took possession of the chief city of Lankā (Ceylon). He was, however, compelled to yield it to his more powerful brother, who reduced Kuvera to a state of servitude, and made him his cash keeper. He did not remain long in this inferior position. By the practice of great austerities he obtained a boon from Brahmā that he should become "the god of wealth," and one of the four guardian deities of the world—a position of great trust and responsibility. The names of these officials are mentioned in the Rāmāyana:

"May he whose hands the thunder wield (Indra)
Be in the East thy guard and shield:
May Yama's care the South befriend,
And Varuna's arm the West defend
Let Kuvera, the lord of gold,
The North with firm protection hold."[1]

Notwithstanding this high dignity, the god of wealth does not occupy a very important position in the estimation of the Hindus. Their scorn of the materialistic spirit, and their conception of the ugliness of mere wealth, and the lack of true refinement in the plutocracy, is strikingly borne out by the names given to this god. The word *Kuvera*, itself means "vile body" alluding to his lack of beauty, and another name, *Ratna-garbha*, is even worse. It means "a belly of jewels." So a demon in very truth he is. He is

[1] Griffith, "*Rāmāyana*," ii. 20.

represented as a gloomy, selfish being of disagreeable countenance, deformed in body, having three legs and only eight teeth. In the Vedas he is represented as a chief of vile spirits, living in the underworld, a sort of Pluto; later he becomes a Pluto in another sense, but he still remains in the underworld and consorts with thieves, misers, and other degraded beings.

"Kuvera married Yakshī, and two of his sons, through a curse of the saint Nārada, became trees, in which condition they remained until Krishna, when an infant, uprooted them. Nārada met them in a forest, in a state of intoxication, bathing with their wives. The wives were ashamed of themselves and fell at Nārada's feet and sought for pardon, but the husbands disregarded the sage, and so suffered the full effects of his curse." [1]

Kuvera's descendants are the Yakshas—a race of demons—into whose forms the souls of men transmigrate who in this life are addicted to sordid and base passions, or are absorbed in mere worldly prosperity. A warning truly to the miserly soul!

Further, on a man becoming a criminal while in pursuit of wealth, he is required to sacrifice to Kuvera's wife, or Śakti, "a black or a one-eyed ass, as a meat offering, by night, in a place where four ways meet." In the Institutes of Manu we have this instruction laid down:

> "Let him daily offer to her in fire the fat of that ass; and at the close of the ceremony, let him offer clarified butter, with the holy text Sem, &c." (ch. xi. v. 119–120).

Kuvera himself receives no worship and has no images erected to his honour. The Hindu, seeking wealth and prosperity, prefers to worship Lakshmī or Ganesha.

[1] Wilkins, *Hindu Mythology*, p. 393.

CHAPTER X

WORSHIP OF THE NINE PLANETS

THE Hindus worship nine planets, or heavenly bodies. Two of these we have already noticed among the Vedic gods—Sūrya the Sun, and Soma (or Chandra) the Moon. Then there are five planets—Mercury (Budha), Venus (Sukra), Mars (Mangala), Jupiter (Vrihaspati), and Saturn (Sani), with the ascending and descending nodes (Rāhu and Ketu).[1] Ward says:[2] "The Hindus, like other idolatrous nations, have gone into the worship of the heavenly bodies. At the great festivals a small offering is presented to all the planets at one time; but except on these occasions they are never worshipped together. They are, however, frequently worshipped separately by the sick or unfortunate, who suppose themselves to be under the baneful influence of some planet."

[1] The Sun is described in the Mahābhārata as "the eye of the universe, the soul of all corporeal existence." The moon is represented as "white, like a sankha (conch-shell), produced from the ocean of milk, gracing the forehead of Mahādeo (Śiva); Mars as bright like lightning, a young man armed with a spear; Mercury as dark, like the blossom of the Priyangu flower, and blessed with the attribute of serenity; Jupiter as shining like gold, the preceptor of the gods and Rishis and the intelligence of the three worlds; Venus as resplendent like the thread of the golden lotus, the preceptor of the demons and the teacher of all the Sāstras (Hindu Scriptures); Sani (Saturn) as possessing a shining body, dark like a blue mountain, the son of the Sun and the brother of Yama; Rāhu as having only half a body possessed of great strength, the destroyer of the light of the sun and moon; and Ketu as red like the palasa flower and of fierce aspect.

[2] P. 54.

At these times they are worshipped one after another in regular succession. The prophet Jeremiah warns the Jews:

> "Learn not the way of the heathen, and be not dismayed at the signs of heaven, for the heathen are dismayed at them."

Quoting Ward's authority, we learn that the image of Sūrya is a round piece of mixed metal twelve inches in diameter; of Soma (Chandra), a piece like a half moon; of Mangala, a triangular piece six fingers in length; of Budha, a golden bow two fingers in breadth; of Vrihaspati, a piece like a lotus; of Sukra, a square piece of silver; of Sani, an iron scimitar; of Rāhu, an iron makara, a fabulous animal, half stag and half fish; and of Ketu, an iron snake.

The planets give their names to the days of the week and each has a special influence in human affairs.

1. *Ravi* or *Sūrya*[1] (the Sun) to Ravibara (Sunday). *The Jyotish-tatwa*, a great work on astrology, says that "a person born under this planet will possess an anxious mind, be subject to disease and other sufferings, be an exile, a prisoner, and suffer the loss of wife, children, and property."

2. *Soma*[2] (the Moon), hence Somavāra (Monday), is more auspicious. The fortunate one born under this planet will have many friends; will possess elephants, horses, and palanquins; be honourable and powerful; will live on excellent food and rest on superb couches.

3. *Mangala* (Mars), hence Mangal (Tuesday), is also, a malignant deity. If a person be born under the planet Mangala, he will be full of anxious thoughts, wounded with offensive weapons, imprisoned, oppressed with fear of robbers, fire, &c., and will lose his lands, trees, and good name.[3] This deity is identical with Kārtikeya (see p. 194).

4. *Budha* (Mercury), hence Budh (Wednesday), was the son of the moon (Soma) by Tārā, wife of Vrihaspati (Jupiter), who was the preceptor to the gods. Ward tells the story that when Tārā confessed that Soma was the father of her child Vrihaspati reduced her to ashes, but Brahmā restored her,

[1] See p. 35. [2] See p. 57. [3] Ward, pp. 56-7.

whereupon Vrihaspati received her back again. Samudra (the sea) father of Soma, was incensed with his son for dishonouring the wife of his spiritual leader, and disinherited him, but his sister Lakshmī[1] (Vishnu's wife) interceded, and the curse was partially removed. He was restored to heaven by being placed on Śiva's forehead, who, thus ornamented, went in to a feast of the gods. Vrihaspati, on seeing Soma again in heaven, was greatly angered, and could only be appeased by Brahmā, ordering that the lascivious god should be excluded from heaven, and placed among the stars, and that the sin which had obscured his glory should remain for ever. This planet is auspicious. " If a person be born under the planet Budha he will be fortunate and obtain an excellent wife." Budha must not be confounded with Buddha, an incarnation of Vishnu.

5. *Vrihaspati* (Jupiter), hence Vrihaspativāra (Thursday), is the spiritual guide or preceptor of the gods. He is a Vedic deity and regarded as identical with Agni (see p. 31). " If a person be born under this planet, he will have an amiable disposition, possess palaces, gardens, lands, and be rich in money and corn. He will possess much religious merit, and have all his wishes gratified."

6. *Sukra* (Venus), hence Sukravāra (Friday), was the preceptor and priest of the demons, and was blind in one eye, the reason for which is related. "Vishnu, in the Dwarf incarnation" (see p. 113), "went to Bali, king of the demons, to solicit a present. Sukra, King Bali's preceptor, forbade the king to give anything. The king, disregarding his advice, obliged his priest to read the necessary formulas, and pour out water from a vessel to ratify the gift. Sukra foresaw that the giving of this gift would be the destruction of his master and entered the water in an invisible form, and by his magic power prevented it from falling, but Vishnu, aware of the device, put a straw into the basin of water, which, entering Sukra's eye, gave him so much pain that he could remain

[1] Lakshmī and Soma were produced together at the churning of the ocean of milk.

there no longer. The water thereupon fell and the gift was ratified, but Sukra lost his eye." [1]

Of the fate of a person born under this planet we read that he will have the faculty of knowing the past, present, and future; will have many wives, and possess a kingly umbrella, elephants, horses, palanquins, and footmen.

7. *Sani* (Saturn), hence Sanichar (Saturday), is said to be the son of Sūrya by Chhāyā, the shade.[2] This planet is of all the most fatal to good fortune. It was Sani who lost Ganesha his original head. Many Hindus refuse to do business and return to their homes when Sani is in the ascendant. The book on Hindu astrology already quoted says: "If a person be born under the planet Sani he will be slandered, his riches dissipated, his son and wife destroyed; he will live at variance with others, and endure many sufferings."

8, 9. The Eclipse demon *Rāhu* is the ascending node, and is classed by the Hindu astronomers as a planet. The name means "seizer" or "looser." He is said to swallow the sun and moon, and at the great Mēlas, which are usually held at the time of the sun's eclipse, crowds of people, watching anxiously the disappearing luminary, cry out "Isko chhor do! Chhor do!" "Loose it, Leave it." He is one of the Asuras, or demons, and, when the gods produced the Amrita (or nectar) at the churning of the ocean, Rāhu disguised himself as one of them, and stole and drank a portion of the precious liquid. The Sun and Moon detected the fraud and told Vishnu, who, with his discus, severed Rāhu's head and four arms from his trunk; but the nectar which he had drunk secured his immortality and the severed parts of his body lived. The head and arms were transferred to the solar system where they now wreak their vengeance on the Sun and Moon by occasionally swallowing them; while the tail has given birth under the name of *Ketu* to a numerous progeny of comets and fiery meteors. Ketu is therefore the descending node, the father of the falling star and meteor.

[1] Ward, pp. 58–9. [2] See p. 36.

In the Vishnu Purāna we read: "Rāhu directs his course from the sun to the moon, and back again from the moon to the sun." Sometimes he covers the sun and moon with his hand, sometimes hides them under his jaw which is 3000 miles deep, sometimes licks them with his tongue. Sometimes he moves them up and down in his mouth like an animal chewing the cud. He is able to swallow them for a while because he is larger than they, but he is not able to keep them in his mouth because of their heat. Hence the phenomena of eclipses.

"Eclipses are believed to be of evil omen. Gloucester summarises admirably the Hindu belief in the passage in *King Lear* (i. 2): 'These late eclipses in the sun and moon portend no good to us . . . love cools, friendship falls off, brothers divide: in cities, mutinies; in countries, discord; in palaces, treason; and the bond cracked 'twixt son and father.' A high-caste Hindu will eat no food which has remained in the house during an eclipse, and all earthen vessels which are in the house at the time must be broken. During an eclipse all household business is suspended, and eating and drinking is prohibited; even sleep at such a time is forbidden, for it is then that demons and devils are most active. The most effectual way of scaring the demon Rāhu and releasing the afflicted planet is to bathe in some sacred stream—and for protection a Brāhman should stand in the water beside the worshipper and recite the Gāyatrī."[1] Bathing during an eclipse also cleanses from sin.

The whole array of these nine planets constitutes a most formidable group of deities whose power over every living person's career from the moment of birth and over the whole course of his life no one for an instant dreams of doubting. The influences of Saturn, Rāhu, and Ketu are most sinister and therefore are most propitiated. If they are in the ascendant when a man is born they are sure to shorten his life and cause him endless trouble.

[1] Crooke, *Popular Religion and Folk-Lore*, i. 19–23.

CHAPTER XI

THE DIVINE RISHIS—THE CONSTELLATION OF THE GREAT BEAR

WHEN Brahmā wished to populate the world he created mind-born sons like to himself. Seven of these are mentioned in the Mahābhārata, but in the Purānas nine are named. These seven are supposed to be visible as the constellation of the Great Bear, while their wives shine as the Pleiades. As there are only six of the latter, many fables became necessary to reconcile the difference, one being the seventh bright star in the Pleiades has since ceased to shine! One piece of great scandal is related concerning these ladies. Agni, the ardent deity of fire, was charitably disposed to communicate some portion of his warmth to them, seeing that they shivered with cold in the Arctic circle. His wife, Swāhā, either through jealousy or because she dreaded the resentment of the holy Rishis, assumed the form and countenance of each dame in succession, and completely deceived her husband. The Rishis, however, heard of the scandal, and with great wrath divorced their sparkling spouses and drove them out into the heavens. They, however, became nurses to Kārtikeya (Mars), the war god, and were placed by him, as a reward, in the zodiac, where they now shine.

Of these Rishis it is only necessary to mention three by name, Daksha, Bhrigu, and Nārada, the others are unimportant.

I. DAKSHA

Daksha is famed as the father of Umā the consort of Śiva. He shines through the greatness of his son-in-law. He in some accounts is said to have sprung from the thumb of Brahmā, in others from his mind. He is one of the chief Prajāpatis, a word formerly given solely to Brahmā, but afterwards employed for the first-formed men from whom the human race sprung. It means "Lord of Creatures" and is used very much in the same way as patriarch is used in Christian Scriptures. The story of his quarrel with his son-in-law, Śiva, and of his daughter's consequent self-afflicted death (Satī), is given under the daughter's name.[1] One sad consequence remained. Śiva during the fray struck off Daksha's head, and the head fell into the fire and was burned. A he-goat was then brought in and his head was struck off and placed on Daksha's lifeless body, who instantly revived. Nevertheless the goat's head remained a perpetual sign of his ignorance and stupidity in warring against so powerful an adversary as Śiva.

II. Bhrigu

Another of the mind-born sons of Brahmā, Bhrigu, officiated as priest at the sacrifice of Daksha which gave such terrible offence to Śiva. He suffered from the wrathful god's displeasure by the loss of his beard. He also was sent to test the character of the three great deities.[2]

Various legends are narrated of him. He on one occasion cursed Agni. The Mahābhārata relates: "A woman named Puloma was betrothed to a demon; Bhrigu, seeing her beauty, married her secretly according to the Vedic rites and carried her off. The demon, by the aid of Agni, discovered the bride's hiding-place and took her away to his home. For rendering the demon assistance Bhrigu cursed Agni and said: 'From this day you shall eat everything.' 'I too can curse,' said Agni, 'but respecting the high dignity of Brāhmans (Bhrigu was descended directly from Brahmā) I restrain my anger. I am really the mouth of the gods and ancestors. When clarified butter is offered to them in

[1] See p. 181.

[2] See story under Vishnu, Part III, ch. iii.

sacrifice they really partake of it through me, their mouthpiece; how then can I be said to eat everything?' Bhrigu, hearing this, consented to modify his curse by saying that 'As the Sun by his light and heat purifies all nature, so Agni should purify all he eats.'" [1]

He also performed a most wonderful deed in making a Kshatriya into a Brāhman by his mere word. The Mahābhārata [2] gives the following account of this occurrence: "Divodāsa, king of Kāsi (Benares) was attacked by the sons of Vitahavya and all his family were slain in battle. The afflicted monarch then resorted to the sage Bharadvaja who performed a sacrifice on his behalf, in consequence of which a son named Pratardana was born to him. Pratardana, becoming an accomplished warrior, was sent by his father to take vengeance on the Vitahavyas. Vitahavya had now to fly to another sage, Bhrigu, who promised his protection. The avenger, Pratardana, however followed and demanded that the refugee should be given up. Bhrigu, filled with compassion, then said: 'There is no Kshatriya here; all these are Brāhmans.' Hearing this assertion of Bhrigu's Pratardana was glad, and gently touching the Sage's feet rejoined: 'Even thus, O glorious saint, I have gained my object, for I have compelled this king to relinquish his caste and he can no more war against me.' In this way Vitahavya became a Brāhman Rishi and an utterer of the Vedas."

Paraśurāma—"Rāma with the axe"—(see p. 114) was one of Bhrigu's most illustrious descendants.

III. Nārada

This sage resembles Mercury, the messenger of the gods. He is wise and eloquent, a musician of exquisite skill and the inventor of the Indian lute, the *vīna*. Unfortunately, too, he

[1] Wilkins, *Hindu Mythology*, pp. 364–7.
[2] Muir, *O.S.T.*, i. 229.

has an unenviable reputation as a gossip, a strife-maker, a quarrelsome, meddling person. It was he who informed Kansa of the approaching birth of Krishna, which led the king to slay the children of Vāsudeva. He was said to have been produced from the thigh of Brahmā. His father was very incensed with him because he dissuaded the other Rishis from peopling the world, and declared that he would have no resting-place; hence his wandering nature.

In the Mahābhārata Nārada figures as a religious teacher, and in the Rāmāyana is a specimen of his teaching: "One day a Brāhman carrying the dead body of his son came to the door of Rāma's house at Ajodhya and, bewailing his loss, said that as he himself was unconscious of any fault, he believed his son's death was owing to some misconduct on the part of the king. Rāma, greatly distressed at the charge, instantly summoned his councillors and put the case before them. Then spake Nārada: 'Hear, O king, how this boy's untimely death occurred; and having heard the truth regarding what ought to be done, do it. A presumptuous *Śūdra* (lowest caste), paying no regard to the fact that the privilege of obtaining merit by self-mortification had not descended to the humble caste to which he belonged, has been guilty of seeking to secure a store of religious merit by practising mortifications.' Rāma at once went in search of the individual and found him engaged in the manner described by Nārada. The śūdra avowed his caste and his desire to obtain for himself the rank of a god by the self-mortification he was undergoing. Rāma instantly cut off the offender's head, and the gods assembled applauded the deed. He then requested them that the Brāhman's boy might be resuscitated. He was informed that this had happened the very moment the śūdra was slain." [1]

Finally, great honour is given to Nārada because he is said to have revealed to Vālmīki the Rāmāyana. Vālmīki, as Nārada related the life of Rāma to him, felt that the task

[1] Muir, *O.S.T.*, i. 117.

of writing it was too great for his powers, but Brahmā himself appeared and encouraged him to proceed :

> "Then come, O best of seers, relate
> The life of Rāma, good and great ;
> The tale that saintly Nārad told
> In all its glorious length unfold."
>
> GRIFFITH'S *Rāmāyana*, I-22.

CHAPTER XII

THE JAIN DEITIES

THE Jains, like the Buddhists, represent a revolt against Brāhmanism which they regarded as a departure from the true primitive religion of India. But when Buddhism declined and finally died out, the Jains, though depleted by persecution, survived. They form a small but wealthy community of merchants and bankers, and number about 750,000. They have much in their religion that resembles Buddhism. Both reject the authority of the Vedas, both disregard caste rules, and profess to believe in the religious and social equality of man. The Jains are considered heretics by orthodox Hindus, although they have so far departed from the tenets of Buddhism as to acknowledge in a general way the more common and modern Hindu deities, and their worship is very similar to that which prevails amongst the Hindus.

The origin of the sect is said to be accounted for in the following way: The innovations of the Brāhmans, who introduced gradually into India such practices as lingam-worship, the worship of the cow and other sacred animals, the wondrous stories of the Avatāras of Vishnu, and certain sacrificial rites of Purānic times, were deeply resented for a long time by a number of influential Hindus of many castes. These men were unwilling to come to an open rupture, but their opposition to what they regarded as dangerous innovations and changes in the true primitive faith, handed down from remote times, never ceased.

A crisis, however, became unavoidable when the Brāhmans introduced the sacrifice of Yajna, in which a living offering, generally a ram, was sacrificed. This violated the most sacred principle, and the hitherto inviolable practice of the

U

Hindus, and "the Jains" withdrew from association with the priestly caste, whom they regarded as corrupters of their primitive faith. The secession included men of all the four main castes, for, to some of the faithful Brāhmans, were joined those from the warrior, merchant, and Śūdra castes, who desired to maintain the purity of their ancient faith. The Brāhmans, however, succeeded in imposing their will upon the body politic, and their innovations were adopted by the majority of the people. Consequently persecution arose and in many parts of the country, the places and objects of Jain worship were demolished, the Jains were deprived of their civil and religious liberty, and were reduced to such absolute subjection that in many provinces not a vestige of them remains.

There are two principal sects among the Jains, the Jaina-Basru and the Kāshta-Sanghi-Swetāmbara (white-robed Jains). The term Jain comes from Jina, "he who has conquered" (*i.e.* human passions or infirmities). A Jina is the deified saint, also called a Tīrthankara, who is the object of Jain worship. Both Jains and Buddhists now worship a succession of deified saints in place of the many gods adored by the Hindus. The Jains divide time into three successive eras and assign twenty-four Jinas to each era. They are now in the second era and the twenty-four saints of the first and second eras are the deities of modern Jainism.

"These twenty-four are represented in the temples as seated in an attitude of contemplation. In features they so resemble each other that in order to distinguish them they are painted in different colours and have their respective names engraved on their pedestals, or some distinguishing sign, commonly an animal, by their side. In the stories of their lives there is little of a distinctive character, but there is this noticeable fact that in height of stature and length of life there has been a steady decline." An example or two in support of the last remark may not be out of place. The first of the second series of twenty-four saints was Vrishabha. His stature was 500 poles in height, and he lived 8,400,000 great years. He was crowned king when 2,000,000 years old and reigned 6,300,000 years, and afterwards spent 100,000 years in the practice of austerities, by which he became qualified for sainthood. The last of the twenty-four saints, called "The Saint," because he is the best known of all, was Mahāvīra. He lost his father when twenty-eight years of age and became king, but resigned after two years reign and entered upon a life of austerity. After forty-two years of preparation he became exempt from pain for ever. In other words he died at the age of seventy-two, obtaining "absorption." This, according to tradition, occurred 2400 years ago![1]

The Jains, according to Abbé Dubois,[2] have a lofty doctrine of God. They acknowledge but one Supreme Being. He is one, indivisible and invisible, a pure Spirit. He has four main attributes: wisdom, infinite knowledge, power, and happiness. This omnipotent Being is wholly absorbed in the contemplation of his own perfections and in the enjoyment of his own blessedness. Virtue and vice, good and evil, are equally indifferent to him.

"The adoration and worship which the Jains offer to their deified saints, the Tīrthankaras, and to other objects of worship held sacred among them, does not detract from the worship of the Supreme Being, for these holy personages, in taking possession after death of the Moksha or Mukti, the supreme felicity, have become intimately united and inseparably incorporated with the Divine."

The Jains are firm believers in the doctrine of the transmigration of the soul from one body into another after death, and hold that the offender may suffer transmigration into the body of an insect, reptile, or bird, or quadruped, according to the degree of his offences. Naturally therefore they hold all life in honour, and their distinctive precept is "ahimsa parama dharma"—*i.e.* "non-killing is the supreme religion." They abhor the taking of life in any form, they show the

[1] Wilkins, *Hindu Mythology*, p. 489.

[2] Dubois, *Description of People of India*, p. 397.

greatest tenderness to animals, and are the best supporters of hospitals and asylums for sick or worn-out beasts.

As to the future of the Jains, there is little doubt that they will gradually be absorbed into Hinduism. As it is they already employ Brāhman priests in their temples and pay inferior homage to such Hindu gods as Brāhma, Śiva, Vishnu, and Ganesha.

GENERAL SUMMARY AND CONCLUSION

In our brief survey of the gods and goddesses of the Hindu Pantheon the painstaking researches of Western scholarship have enabled us to read the character, and narrate from authentic sources the life-story, and in some measure define the position and importance, of certain deities whom tradition asserts were potent forces in the dim ages when history began to be. Our wonder in being able to do so, becomes the greater, when we realise that they are the product, the devotional and imaginative outcome, of a religious and social system which is one of the oldest known to man; and which has exhibited a cohesion and adaptiveness and a power of recovery that no other faith can claim. Still more do we marvel when we trace the roots of this all-embracing and closely-knit mythology back to its original sources in the ancient Vedas, amongst the oldest Scriptures of the world. The importance, the overwhelming practical bearing of our survey of Hindu mythology becomes manifest when we remember that the people who worship these time-worn deities, and are moulded and controlled by that ancient system of thought, and who honour supremely the Vedic poems, form a population second only to one on the world's surface, an incalculable and yet determining force for good or evil on the world's moral battlefield.

It is therefore of first importance that we should estimate rightly, and weigh with judgment, the moral and intellectual value of Hindu mythology. What part does it play in the upbuilding of the great Hindu community, what consolation, what hope, what inspiration in living has it given to the dim wandering millions who have turned to it in their times of crisis and need? Can Hindu mythology be said to have a moral value? Does it not tend to obscure the moral sense? The testimony of European savants is well-nigh unanimous that it does. It would be comparatively easy to quote *in extenso* from many authorities named in these pages; but our hesitancy arises from the fact that we consider it extremely difficult for the most sympathetic and learned European scholar to understand the mental position (the *penetralia*) of the devout Hindu, who implicitly believes the wildest and most contradictory myths, and worships with utter abandon at the shrine of some strange conception of deity. And if a Hindu is "born and not made," and the inwardness of his religious ideals is not easily understood by our best Western scholars, how then are they capable of guiding us as to the correct moral value of Hindu mythology?

Still, even when viewed from our Western standpoint, it must surely be conceded that the mythology of so preeminently religious a race as the Hindu has important lessons to teach us. For one thing, it constantly emphasizes the superiority of the spiritual over the intensely material conceptions of our present-day Western life. Plutocracy will not feel flattered by the Hindu conception of the "God of wealth" as a demon of a most unpleasant type, or the "God of prosperity," Ganesha, who has a most repulsive appearance, and who is depicted as lord of an inferior type of goblins. Then, again, how marvellously these multitudinous deities cover every possible activity and every phase of human life. The contribution the Hindu will ultimately make to the religious consciousness of the world will be no slight one, for Hindu mythology and the practice of Hinduism teach us that to the Hindu, religion is taken into the very core and centre of daily life. For our Western externalism in religion the Hindu has uncompromising disdain; and instead of a faith which is in so many instances fading from the horizon of the West, the Hindu offers a real ardour of faith. Nothing is more wonderful in the world to-day than the sight of those countless thousands crowding the Benares Ghāts, swarming into the sacred stream for cleansing of the soul, fighting their way with good-humoured zest in such numbers into the principal temples, that the city police have to erect barriers and regulate the number admitted at one time. These worshippers, it must be remembered, have travelled long distances, borne great discomforts, and even privations, in order to propitiate some weird, grotesque deity. Though it may not be a faith which appeals to our Western reason, or to our sense of helpful religion, no one, not even Professor Max Müller, would question the reality of such a faith. Hindu mythology, even to-day, is instinct with this wondrous faith, nay, is often transfigured by it, for it bears the mark of a supreme and very real religious consciousness.

Having said so much, let us summarise the testimony of western scholarship as to the moral worth of Hindu mythology. We quote only one or two leading names of the large number of those who have striven for years to navigate the difficult sea of eastern thought. They warn us of dangers in Hindu mythology, due to the existence of mighty currents, steadily setting towards treacherous moral reefs or sandbanks. We may surely admit that they are able to realise the presence of such forces; although they cannot probe into the depths of the Oriental mind, or trace these currents to their primal sources. In other words, it may be possible to estimate the moral worth of our subject without solving the mystery of its confused and often self-contradictory data.

Sir Alfred Lyall, who had wide experience of Indian life and was a trusted Government official, sums up his point of view in a striking illustration:

"The whole panorama of religious ideas and practices in polytheistic India may be compared to the entangled confusion of a primeval forest, where one sees trees of all kinds, ages, sizes, interlacing and contending with each other; some falling into decay, others shooting up vigorously and overtopping the crowd—while the glimpse of blue sky above the tree-tops may symbolise the illimitable transcendental ideas above and apart from the earth-born conceptions."[1]

[1] Lyall, *Asiatic Studies*, ii. p. 318.

Other great savants are even less favourable to the moral value of Hindu mythology.

In a lecture on missions delivered in the nave of Westminster Abbey on December 3, 1873, Max Müller declares that "Brāhmanism as a religion cannot stand the light of day. The worship of Śiva, of Vishnu, and of other popular deities, is of the same, nay, in many cases of a more degraded and savage character than the worship of Jupiter, Apollo, and Minerva; it belongs to a stratum of thought which is long buried beneath our feet; it may live on, like the lion and tiger, but the mere air of free thought and civilised life will extinguish it. . . .

"It is true that there are millions of men, women, and children in India who fall down before the stone images of Vishnu with his four arms, riding on a creature half bird, half man, or sleeping on a serpent; who worship Śiva, a monster with three eyes, riding naked on a bull, with a necklace of skulls for his ornament. There are human beings who still believe in a god of War, Kārtikeya, with six faces, riding on a peacock, and holding bow and arrow in his hands; and who invoke a god of Success, Ganesha, with four hands and an elephant's head, sitting on a rat. Nay, it is true that in the broad daylight of the Nineteenth Century, the figure of the goddess Kālī is carried through the streets of her own city, Calcutta, her wild dishevelled hair reaching to her feet, with a necklace of human heads, her tongue protruded from her mouth, her girdle stained with blood. All this is true; but ask any Hindu who can read, write, and think, whether these are the gods he believes in, and he will smile at your credulity. How long this living death of national religion in India may last no one can tell."

There are a few simple and quite elementary reasons to support these opinions on the absence of moral worth in Hindu mythology. Its very luxuriance of growth—the tangled confusion of a multiplicity of contending deities—undoubtedly diminishes the force of the moral law, for that law depends on a *central* authority, who with unchallengeable clearness and dignity can order its concerns. Then again, although not originally the case, *idolatry* is now an integral part of Hinduism and is more especially associated with Hindu mythology, and idolatry as such is degrading to character. The type of popular idolatry which the photographs illustrating these pages portray, suffices to reveal my meaning. The land is full of the stories of the reputed lives of the gods these photographs and pages speak of, and one does not need to labour the point that impure conceptions of deity, clothed in idols, ugly and repulsive, must necessarily degrade the minds and lives of the worshippers.

And from the intellectual standpoint, can mythology be said to refine and elevate the Hindu? Mythology exalts conceptions which are often false and puerile, and, although strange gleams of beauty run through it, its teaching is really calculated to keep the mind in a state of perpetual ignorance. Sir Monier Williams says of Brāhmanism: " Its policy being to check the development of intellect, and to keep the inferior castes in perpetual childhood, it encouraged an appetite for exaggeration more monstrous and more absurd than would be tolerated in the most extravagant European fairy tales. The more improbable the statement, the more childish delight it was calculated to awaken. Time is measured by millions of years; space by millions of miles; and if a battle is to be described, nothing is thought of unless millions of soldiers, elephants, and horses are brought into the field."

Lord Macaulay similarly says, "The Brāhminical mythology is so absurd that it necessarily debases every mind that receives it as truth."

If, however, the student of Hindu mythology will leave such considerations outside his purview, and approach its study with unbiassed mind, it will prove to be one of undoubted fascination. There are whole realms of Hindu mythological thought still to be surveyed. The study of origins; the influence on Hindu mythological conceptions of aboriginal deities on the one hand, and of the gods of nations outside India on the other hand; and the close relationship of Hindu mythology with the ancient Persian, Greek, and Roman deities, are themes replete with interest, and should present a strong call to men of scholarship and leisure. Such study would open out questions, and possibly solve problems, of the deepest importance to students of ethnology and comparative religions.

We must draw to a conclusion in our brief survey of an engrossing subject, by a few words on the scope of mythology, and its underlying and controlling idea.

Ruskin has laid down this dictum, that in mythology you have to discern three structural parts.

I. The *root* in physical existence :
i.e. the sun, sky, cloud or sea.

II. *Two branches :*
(*a*) the *personal incarnation* of that, becoming a trusted and companionable deity with whom you may walk hand in hand as a child with its brother or its sister ;
(*b*) the *moral significance and idea* expressed by the incarnation.

Applying this rule to Aryan myths, their roots in physical existence, with their trunks, bearing the two branches, can be clearly traced in many of the Vedic and Purānic conceptions. Varuna is god of the illimitable firmament. His physical background is the vast starry expanse of heaven. Incarnated, his omniscient eyes watch over the seething world below him. He punishes the evil-doer and rewards the good :

> " Whate'er exists in heaven and earth, whate'er beyond the skies,
> Before the eye of Varuna the thing unfolded lies."

Then the moral significance of this omniscient deity comes into view. Men, realising his knowledge and power, cry to him for pardon. " Release us," they say, " from the sins of our fathers and from those which we have committed."

Similarly Indra represents the angry sweep of the

storm. The crash of his thunderbolt is still heard in the bursting of the monsoon after the long Indian drought. Incarnated, he vanquishes the demon Vritra, who withholds the precious rain-bearing clouds from the parched ground and perishing people, who plead to the Rain-god on those sultry Gangetic plains. His moral significance is seen in the Vedic prayer to this, the chief of the later Vedic deities :

> "Thou art our guardian, advocate and friend,
> A brother, father, mother—all combined ;
> Most fatherly of fathers, we are thine
> And thou art ours. Oh ! let thy pitying soul
> Turn to us in compassion when we praise thee,
> And slay us not for one sin or for many."

The Rain-giver, who sends the genial showers which water the earth and give life and hope to thousands, becomes at one step, the saviour and friend of the people.

Passing onward to Purānic times in our necessarily brief survey, we find the root, not in some object having physical existence, but in a fundamental principle, controlling and underlying physical existence. "The august and terrible Śiva," says Lyall, "represents in all probability the earliest and most general impression of Nature on man—the impression of endless and pitiless change, the recurrent ebb and flow of life. Incarnated, he becomes the dread agent of Destruction, and at the same time the lord and giver of life. For though by inexorable law all things are liable to decay and disintegration, yet Nature is endlessly reproducing herself in various forms of life. The whole circle of animated creation is therefore his. He presides over incessant round of birth and death in which Nature eternally revolves. The moral significance and mighty sway of this deity, lord of time, ruler of life and death, can only be even dimly estimated by those who have seen the thousands of temples scattered up and down the length and breadth of India. He is more worshipped as he is more dreaded than any single incarnation in India.

"Vishnu, on the other hand, impersonates the higher evolution; the upward tendency of the human spirit. He represents several great and far-reaching religious ideas. In the increasing flux and change of all things he is their Preserver; and although he is one of the highest gods he has constantly revisited the earth either in animal or human shape. . . . Most of the famous saints, heroes, demigods of poetry and romance, with many of the superior divinities, are recognised as having been the sensible manifestations of Vishnu; their bodies were only the mortal vesture that he assumed for the purpose of interposing decisively at some great emergency, or whenever he condescended to become again an actor in the world's drama. This theory of divine embodiment is one of the most essential and effective doctrines of Hinduism; it links together and explains the various phases of the religion, connecting the lower with the higher ideas, and providing them with a common ground or method of reconciliation. It serves to show, for instance, that the sacred animal of a wild tribe is merely the great Brāhmanic deity in disguise, or it may prove that the worshippers of some obscure or local hero have been adoring Vishnu unawares. It thus accommodates and absorbs the lower deities; and while it draws them up to the sky and completes their apotheosis, it also brings the higher gods constantly down again from heaven to take part in human affairs."[1]

The conclusion that is reached from tracing thus the evolution of Śiva and Vishnu, the great gods of the Brāhmanic Triad, as from the earlier and less complex Vedic deities, is that the principal cause for the rise of myths is a belief in the *animation of Nature.* In its humblest form it is found in local Animism, with its village fetish and its wayside godling, but it rises to its height in the personification and afterwards deification of the controlling and underlying principles of Nature, as seen in the great creations of Śiva and Vishnu. It is not a mere poetic fancy, but a thoughtful and serious, if crude, philosophy of Nature. It fails because it does not

[1] Lyall, *Asiatic Studies*, pp. 306–7.

realise to any great extent that Nature is only the vestibule through which the devout spirit approaches the Eternal, and that the Creator is an entity, distinct from, and immeasurably above the work of His hands. It draws its strength, and perhaps the secret of its marvellous longevity, from the measure in which it has faintly apprehended this truth. That it is constantly present in Hindu thought is proved by the ceremony performed by the Brāhmans of *adhivāsa* or "inhabitation," whereby they invite the deity to dwell in the idol which they have made. The conclusion of this ceremony is when the *prāna*, *i.e.* "breath, life or soul," is given to the idol, and the figure which previously had received no veneration becomes an object of worship because the Supreme Spirit is believed to have entered it. This Supreme Spirit or essence, Brahma, is believed to pervade the whole universe and animate all things.

And this, which we may describe as the controlling idea of mythology, is not limited in scope to this present life. It develops into a belief in personal souls animating the unseen world, and by the doctrine of the Transmigration of souls, which has its origin in this belief, it extends itself into eternity.

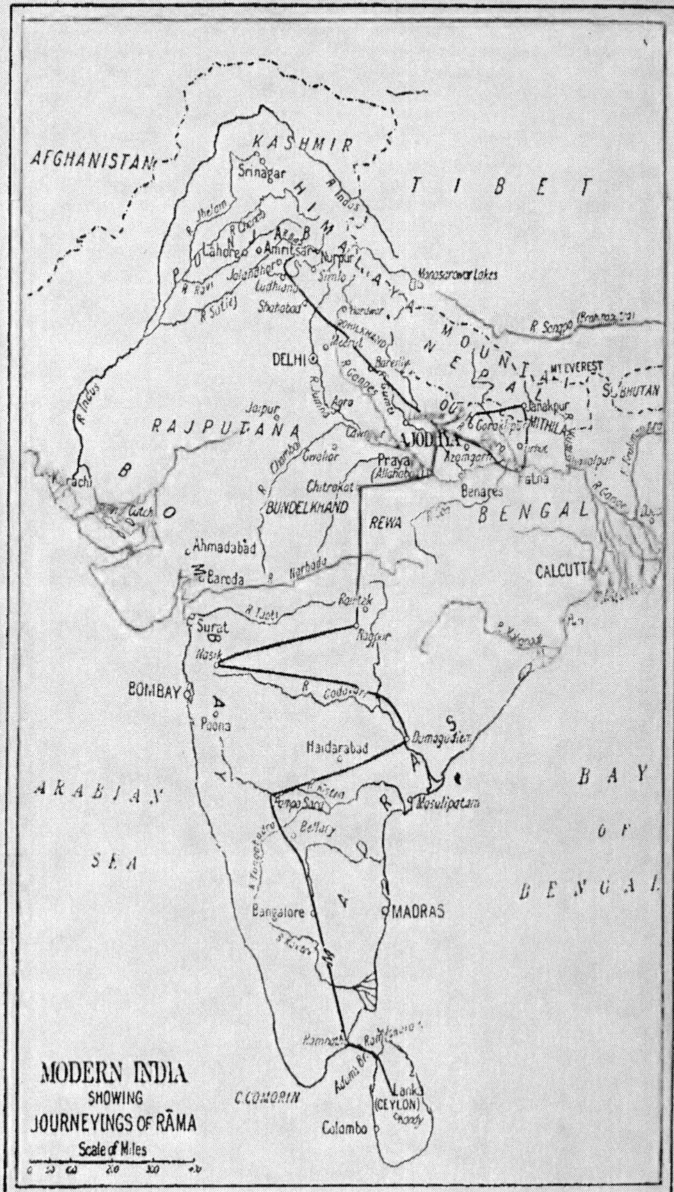

MODERN INDIA
SHOWING
JOURNEYINGS OF RĀMA

INDEX

The chief references are in heavy type; words that are not proper names have been put in italics; q.=quoted; *n.*=note.